Developing with Docker

Change the way your organization deploys software at
scale with this fast-paced guide to the world of Docker

Jarosław Krochmalski

BIRMINGHAM - MUMBAI

Developing with Docker

First published: November 2016

Production reference: 2011216

Published by Packt Publishing Ltd.
Livery Place
35 Livery Street
Birmingham
B3 2PB, UK.
ISBN 978-1-78646-990-8

www.packtpub.com

Credits

Author
Jarosław Krochmalski

Reviewer
Jeeva S. Chelladhurai

Commissioning Editor
Kartikey Pandey

Acquisition Editors
Narsimha Pai
Rahul Nair

Content Development Editor
Trusha Shiryan

Technical Editor
Naveenkumar Jain

Copy Editors
Laxmi Subramanium
Sneha Singh

Project Coordinator
Kinjal Bari

Proofreader
Safis Editing

Indexer
Pratik Shirodhkar

Graphics
Kirk D'Penha

Production Coordinator
Shantanu N. Zagade

About the Author

Jarosław Krochmalski is a passionate software designer and developer who specializes in the financial business domain. He has over 12 years of experience in software development. He is a clean-code and software craftsmanship enthusiast. He is a Certified Scrum Master and a fan of Agile. His professional interests include new technologies in web application development, design patterns, enterprise architecture, and integration patterns.

He has been designing and developing software professionally since 2000 and has been using Java as his primary programming language since 2002. In the past, he worked for companies such as Kredyt Bank (KBC) and Bank BPS on many large-scale projects such as international money orders, express payments, and collection systems. He currently works as a consultant at Danish company 7N as an infrastructure architect for the Nykredit bank. You can reach him via Twitter at @jkroch or by e-mail at jarek@finsys.pl.

I would like to say hello to my friends at 7N and Nykredit—keep up the great job!

About the Reviewer

Jeeva S. Chelladhurai has been working as a DevOps specialist at the IBM Global Cloud Center of Excellence (CoE) for the last 8 years. He is the co-author of *Learning Docker* published by PacktPub, UK. He has more than 20 years of IT industry experience. He has technically managed and mentored diverse teams across the globe in envisaging and building pioneering telecommunication products. He specializes in DevOps and cloud solution delivery, with a focus on data center optimization, software-defined environments (SDEs), and distributed application development, deployment, and delivery using the newest Docker technology. Jeeva is also a strong proponent of the agile methodologies, DevOps, and IT automation. He holds a master's degree in computer science from Manonmaniam Sundaranar University and a graduation certificate in project management from Boston University, USA. Besides his official responsibilities, he writes book chapters and authors research papers. He has been instrumental in crafting reusable technical assets for IBM solution architects and consultants. Currently, he is contributing for the second edition of the Docker book. He speaks in technical forums on DevOps technologies and tools. His Linked in profile can be found at `https://www.linkedin.com/in/JeevaChelladhurai`.

www.PacktPub.com

For support files and downloads related to your book, please visit www.PacktPub.com.

Did you know that Packt offers eBook versions of every book published, with PDF and ePub files available? You can upgrade to the eBook version at www.PacktPub.com and as a print book customer, you are entitled to a discount on the eBook copy. Get in touch with us at service@packtpub.com for more details.

At www.PacktPub.com, you can also read a collection of free technical articles, sign up for a range of free newsletters and receive exclusive discounts and offers on Packt books and eBooks.

https://www.packtpub.com/mapt

Get the most in-demand software skills with Mapt. Mapt gives you full access to all Packt books and video courses, as well as industry-leading tools to help you plan your personal development and advance your career.

Why subscribe?

- Fully searchable across every book published by Packt
- Copy and paste, print, and bookmark content
- On demand and accessible via a web browser

Table of Contents

Preface   1

Chapter 1: Introduction to Docker   7

    The basic idea   8
    Containerization versus virtualization   8
        Traditional virtualization   8
        Containerization   9
    Benefits of using Docker   10
        Speed and size   10
        Reproducible and portable builds   10
        Immutable and agile infrastructure   11
        Tools and APIs   12
    Tools overview   12
        Docker Engine and Docker Engine client   13
        Docker Machine   13
        Kitematic   15
        Docker compose   15
        Oracle VirtualBox   16
        Git   17
    Summary   18

Chapter 2: Installing Docker   19

    Hardware requirements   20
    Installing on Windows   21
    Installing on Mac OS   30
    Installing on Linux   35
    Installing on the cloud — AWS   38
    Summary   44

Chapter 3: Understanding Images and Containers   45

    Images   46
    Layers   48
    Containers   54
        Saving changes to a container   56
    Docker registry, repository and index   60
    Summary   63

Chapter 4: Networking and Persistent Storage   65

   Docker networking   66
      Default networks   67
      No networking   68
      Host network   69
      Bridged network   70
      Creating a network   71
      Running a container in a network   72
      Creating multi-host networking   76
        Swarm mode   76
        Key-value store overlay networking   78
      Exposing and mapping ports   85
      Linking containers   90
      Networking plugins   93
   Docker volumes   93
      Creating a volume   94
      Removing a volume   100
      Volume drivers   101
   Summary   102

Chapter 5: Finding Images   105

   The Docker Hub   106
      Docker Hub account   108
      Organization account and teams   110
      Collaborators   111
      Private Repositories   112
      Logging into Docker Hub   113
   Searching for images   116
      Image naming and tags   116
      Searching through the web interface   118
      Searching using the command line   120
   Docker Hub and docker registry REST API   122
   Summary   127

Chapter 6: Creating Images   129

   Dockerfile instructions   131
      FROM   132
      MAINTAINER   133
      ADD   133
      COPY   136

CMD	137
ENTRYPOINT	140
LABEL	143
EXPOSE	146
RUN	147
USER	150
VOLUME	151
WORKDIR	152
ARG	152
ONBUILD	153
STOPSIGNAL	154
HEALTHCHECK	155
SHELL	156
Using Dockerfiles	157
Summary	160
Chapter 7: Running Containers	163
Runtime modes – detached and foreground	165
Detached	165
Foreground	166
Identifying images and containers	167
PID settings	168
UTS settings	169
Overriding default commands from Dockerfile	170
Overriding the CMD	170
Overriding the ENTRYPOINT	171
Executing arbitrary commands with exec	172
Monitoring containers	173
Viewing logs	174
Container events	176
Inspecting a container	177
Statistics	179
Container exit codes and restart policies	180
no	182
always	182
on-failure	182
unless-stopped	183
Updating a restart policy on a running container	184
Runtime constraints on resources	186
Memory	186

Processors   188
Updating constraints on a running container   190
Docker Swarm mode   192
The purpose   192
Terminology   192
Swarm mode commands   193
Summary   196

Chapter 8: Publishing Images   197

Publishing images   197
Tagging   198
Untagging the image   198
Pushing the image   199
Webhooks and automated builds   200
Setting up the automated build   200
Build Triggers   206
Webhooks and continuous deployments   208
Summary   215

Chapter 9: Using Docker in Development   217

Using Docker with Maven   218
Spotify's Maven Docker plugin   219
fabric8io Maven Docker plugin   220
Spring Boot application in Docker container   225
Packaging Angular.js application   234
Summary   242

Appendix A: More Resources   243

Official documentation   243
Awesome Docker   244
Training   245

Index   247

Preface

Docker has got a lot of attention in the last few years. Today it has thousands of community contributors, countless numbers of containers downloads, and more and more third party projects using it. It seems that its acclaim will grow even more in the next few years. In this book, we will try to explain this extraordinary popularity and show how you can benefit from faster and simpler application development, testing, and deployment. We will learn Docker from a developer's perspective mostly and focus on creating, running, and publishing Docker images, rather than managing and clustering them. We will begin with the basic ideas and advantages which Docker brings to the developer's tool set.

What this book covers

Chapter 1, *Introduction to Docker*, briefly describes what Docker is and how it can be useful in modern software development and deployment. We will point out what advantages come with the tool and why it is helpful. This chapter will also demonstrate how the containers containing code, runtime, system tools, and libraries can speed up the development and deployment, at the same time making it a more enjoyable experience.

Chapter 2, *Installing Docker*, contains the brief description of the available tools, such as Docker CLI or Kinematic (Docker GUI). Next, we will go straight to the action--installing the tools. The chapter will give precise and practical instructions on how to install the Docker Toolbox on Mac, Linux, and Windows. The chapter will also describe the process of installing Docker in the cloud, such as Amazon AWS.

Chapter 3, *Understanding Images and Containers*, talks about the Docker's architecture. We will explain the terminology related to working with it. After reading this chapter you will understand the concepts and architecture behind Docker; it is a must when going through the next chapters.

Chapter 4, *Networking and Persistent Storage*, describes the Dockers networking and storage concepts. The chapter will introduce the reader to containers networking and present different kind of containers (open, closed, bridged and joined). The reader will also get familiar with the idea of volumes and their types. Additionally, the reader will learn how to manage, mount, and share Docker volumes.

Chapter 5, *Finding Images*, describes the process of identifying software, finding and installing it with the Docker Hub, and the alternative sources. After reading this chapter, the reader will be able to find a specified image in the Docker repository and then install it.

Chapter 6, *Creating Images*, tells the reader how to write a Dockerfile, how to build an image from it, and get familiar with the image build process. The chapter will contain the best practices for writing Dockerfiles and useful tips and tricks for dealing with the images.

Chapter 7, *Running Containers*, tells us how to run programs within containers. The chapter will describe the concept of starting, stopping, restarting, listing, and viewing the container output. The reader will run multiple programs in a container and get familiar with injecting the configuration into the container. We will also describe the container life cycle and the cleanup process.

Chapter 8, *Publishing Images*, familiarizes us with the process of packaging software for distribution. After reading this chapter, the reader will be able to create a Docker Hub account & repository. Then, he will push his image up to it so other people with Docker Engine can run it. The chapter will also describe the process of private software distribution. At the end of the chapter, the reader will pull his own image from the repository to test the process.

Chapter 9, *Using Docker in Development*, discusses how to incorporate building Docker images into the Maven build process. To do that, we will utilize docker-maven plugins. We will also package a Java web application running on Spring Boot embedded server. To demonstrate the process of packaging a static web application into Docker container we will also run angular.js application with node.js backend from inside the Docker container.

Appendix A, *More resources*, directs you to some more useful resources for further reading, such as forums, blogs, and websites related to Docker. The chapter will also mention some useful third party tools related to Docker and show how they can be useful when working with Docker.

What you need for this book

You will need a Mac or PC, running OS X, MS Windows or Linux to be able to setup and run Docker. You can download Docker for free. You can read how to get and install it in Chapter 2, *Installing Docker*.

Who this book is for

This book is aimed at being a fast-paced and practical guide to get you up and running with Docker. It targets developers, IT professionals, DevOps, or anyone looking to quickly develop and deploy software to production at scale. If you are interested in Docker, DevOps, or containers in general, don't look any further.

You will start with installing Docker and start working with images and containers. We will present different types of containers, their applications and show how to find and build images. This will allow you to familiarize with the image building process and you will be able to successfully run your programs within containers. By finishing this book, you will be well equipped in deploying your applications using Docker and will have a clear understanding of concepts, techniques, and practical methods to get it running in production systems.

Conventions

In this book, you will find a number of text styles that distinguish between different kinds of information. Here are some examples of these styles and an explanation of their meaning.

Code words in text, database table names, folder names, filenames, file extensions, pathnames, dummy URLs, user input, and Twitter handles are shown as follows: "Mount the downloaded WebStorm-10*.dmg disk image file as another disk in your system."

A block of code is set as follows:

```
html, body, #map {
  height: 100%;
  margin: 0;
  padding: 0
}
```

Any command-line input or output is written as follows:

```
$ mkdir css
$ cd css
```

New terms and **important words** are shown in bold. Words that you see on the screen, for example, in menus or dialog boxes, appear in the text like this: "The shortcuts in this book are based on the Mac OS X 10.5+ scheme."

Warnings or important notes appear in a box like this.

Tips and tricks appear like this.

Reader feedback

Feedback from our readers is always welcome. Let us know what you think about this book--what you liked or disliked. Reader feedback is important for us as it helps us develop titles that you will really get the most out of. To send us general feedback, simply e-mail feedback@packtpub.com, and mention the book's title in the subject of your message. If there is a topic that you have expertise in and you are interested in either writing or contributing to a book, see our author guide at www.packtpub.com/authors.

Customer support

Now that you are the proud owner of a Packt book, we have a number of things to help you to get the most from your purchase.

Errata

Although we have taken every care to ensure the accuracy of our content, mistakes do happen. If you find a mistake in one of our books-maybe a mistake in the text or the code-we would be grateful if you could report this to us. By doing so, you can save other readers from frustration and help us improve subsequent versions of this book. If you find any errata, please report them by visiting http://www.packtpub.com/submit-errata, selecting your book, clicking on the **Errata Submission Form** link, and entering the details of your errata. Once your errata are verified, your submission will be accepted and the errata will be uploaded to our website or added to any list of existing errata under the Errata section of that title.

To view the previously submitted errata, go to https://www.packtpub.com/books/content/support and enter the name of the book in the search field. The required information will appear under the **Errata** section.

Piracy

Piracy of copyrighted material on the Internet is an ongoing problem across all media. At Packt, we take the protection of our copyright and licenses very seriously. If you come across any illegal copies of our works in any form on the Internet, please provide us with the location address or website name immediately so that we can pursue a remedy.

Please contact us at copyright@packtpub.com with a link to the suspected pirated material.

We appreciate your help in protecting our authors and our ability to bring you valuable content.

Questions

If you have a problem with any aspect of this book, you can contact us at questions@packtpub.com, and we will do our best to address the problem.

1
Introduction to Docker

At the beginning, Docker was created as an internal tool by a Platform as a Service company called **dotCloud.** Later on, in March 2013, it was released as open source. Apart from the Docker Inc. team, which is the main sponsor, there are some other big names contributing to the tool—Red Hat, IBM, Microsoft, Google, and Cisco Systems, just to name a few. Software development today needs to be agile and react quickly to changes. We use methodologies such as Scrum, estimate our work in story points, and attend the daily stand-ups. But what about preparing our software for shipment and the deployment? Let's see how Docker fits into that scenario and can help us to be agile.

In this chapter, we will cover the following topics:

- The basic idea behind Docker
- A difference between virtualization and containerization
- Benefits of using Docker
- Components available to install

We will begin with the basic idea behind this wonderful tool.

The basic idea

The basic idea behind Docker is to pack an application with all of its dependencies (let it be binaries, libraries, configuration files, scripts, jars, and so on) into a single, standardized unit for software development and deployment. Docker containers wrap up a piece of software in a complete filesystem that contains everything it needs to run: code, runtime, system tools, and system libraries-anything you can install on a server. This guarantees that it will always run in the same way, no matter what environment it will be deployed in. With Docker, you can build a Node.js or Java project (but you are of course not limited to those two) without having to install Node.js or Java on your host machine. Once you're done with it, you can just destroy the Docker image, and it's as though nothing ever happened. It's not a programming language or a framework; rather, think of it as a tool that helps solve common problems such as installing, distributing, and managing the software. It allows programmers and DevOps to build, ship, and run their code anywhere.

You may think that Docker is a virtualization engine, but it's far from it as we will explain in a while.

Containerization versus virtualization

To fully understand what Docker really is, first we need to understand the difference between traditional virtualization and containerization. Let's compare those two technologies now.

Traditional virtualization

A traditional virtual machine, which represents the hardware-level virtualization, is basically a complete operating system running on top of the host operating system. There are two types of virtualization hypervisor: **Type 1** and **Type 2**. Type 1 hypervisors provide server virtualization on bare metal hardware—there is no traditional end user's operating system. Type 2 hypervisors, on the other hand, are commonly used as a desktop virtualization—you run the virtualization engine on top of your own operating system. There are a lot of use cases that would take advantage of using virtualization—the biggest asset is that you can run many virtual machines with totally different operating systems on a single host.

Virtual machines are fully isolated, hence very secure. But nothing comes without a price. There are many drawbacks—they contain all the features that an operating system needs to have: device drivers, core system libraries, and so on. They are heavyweight, usually resource-hungry, and not so easy to set up—virtual machines require full installation. They require more computing resources to execute. To successfully run an application on a virtual machine, the hypervisor needs to first import the virtual machine and then power it up, and this takes time. Furthermore, their performance gets substantially degraded. As a result, only a few virtual machines can be provisioned and made available to work on a single machine.

Containerization

The Docker software runs in an isolated environment called a **Docker container**. A Docker container is not a virtual machine in the popular sense. It represents operating system virtualization. While each virtual machine image runs on an independent guest OS, the Docker images run within the same operating system kernel. A container has its own filesystem and environment variables. It's self-sufficient. Because of the containers run within the same kernel, they utilize fewer system resources. The base container can be, and usually is, very lightweight. It's worth knowing that Docker containers are isolated not only from the underlying operating system, but from each other as well. There is no overhead related to a classic virtualization hypervisor and a guest operating system. This allows achieving almost bare metal, near native performance. The boot time of a **dockerized** application is usually very fast due to the low overhead of containers. It is also possible to speed up the roll-out of hundreds of application containers in seconds and to reduce the time taken provisioning your software.

the traditional virtualization engines. Be aware that containers cannot substitute virtual machines for all use cases. A thoughtful evaluation is still required to determine what is best for your application. Both solutions have their advantages. On one hand we have the fully isolated, secure virtual machine with average performance and on the other hand, we have the containers that are missing some of the key features (such as total isolation), but are equipped with high performance that can be provisioned swiftly. Let's see what other benefits you will get when using Docker containerization.

As you can see, Docker is quite different from the traditional virtualization engines. Be aware that containers are not substitutes for virtual machines for all use cases. A thoughtful evaluation is still required to determine what is best for your application. Both solutions have their advantages. On one hand we have the fully isolated, secure virtual machine with average performance, and on the other hand, we have containers that are missing some of the key features (such as total isolation), but are equipped with high performance and can be provisioned swiftly.

Let's see what other benefits you will get when using Docker containerization.

Benefits of using Docker

When comparing the Docker containers with traditional virtual machines, we have mentioned some of its advantages. Let's summarize them now in more detail and add some more.

Speed and size

As we have said before, the first visible benefit of using Docker will be very satisfactory performance and short provisioning time. You can create or destroy containers quickly and easily. Docker shares only the Kernel, nothing less, nothing more. However, it reuses the image layers on which the specific image is built upon. Because of that, multiple versions of an application running in containers will be very lightweight. The result is faster deployment, easier migration, and nimble boot times.

Reproducible and portable builds

Using Docker enables you to deploy ready-to-run software, which is portable and extremely easy to distribute (we will cover the process of creating an image in `Chapter 6`, *Building Images*). Your containerized application simply runs within its container: there's no need for traditional installation. The key advantage of a Docker image is that it is bundled with all the dependencies the containerized application needs to run. The lack of installation of dependencies has a huge advantage. This eliminates problems such as software and library conflicts or even driver compatibility issues. Because of Docker's reproducible build environment, it's particularly well suited for testing, especially in your continuous integration flow. You can quickly boot up identical environments to run the tests. And because the container images are identical each time, you can distribute the workload and run tests in parallel without a problem. Developers can run the same image on their machine that will be run in production later, which again has a huge advantage in testing. The use of Docker containers speeds up continuous integration. There are no more endless build-test-deploy cycles. Docker containers ensure that applications run identically in development, test, and production environments.

One of Docker's greatest features is the portability. Docker containers are portable – they can be run from anywhere: your local machine, a nearby or distant server, and private or public cloud. When speaking about the cloud, all major cloud computing providers, such as Amazon Web Services and Google's Compute Platform have perceived Docker's availability and now support it. Docker containers can be run inside an Amazon EC2 instance or a Google Compute Engine instance, provided that the host operating system supports Docker. A container running on an Amazon EC2 instance can easily be transferred to some other environment, achieving the same consistency and functionality. Docker works very well with various other **IaaS** (**Infrastructure-as-a-Service**) providers such as Microsoft's Azure, IBM SoftLayer, or OpenStack. This additional level of abstraction from your infrastructure layer is an indispensable feature. You can just develop your software without worrying about the platform it will be run later on. It's truly a *write once run everywhere* solution.

Immutable and agile infrastructure

Maintaining a truly idempotent configuration management code base can be tricky and a time-consuming process. The code grows over time and becomes more and more troublesome. That's why the idea of an immutable infrastructure is becoming more and more popular nowadays. Containerization comes to the rescue. By using containers during the process of development and deployment of your applications, you can simplify the process. Having a lightweight Docker server that needs almost no configuration management, you manage your applications simply by deploying and redeploying containers to the server. And again, because the containers are very lightweight, it takes only seconds of your time.

As a starting point, you can download a prebuilt Docker image from the Docker Hub, which is like a repository of ready-to-use images. There are many choices of web servers, runtime platforms, databases, messaging servers, and so on. It's like a real gold mine of software you can use for free to get a base foundation for your own project. We will cover the Docker Hub and looking for images in Chapter 5, *Finding Images*.

The effect of the immutability of Docker's images is the result of the way they are created. Docker makes use of a special file called a Dockerfile. This file contains all the setup instructions on how to create an image, such as must-have components, libraries, exposed shared directories, network configuration, and so on. An image can be very basic, containing nothing but the operating system foundations, or—something that is more common—containing a whole prebuilt technology stack that is ready to launch. You can create images by hand, but it can be an automated process as well.

Docker creates images in a layered fashion: every feature you include will be added as another layer in the base image. This is another serious speed boost compared to the traditional virtualization techniques.

We will get into the details of creating images later, in Chapter 6, *Creating Images*.

Tools and APIs

Of course, Docker is not just a Dockerfile processor and runtime engine. It's a complete package with a wide selection of tools and APIs that are helpful during the developer's and DevOp's daily work. First of all, there's The Docker Toolbox, which is an installer to quickly and easily install and setup a Docker environment on your own machine. The Kinematic is desktop developer environment for using Docker on Windows and Mac OS X. Docker distribution also contains a whole bunch of command-line tools that we will be using through out the book. Let's look at them now.

Tools overview

On Windows, depending on the Windows version you use, there are two choices. It can be either Docker for Windows if you are on Windows 10 or later, or Docker Toolbox for all earlier versions of Windows. The same applies to MacOS. The newest offering is Docker for Mac, which runs as a native Mac application and uses xhyve to virtualize the Docker Engine environment and Linux Kernel. For earlier version of Mac that doesn't meet the Docker for Mac requirements (we are going to list them in Chapter 2, *Installing Docker*) you should pick the Docker Toolbox for Mac. The idea behind Docker Toolbox and Docker native applications are the same—to virtualize the Linux kernel and Docker Engine on top of your operating system. For the purpose of this book, we will be using Docker Toolbox, as it is universal; it will run in all Windows and MacOS versions. The installation package for Windows and Mac OS is wrapped in an executable called the Docker Toolbox. The package contains all the tools you need to begin working with Docker. Of course there are tons of additional third-party utilities compatible with Docker, and some of them very useful. We will present some of them briefly in Chapter 9, *Using Docker in Development*. But for now, let's focus on the default toolset. Before we start the installation, let's look at the tools that the installer package contains to better understand what changes will be made to your system.

Docker Engine and Docker Engine client

Docker is a client-server application. It consists of the daemon that does the important job: builds and downloads images, starts and stops containers and so on. It exposes a REST API that specifies interfaces for interacting with the daemon and is being used for remote management. Docker Engine accepts Docker commands from the command line, such as `docker` to run the image, `docker ps` to list running containers, `docker images` to list images, and so on.

The Docker client is a command-line program that is used to manage Docker hosts running Linux containers. It communicates with the Docker server using the REST API wrapper. You will interact with Docker by using the client to send commands to the server.

Docker Engine works only on Linux. If you want run Docker on Windows or Mac OS, or want to provision multiple Docker hosts on a network or in the cloud, you will need Docker Machine.

Docker Machine

Docker Machine is a fairly new command-line tool created by the Docker team to manage the Docker servers you can deploy containers to. It deprecated the old way of installing Docker with the **Boot2Docker** utility. Docker Machine eliminates the need to create virtual machines manually and install Docker before starting Docker containers on them. It handles the provisioning and installation process for you behind the scenes. In other words, it's a quick way to get a new virtual machine provisioned and ready to run Docker containers. This is an indispensable tool when developing **PaaS** (**Platform as a Service**) architecture. Docker Machine not only creates a new VM with the Docker Engine installed in it, but sets up the certificate files for authentication and then configures the Docker client to talk to it. For flexibility purposes, the Docker Machine introduces the concept of drivers. Using drivers, Docker is able to communicate with various virtualization software and cloud providers. In fact, when you install Docker for Windows or Mac OS, the default VirtualBox driver will be used. The following command will be executed behind the scenes:

```
docker-machine create --driver=virtualbox default
```

Another available driver is amazonec2 for Amazon Web Services. It can be used to install Docker on the Amazon's cloud—we will do it later in this chapter. There are a lot of drivers ready to be used, and more are coming all the time. The list of existing official drivers with their documentation is always available at the **Docker Drivers** website: https://docs.docker.com/machine/drivers.

The list contains the following drivers at the moment:

- Amazon Web Services
- Microsoft Azure
- Digital Ocean
- Exoscale
- Google Compute Engine
- Generic
- Microsoft Hyper-V
- OpenStack
- Rackspace
- IBM Softlayer
- Oracle VirtualBox
- VMware vCloud Air
- VMware Fusion
- VMware vSphere

Apart from these, there are also a lot of third-party driver plugins available freely on Internet sites such as GitHub. You can find additional drivers for different cloud providers and virtualization platforms, such as OVH Cloud or Parallels for Mac OS, for example, you are not limited to Amazon's AWS or Oracle's VirtualBox. As you can see, the choice is very broad.

 If you cannot find a specific driver for your cloud provider, try looking for it on the GitHub.

When installing the Docker Toolbox on Windows or Mac OS, Docker Machine will be selected by default. It's mandatory and currently the only way to run Docker on these operating systems. Installing the Docker Machine is not obligatory for Linux—there is no need to virtualize the Linux kernel there. However, if you want to deal with the cloud providers or just want to have common runtime environment portable between Mac OS, Windows, and Linux, you can install Docker Machine for Linux as well. We will describe the process later in this chapter. Docker Machine will be also used behind the scenes when using the graphical tool Kitematic, which we will present in a while.

After the installation process, Docker Machine will be available as a command-line tool: docker-machine.

Kitematic

Kitematic is the software tool you can use to run containers through a plain, yet robust graphical user interface (GUI). In 2015, Docker acquired the Kitematic team, expecting to attract many more developers and hoping to open up the containerization solution to more developers and a wider, more general public.

Kitematic is now included by default when installing Docker Toolbox on Mac OS and MS Windows. You can use it to comfortably search and fetch the images you need from Docker Hub. The tool can also be used to run your own app containers. Using the GUI, you can edit environment variables, map ports, configure volumes, study logs, and have command-line access to the containers. It is worth mentioning that you can seamlessly switch between the Kitematic GUI and command-line interface to run and manage application containers. Kitematic is very convenient, however, if you want to have more control when dealing with the containers or just want to use scripting – the command line will be a better solution. In fact, Kitematic allows you to switch back and forth between the Docker CLI and the GUI. Any changes you make on the command-line interface will be directly reflected in Kitematic. The tool is simple to use, as you will see at the end of this chapter, when we are going to test our setup on Mac or Windows PC. For the rest of the book, we will be using the command-line interface for working with Docker.

Docker compose

Compose is a tool, executed from the command line as `docker-compose`. It replaces the old *fig* utility. It's used to define and run multicontainer Docker applications. Although it's very easy to imagine a multi-container application (such as a web server in one container and a database in the other), it's not mandatory. So if you decide that your application will fit in a single Docker container, there will be no use for `docker-compose`. In real life, it's very likely that your application will span into multiple containers. With `docker-compose`, you use a compose file to configure your application's services, so they can be run together in an isolated environment. Then, using a single command, you create and start all the services from your configuration. When it comes to multicontainer applications, `docker-compose` is great for development and testing, as well as continuous integration workflows.

We will use `docker-compose` to create `multicontainer` applications in `Chapter 6`, *Creating Images*, later in this book.

Oracle VirtualBox

Oracle VM VirtualBox is a free and open source hypervisor for x86 computers from Oracle. It will be installed by default when installing the Docker Toolbox. It supports the creation and management of virtual machines running Windows, Linux, BSD, OS/2, Solaris, and so on. In our case, the Docker Machine using VirtualBox driver, will use VirtualBox to create and boot a bitsy Linux distribution capable of the running `docker-engine`. It's worth mentioning that you can also run the teensy-weensy virtualized Linux straight from the VirtualBox itself.

Every Docker Machine you have created using the `docker-machine` or `Kitematic`,will be visible and available to boot in the VirtualBox, when you run it directly, as shown in the following screenshot:

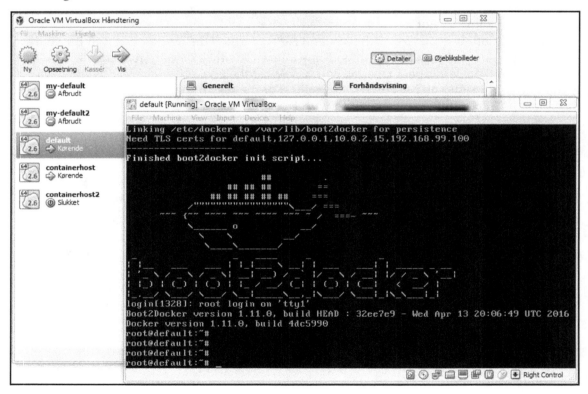

You can start, stop, reset, change settings, and read logs in the same way as for other virtualized operating systems.

You can use VirtualBox in Windows or Mac for other purposes than Docker.

Git

Git is a distributed version control system that is widely used for software development and other version control tasks. It has emphasis on speed, data integrity, and support for distributed, non-linear workflows. Docker Machine and Docker client follows the pull/push model of Git for fetching the needed dependencies from the network. For example, if you decide to run the Docker image that is not present on your local machine, Docker will fetch this image from Docker Hub. Docker doesn't internally use Git for any kind of resource versioning. It does, however, rely on hashing to uniquely identify the filesystem layers, which is very similar to what Git does. Docker also takes initial inspiration in the notion of commits, pushes, and pulls. Git is also included in the Docker Toolbox installation package.

From a developer's perspective, there are tools especially useful in a programmer's daily job, be it IntelliJ IDEA Docker Integration Plugin for Java fans or Visual Studio 2015 Tools for Docker for those who prefer C#. They let you download and build Docker images, create and start containers, and carry out other related tasks straight from your favorite IDE. We will cover them in more detail in the next chapters.

Apart from the tools included in the Docker's distribution package (it will be Docker Toolbox for older versions of Windows or Docker for Windows and Docker for Mac), there are hundreds of third-party tools, such as Kubernetes and Helios (for Docker orchestration), Prometheus (for monitoring of statistics), or Swarm and Shipyard for managing clusters. As Docker captures higher attention, more and more Dockerrelated tools pop up almost every week. We will try to briefly cover the most interesting ones in Chapter 9, *Using Docker in Development*, and more resources.

But these are not the only tools available for you. Additionally, Docker provides a set of APIs that can be very handy. One of them is the Remote API for the management of the images and containers. Using this API, you will be able to distribute your images to the runtime Docker engine. The container can be shifted to a different machine that runs Docker, and executed there without compatibility concerns. This may be especially useful when creating PaaS (Platform-as-a-Service) architectures. There's also the Stats API that will expose live resource usage information (such as CPU, memory, network I/O, and block I/O) for your containers. This API endpoint can be used to create tools that show how your containers behave, for example, on a production system.

Summary

By now, we understand the difference between the virtualization and containerization and also, I hope, we can see the advantages of using the latter. We also know what components are available for us to install and use. Let's begin our journey to the world of containers and go straight to the action by installing the software.

2
Installing Docker

In this chapter, we will find out how to install Docker on Windows, Mac OS, and Linux operating systems. There will also be step-by-step instructions on how to set up Docker in the cloud and Amazon EC2 will be used as an example. Next, we will run the sample `hello-world` image to verify the setup and check whether everything works fine after the installation process. We are going to cover the following topics in this chapter:

- Hardware requirements for running Docker
- Installing on Windows
- Installing on Mac OS
- Installing on Linux
- Installing on the Amazon AWS cloud

Docker installation is quite straightforward, but there are some things you will need to focus on to make it run. We will point them out to make the installation process painless.

 It's worth mentioning that Linux is the natural environment for Docker. The Docker engine is built on top of the Linux kernel. To make it run on Windows or Mac OS, the Linux kernel needs to be virtualized.

The Docker Engine could be run on the Mac and MS Windows operating systems by using the lightweight Linux distribution, made specifically to run Docker containers. It runs completely from RAM, weighs just several dozens of megabytes, and boots in a couple of seconds. During the installation of the main Docker package—the Docker Toolbox—the virtualization engine VirtualBox will also be installed by default. Therefore, there are some special hardware requirements for your machine.

Hardware requirements

To use Docker, you will need some reasonably new machine, that supports hardware-level virtualization: VT-x for Intel-based PCs and AMD-V for AMD processors. Most of the Mac machines support it out of the box, but for PC you will need to make sure it's turned on and perhaps enable it in the BIOS settings. It will be different for different BIOS, just look for VT-x / AMD-V switch.

In Windows 8, you can check virtualization support in the task manager in the **Performance** tab:

Virtualization:	Enabled
L1 cache:	256 KB
L2 cache:	2.0 MB

If you want to check whether your PC supports the hardware level virtualization in Windows 7, look for **Microsoft Hardware-Assisted Virtualization Detection Tool**. Its free, tiny utility is used to check whether your system supports virtualization. Download and run it to see the report:

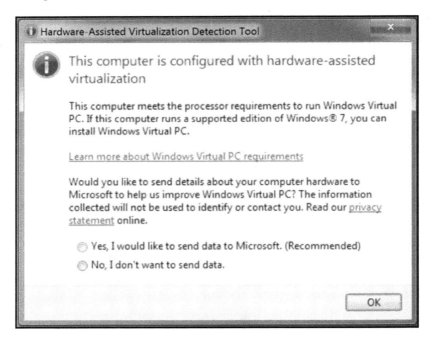

If the report is different for you, saying that hardware-assisted virtualization is not enabled, you will need to check the BIOS settings on your machine, maybe the hardware-assisted virtualization support is just switched off. In such a case, switch it on and re-run the tool.

If your PC doesn't support hardware-assisted virtualization and you decide to install Docker anyway, it will result in an error during the start of the virtualized Linux distribution.

Additionally, when installing on Windows PC, you need to make sure your Windows OS is 64-bit (x64). Docker will not run on the 32-bit system by default.

We already know from `Chapter 1`, *Introduction to Docker*, which Docker components are available to install in the default installation package.

Knowing the hardware requirements, let's download it and install the software.

Installing on Windows

Docker up-to-date installation guides are always available on the `https://www.docker.com/` website. Head to the *Get started with Docker* section and pick the installation guide according to your operating system: Windows, Mac OS, or Linux.

As it was already mentioned in the previous chapter, you have two options for installing Docker on Windows, it will be the Docker Toolbox, running on almost all versions of Windows or Docker For Windows, which will run only on Windows 10 or later. Also, even if you are running Windows 10, there are some additional requirements: it must be a 64-bit Windows 10 Pro, Enterprise and Education (1511 November update, Build 10586 or later). With native versions of Docker installation packages (either Docker for Windows or Docker for Mac), you can go with the stable channel, which is fully tested and reliable or the beta channel, and contains some experimental features that the Docker team currently works on, but can be a little unstable and buggy. I recommend to pick the stable channel. The installation package is just a single `installDocker.msi` package. Just run it—it's rather a no-questions-asked type of installation. However, take note that you will need to have administrative rights on your Windows machine.

After the installation ends, you will be notified about its completion and asked to run Docker, as you can see in the following screenshot:

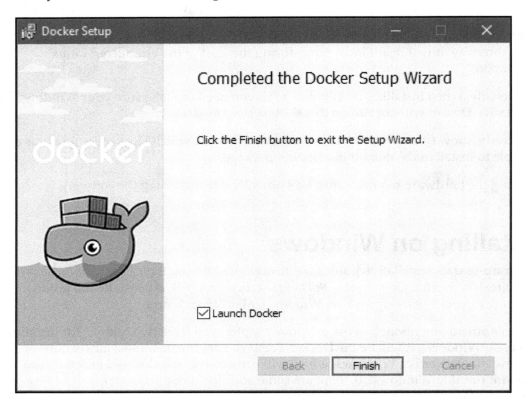

You can run Docker now, or later, from your Windows menu. If you run it, after a while you should see the animated Docker icon in tray, saying that Docker is starting. If so, you should see a popup message saying it's ready to work with:

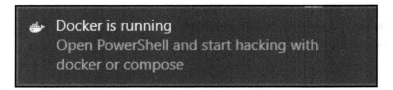

From now on, you can interact with the Docker Engine using the whale icon in the tray area. You should be advised that the Kitematic tool we described in `Chapter 1`, *Introduction to Docker*, is no longer part of Docker for Windows installation package (as it is with the Docker Toolbox). However, Kitematic is compatible with Docker for Windows and can also be used. You can download it separately and unpack it into `C:\Program Files\Docker\Kitematic`.

The setup of the Docker Toolbox is a little bit different. The Toolbox packages for Windows and Mac OS are available at `https://www.docker.com/products/docker-toolbox`.

After downloading the **Docker Toolbox** package, run it. The first screen will ask you permission to provide anonymous usage statistics to help Docker developers improve their software. It's up to you whether you allow it or not depending on your privacy concerns. The next screen presents the components available for installation:

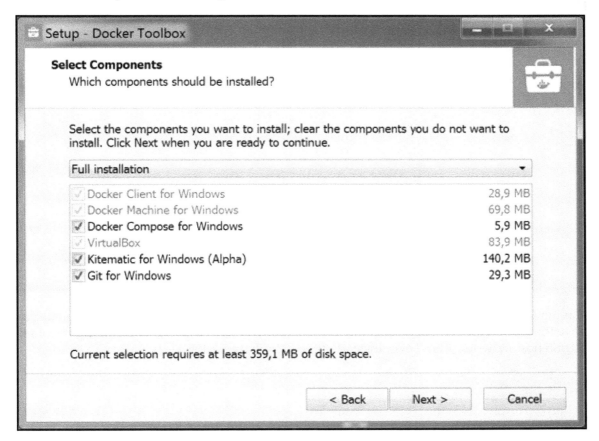

Docker Client for Windows and **Docker Machine for Windows** are mandatory—you will be able to do nothing without them. For the initial setup, it's better to leave all of the options checked. The Kitematic tool is in the alpha version at the time of writing , but don't worry, it behaves just fine. The last installation screen will ask if you would like to add Docker's binaries to path or create the desktop shortcuts, as shown in the following screenshot:

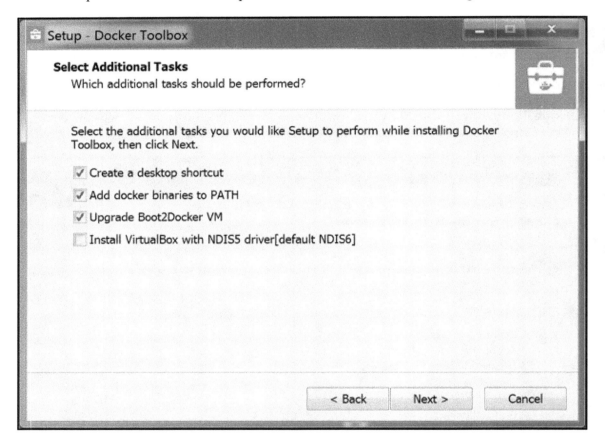

Having Docker command-line tools on path will be very handy in the future, so it's better to have this option marked. It's worth mentioning that you have a choice of installing the older NDIS5 host network filter driver instead of the default one, NDIS6.

If you happen to use an older version of Windows, older than Windows Vista, this may help with some problems such as slowdown or network issues. If you choose NDIS6 and notice problems later, just execute the installer again and then pick NDIS5 instead.

After the installation, run the Kitematic tool we described earlier. It will present the progress window while starting the Docker Linux VM. After a successful start, Kitematic will ask you for your Docker Hub credentials. You may log into **Docker Hub** now, create the Docker Hub account, or skip this process at this time. It's not mandatory for searching and running images. We will use it to create the account and will be using Docker Hub heavily in Chapter 5, *Finding Images*.

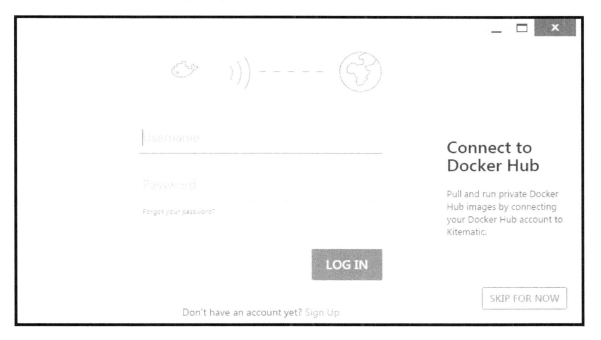

No matter whether you decide to do or skip the login process, you will be presented with the main window of Kitematic. Let's discuss it briefly. On the lef-thand side, there is a list of containers available to run-empty if you are runing Kitematic for the first time. Let's find a simple image to run. Just start typing `hello-world` in the search box to list Docker Hub images containing such a phrase in the name. Experiment with different searches to see what's available in the Hub. You can download and run databases such as MySQL or Mongo, web servers such as nginx, and many, many more, all in a couple of mouse clicks! And best of all no, dependencies are required to be installed on your machine. For example, you don't even need to have Java installed on your machine to be able to run Jboss or Tomcat. This is the magic of containerization and this is just the beginning.

One of the images from the official repository is the famous **hello-world** image. Click on **CREATE** next to it:

Now the magic happens. Docker will fetch the selected image from the Hub and execute it. From now on, you can use Kitematic to start, stop, restart, and configure your container:

As you can see in the **Container** logs section, a lot has happened behind the scenes just to print the Hello from Docker message. But of course, it's not the usual message. It comes from containerized software and makes a huge difference compared to the standard hello world programs. First, it checks whether the Docker daemon is running on your system and connects to it if so. Next, it looks if the hello-world image is present on your local systems. If not—and it will be in your case when running for the first time—it fetches the image from the Docker Hub. Docker runs the image and streams its output back to you to see.

Let's do the same from the Docker CLI. Click on the **Docker CLI** icon in Kitematic to execute the Windows PowerShell command prompt. You should not worry about the command-line syntax at the moment—we will explain it in the next chapters. Also, we will be using command-line tools throughout the book, so you will easily get familiar with the syntax.

At first, let's verify if the virtualized Linux machine is working properly, by executing the command:

```
docker-machine ls
```

`ls` stands for list command and lists the virtual machines configured on your Windows. The currently running machine will have a star in the `ACTIVE` column and the status `Running` in the `STATUS` column:

Next, execute the following command to run the image:

```
docker run hello-world
```

This will give you the same output as in Kitematic:

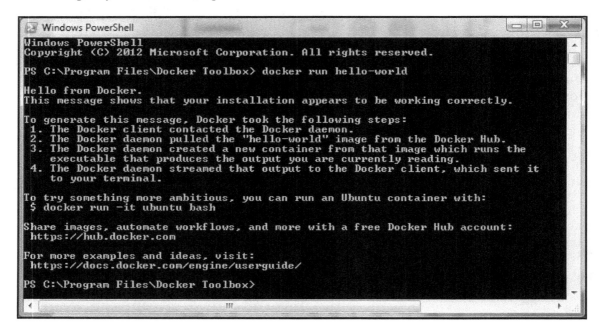

As we have said before, Docker CLI and Kitematic are seamlessly connected, and everything you do in the command line will be reflected in Kitematic. You can notice that the image you just have run shows up in the GUI of Kitematic. It's worth noticing that when you create a new Docker container and don't give it a custom name (by passing the -name option with the Docker CLI), Docker generates a name for you:

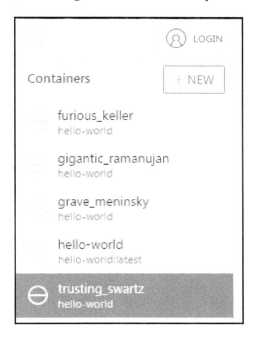

These autogenerated names may be entertaining, but they can also be very useful later, when you will need to distinguish the container by name. It's easier to remember furious_keller than 3955c5396595, isn't it?

Docker will automatically generate a container's name if you forget to do so.

Now we have Docker up and running on Windows, let's explain the installation process on Mac machines.

Installing on Mac OS

Docker installation on Mac OS is very similar to the installation on a Windows PC. Again, you have two options here. If your Mac is from 2010 or later and runs Yosemite or newer Mac OS, you can pick the Docker for Mac installation. Again, the same as with native Docker for Windows, you can select the stable or beta channel. Unless you want to experience the excitement of new features and bugs available in Beta, you should pick the Stable version. Docker for Mac is a native application, you just copy it to your /Applications folder, just like any other Mac application, as can be seen in the following screenshot:

If you run the installed Docker.app, you will see a whale icon in the menu toolbar of your Mac OS:

The same note as for native Docker for Windows applies also for Docker for Mac: Kitematic is no longer part of the installation package. However, it's still compatible with Docker for Mac—you just need to download it separately and put it into the /Applications folder.

If you work on an older Mac or an older Mac OS, you will need the Docker Toolbox. However, you will need at least Mac OS 10.8 *Mountain Lion* to install the Docker Toolbox. The Docker Toolbox package, the same as in Windows, contains all the tools to get you started. It contains Docker Client, Machine, Compose, Kinematic, and VirtualBox. Head straight to the Docker Toolbox website at https://www.docker.com/products/docker-toolbox and download the Mac OS version. Docker Toolbox for Mac is wrapped into a pkg package, so you need to run it, instead of just moving it into the /Applications folder. Similar to the Windows version, you would like to give it permission to report usage statistics to improve the future releases. After the installation, the **Quick Start** page will give you the choice to quickly execute the Terminal or the Kitematic tool:

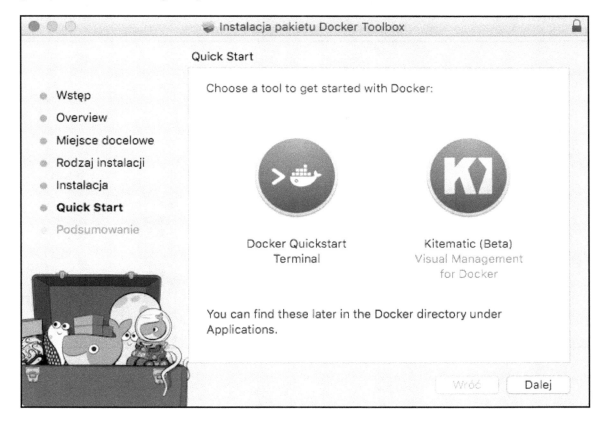

You will also be able to find Docker tools and VirtualBox in the `Applications` folder and **Launchpad** menu later:

To verify the setup, execute **Kitematic**, skip **Docker Hub login** and type `hello-world` in the search field:

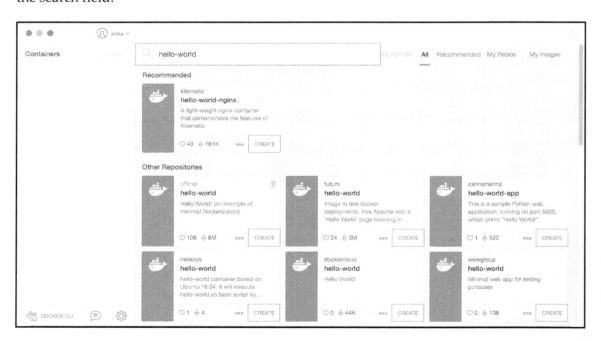

Next, click on the **CREATE** button next to the **hello-world** image. Kitematic (docker-machine to be precise) will download the image from the Docker Hub and present you with the output:

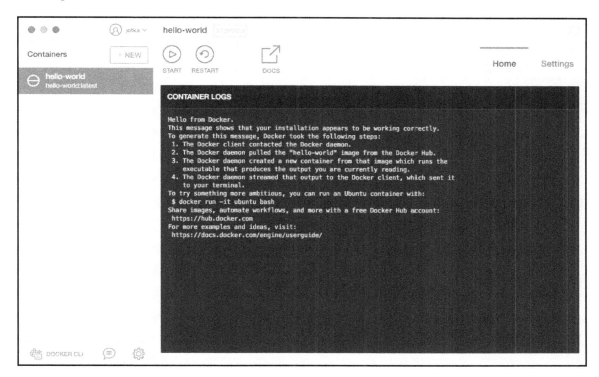

From now on, Docker's command-line tools are also at your disposal. Opening the Terminal from Kitematic will automatically set all the required environment variables and connect you to the default machine. But if you would like to be able to work from your own Terminal session, you may get a message saying that Docker client cannot connect to the Docker daemon. The reason is that the client doesn't know what machine it should control. To attach your client to the specific machine, type the following command in your Terminal session:

```
eval "$(docker-machine env default)"
```

The `eval` command sets environment variables to dictate that `docker` should run a command against a particular machine, which is the `default` machine in our example.

To see the list of Docker-related environment variables, use the `env` command:

```
env | grep DOCKER
```

The output will contain Docker variables, such as machine name, host, and certificate path:

```
DOCKER_TLS_VERIFY=1
DOCKER_HOST=tcp://192.168.99.100:2376
DOCKER_CERT_PATH=/Users/jarek/.docker/machine/machines/default
DOCKER_MACHINE_NAME=default
```

 Always check environment variables when having Docker daemon connection issues.

Another way of testing the setup is the `docker info` command. Execute the following from the command-line shell:

```
docker info
```

The output will contain a lot of useful information about the server's kernel version, memory available, the number of running containers, the name of the machine, and so on.

Let's now type the following command to run the `hello-world` image straight in the Terminal:

```
docker run hello-world
```

If you can see the output from the image, you are all set and have a working Docker set up on your Mac:

```
06:52:22  jarek@MacBook-Pro-Jarek
$ docker run hello-world

Hello from Docker.
This message shows that your installation appears to be working correctly.

To generate this message, Docker took the following steps:
 1. The Docker client contacted the Docker daemon.
 2. The Docker daemon pulled the "hello-world" image from the Docker Hub.
 3. The Docker daemon created a new container from that image which runs the
    executable that produces the output you are currently reading.
 4. The Docker daemon streamed that output to the Docker client, which sent it
    to your terminal.

To try something more ambitious, you can run an Ubuntu container with:
 $ docker run -it ubuntu bash

Share images, automate workflows, and more with a free Docker Hub account:
 https://hub.docker.com

For more examples and ideas, visit:
 https://docs.docker.com/engine/userguide/

06:52:23  jarek@MacBook-Pro-Jarek
```

Installing on Linux

As we have said before, Linux is the natural habitat for Docker. Therefore, there is no need to virtualize the Linux kernel. You can run Docker without VT-x or similar technologies in your processor, since Docker only requires `cgroups` to be available on the kernel to get the majority of its features working. Cgroups (control groups) is a Linux kernel feature that limits, accounts for, and isolates the resource usage (CPU, memory, disk I/O, network, and so on) of a collection of processes. Docker will simply use the kernel of your own operating system. This also makes the installation package smaller—there is no need for a virtualization engine and another virtualized operating system. This is the reason that the installation process is a little bit different from the one on Mac OS or Windows. First, there is no Docker Machine included in the installation—it's simply not mandatory for Linux. Second, there is no fancy GUI installer. You will need to perform most of the tasks from the command line, but this should not be a problem for a Linux user. And last but not least, there is no Kitematic tool available for Linux.

On the Docker website, you can find the installation steps for the specific Linux distribution (this will be the `yum` package manager for Red Hat or `apt-get` for Ubuntu, for example). If you are not willing to use the package manager directly, you can use the installation script provided by the Docker team. In fact, the script will execute the package manager valid for your Linux OS and then install the software using packages. To get the most recent Docker release for Linux, type the following in the shell:

```
$ curl -fsSL https://get.docker.com/ | sh
```

Alternatively, you can install Docker using the `wget` command by executing the following command:

```
$ wget -qO- https://get.docker.com/ | sh
```

The process of downloading the required package will begin and you will observe keys, packages, and their dependencies being downloaded. At the end of the output, the installer will print out the version of the installed Docker client and server:

```
Unpacking docker-engine (1.11.1-0~xenial) ...
Processing triggers for libc-bin (2.23-0ubuntu3) ...
Processing triggers for man-db (2.7.5-1) ...
Processing triggers for ureadahead (0.100.0-19) ...
Processing triggers for systemd (229-4ubuntu5) ...
Setting up aufs-tools (1:3.2+20130722-1.1ubuntu1) ...
Setting up cgroupfs-mount (1.2) ...
Setting up docker-engine (1.11.1-0~xenial) ...
Processing triggers for libc-bin (2.23-0ubuntu3) ...
Processing triggers for systemd (229-4ubuntu5) ...
Processing triggers for ureadahead (0.100.0-19) ...
+ sudo -E sh -c docker version
Client:
 Version:      1.11.1
 API version:  1.23
 Go version:   go1.5.4
 Git commit:   5604cbe
 Built:        Tue Apr 26 23:43:49 2016
 OS/Arch:      linux/amd64

Server:
 Version:      1.11.1
 API version:  1.23
 Go version:   go1.5.4
 Git commit:   5604cbe
 Built:        Tue Apr 26 23:43:49 2016
 OS/Arch:      linux/amd64
```

Installing this way will make the Docker service available to be run from root. It's not always a good idea to run software as a root, so you will probably want to make it runnable also for your user. First, you will need to create the `docker` group:

```
$ sudo groupadd docker
```

Then add your current user to the group (assuming that `yourUsername` is the login name for your user:

```
$ sudo usermod -aG docker yourUsername
```

If you are going to deal with the cloud setup using your Linux, you will want to install the Docker Machine as well. To do this, execute this script:

```
$ curl -L https://github.com/docker/machine/releases/download/
  v0.7.0/docker-machine-`uname -s`-`uname -m` > /usr/local/bin/
  docker-machine
$ chmod +x /usr/local/bin/docker-machine
```

You can also go to the Linux releases page directly and pick your desired version at `https
://github.com/docker/machine/releases/`.

To test the installation, let's print out the Docker service status by executing the script (this is an example for the latest Ubuntu Linux, which I will be using for the rest of the book):

```
$ sudo service docker status
```

If the service responds properly, it will show the running status and also some statistics, lsuch as memory available for the service and some recent log lines:

```
jarek@ubuntu: ~
jarek@ubuntu:~$ sudo service docker status
● docker.service - Docker Application Container Engine
   Loaded: loaded (/lib/systemd/system/docker.service; enabled; vendor preset: enabled)
   Active: active (running) since Mon 2016-05-16 19:00:04 CEST; 2min 25s ago
     Docs: https://docs.docker.com
 Main PID: 822 (docker)
    Tasks: 19 (limit: 512)
   Memory: 69.3M
      CPU: 501ms
   CGroup: /system.slice/docker.service
           ├─822 /usr/bin/docker daemon -H fd://
           └─970 docker-containerd -l /var/run/docker/libcontainerd/docker-containerd.sock --runtime docker-runc

May 16 19:00:03 ubuntu docker[822]: time="2016-05-16T19:00:03.954075716+02:00" level=warning msg="Your kernel does not support swap memory limit."
May 16 19:00:03 ubuntu docker[822]: time="2016-05-16T19:00:03.955732266+02:00" level=info msg="Loading containers: start."
May 16 19:00:03 ubuntu docker[822]: .....
May 16 19:00:03 ubuntu docker[822]: time="2016-05-16T19:00:03.980041988+02:00" level=info msg="Loading containers: done."
May 16 19:00:03 ubuntu docker[822]: time="2016-05-16T19:00:03.980260811+02:00" level=info msg="Daemon has completed initialization"
May 16 19:00:03 ubuntu docker[822]: time="2016-05-16T19:00:03.980464035+02:00" level=info msg="Docker daemon" commit=5604cbe graphdriver=aufs versi
May 16 19:00:04 ubuntu systemd[1]: Started Docker Application Container Engine.
May 16 19:00:04 ubuntu docker[822]: time="2016-05-16T19:00:04.027083522+02:00" level=info msg="API listen on /var/run/docker.sock"
May 16 19:00:48 ubuntu docker[822]: time="2016-05-16T19:00:48.770101021+02:00" level=info msg="No non-localhost DNS nameservers are left in resolv."
May 16 19:00:48 ubuntu docker[822]: time="2016-05-16T19:00:48.770388884+02:00" level=info msg="IPv6 enabled; Adding default IPv6 external servers :
jarek@ubuntu:~$
```

The service seems to be working fine, so the next thing we are going to do will be running the simple hello-world image. This is where the fun begins—if Docker will not be able to find the image on your local machine, it will fetch if from the Docker Hub and then run it. We will talk a lot more about finding images and the Docker Hub later, in `Chapter 5`, *Finding Images*. To execute the sample `hello-world` image, type the following command in your shell after logging out and logging in again:

docker run hello-world

After executing the command, the correct result will be just a `Hello from Docker` message along with some more interesting facts:

```
jarek@ubuntu: ~
jarek@ubuntu:~$ docker run hello-world

Hello from Docker.
This message shows that your installation appears to be working correctly.

To generate this message, Docker took the following steps:
 1. The Docker client contacted the Docker daemon.
 2. The Docker daemon pulled the "hello-world" image from the Docker Hub.
 3. The Docker daemon created a new container from that image which runs the
    executable that produces the output you are currently reading.
 4. The Docker daemon streamed that output to the Docker client, which sent it
    to your terminal.

To try something more ambitious, you can run an Ubuntu container with:
 $ docker run -it ubuntu bash

Share images, automate workflows, and more with a free Docker Hub account:
 https://hub.docker.com

For more examples and ideas, visit:
 https://docs.docker.com/engine/userguide/

jarek@ubuntu:~$
```

This is the same output you will get when running the image using Kitematic for Windows or Mac OS. Docker prints out the steps that it needed to do to run the image. Again, a lot has happened in the background just to print the simple message, but running the sample image is a great way of testing the setup.

Installing on the cloud — AWS

In the next chapters, we will show how to create the Docker instance remotely, using the Docker Machine. This time we will just install Docker and run the sample image on Amazon EC2 cloud manually. If you have a running Linux on the EC2 Cloud, the Docker installation procedure is almost identical as for any Linux system. Let's begin with creating the first Linux instance.

To use the EC2 cloud, you will need to create an account. It's free for basic purposes, so go to `http://aws.amazon.com` and fill out the registration form. Also, the basic `t2.micro` instance is free for you to use and is enough for testing the Docker installation. After creating the account, log into **AWS Console** and select **EC2** from the list of available services:

Next, launch the instance using the **Launch Instance** button:

The next page asks what operating system should be available on your new EC2 instance. For our purposes, **Amazon Linux** will be fine. It's first on the list, select it:

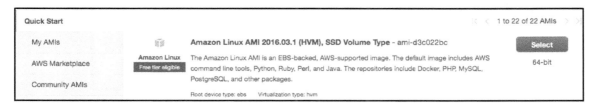

Next, you need to pick the **Instance Type**, which determines what kind of CPU, memory, storage, and network capacity your server will have. Stick with the default option, t2.micro (it's free of charge) and click on gray. Next, click on the **Configure Instance Details** button.

The Amazon EC2 wizard will then present the instance of the configuration page, with the SSH port (22) that is open by default. Depending on your needs, you can add or open more ports, such as HTTP (80) if you plan to run a web application accessible through a web browser:

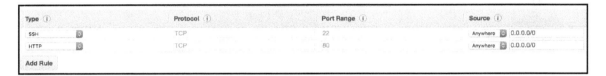

Now comes the important part. To be able to remotely log into your instance, you will need a key pair. It consists of a public and private key file that you must use to connect to your EC2 instance over SSH. Select **Create a new key pair** from the drop-down list, give it a name such as MY_EC2, for example, and click on the **Download Key Pair** button:

If you click on the **Launch Instances** button, the start process begins and the status will be shown:

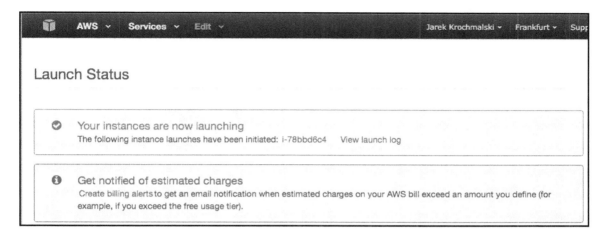

You can also check the status of your AWS instance by picking **Instances** from the **Management Console** menu. It's a handy page, useful to manage all your instances. The status page will list all your cloud machines, their status such as running or stopped, and also their public IP that you can use to log into the instance:

Our newly created instance seems to be running fine, so let's try to log into its shell. Head to the directory you previously saved the keys to that was generated by Amazon, and execute the following commands:

```
chmod 400 MY_EC2.pem.txt
ssh -i MY_EC2.pem.txt ec2-user@52.58.22.247
```

Here, `MY_EC2.pem.txt` is the filename of the generated keys, and `52.58.22.247` is the public IP address of your remote instance—these two will be different for you, of course. After running the SSH login, you will be greeted by Amazon Linux:

```
● ● ●                    1. ec2-user@ip-172-31-28-195:~ (ssh)
 07:12:25   jarek@MacBook-Pro-Jarek    ~/Downloads/keys
 ssh -i MY_EC2.pem.txt ec2-user@52.58.22.247
The authenticity of host '52.58.22.247 (52.58.22.247)' can't be established.
ECDSA key fingerprint is SHA256:bsAlb2HXSQlRB3nlU0SJEIIFqan4GcK9Ca5HtVLDxtg.
Are you sure you want to continue connecting (yes/no)? yes
Warning: Permanently added '52.58.22.247' (ECDSA) to the list of known hosts.

       __|  __|_  )
       _|  (     /    Amazon Linux AMI
      ___|\___|___|

https://aws.amazon.com/amazon-linux-ami/2016.03-release-notes/
9 package(s) needed for security, out of 17 available
Run "sudo yum update" to apply all updates.
[ec2-user@ip-172-31-28-195 ~]$ ▮
```

From now on, the Docker installation process doesn't differ much from any Linux setup. At first, it's good to upgrade the operating system software to ensure the bug fixes are in place. To do this on Amazon Linux, execute the following command:

```
sudo yum update -y
```

Next, install Docker using the `yum` package manager and add your user to the `docker` group:

```
sudo yum install -y docker
sudo usermod -a -G docker ec2-user
```

> After adding your user to the `docker` Linux group, you will need to log out and log in again, to be able to run Docker as a normal, non-root user.

After installing Docker, let's check directly whether it's running or not. We will do it by firing up the `hello-world` image. Execute the following command:

```
docker run hello-world
```

Docker will fetch the image from the Docker Hub and then run it:

```
● ● ●                    1. ec2-user@ip-172-31-28-195:~ (ssh)
[ec2-user@ip-172-31-28-195 ~]$ docker run hello-world
Unable to find image 'hello-world:latest' locally
latest: Pulling from library/hello-world

79112a2b2613: Pull complete
4c4abd6d4278: Pull complete
Digest: sha256:4f32210e234b4ad5cac92efacc0a3d602b02476c754f13d517e1ada048e5a8ba
Status: Downloaded newer image for hello-world:latest

Hello from Docker.
This message shows that your installation appears to be working correctly.

To generate this message, Docker took the following steps:
 1. The Docker client contacted the Docker daemon.
 2. The Docker daemon pulled the "hello-world" image from the Docker Hub.
 3. The Docker daemon created a new container from that image which runs the
    executable that produces the output you are currently reading.
 4. The Docker daemon streamed that output to the Docker client, which sent it
    to your terminal.

To try something more ambitious, you can run an Ubuntu container with:
 $ docker run -it ubuntu bash

Share images, automate workflows, and more with a free Docker Hub account:
 https://hub.docker.com

For more examples and ideas, visit:
 https://docs.docker.com/engine/userguide/

[ec2-user@ip-172-31-28-195 ~]$ 
```

The famous `Hello from Docker` message simply says that now you are successfully running a Docker container in the AWS cloud!

Now we have finished the installation process, and hopefully you were able to run the sample `hello-world` image on the operating system of your choice. Let's dive a little bit deeper into the world of containerization and learn more about containers and images in the next chapter.

Summary

In this chapter, we have covered the process of installing Docker on various operating systems and in the Amazon cloud. By far, you should have your Docker installation verified, up, and running. We also know the tools that are available for us to use and what their purpose is. Let's leave it for now and learn some theory.

In the next chapter, we will dive deeper into Docker's images and containers architecture. It's mandatory to understand some concepts prior to running Docker containers or creating your own images.

3
Understanding Images and Containers

In previous chapter, we learned how to install Docker on Windows, Mac OS, Linux, and Amazon EC2 cloud. So far, you should have Docker running on your machine and should be able to run the hello-world image in a container. In this chapter, we will dive deeper into the world of images and containers. Later, we will also cover image distribution-related terms, such as Docker repository, registry, and index. We are going to cover the following topics in this chapter:

- Images
- Layers
- Containers
- Saving changes to containers
- Docker registry, repository, and index

Note that we will mainly use the shell (or command prompt in Windows) to execute Docker commands. You can always execute `docker help` to get a description of the available commands. Executing `docker help` with the name of specific command `docker help pull`, for example, will display information about this command with a brief description of the available options:

```
1. jarek@MBP-Jarek: ~ (zsh)
~ (zsh)        ⌘1    ✕    docker (docker)    ⌘2

07:29:38    jarek@MBP-Jarek    ~
$ docker help pull

Usage:  docker pull [OPTIONS] NAME[:TAG|@DIGEST]

Pull an image or a repository from a registry

  -a, --all-tags                 Download all tagged images in the repository
  --disable-content-trust=true   Skip image verification
  --help                         Print usage

07:29:42    jarek@MBP-Jarek    ~
$
```

Let's start by explaining in detail what images, layers, and containers are.

Images

You can think of an image as a read-only template, which is the base foundation to run a container on. It's like a template that contains everything your application needs to operate. It can be Ubuntu Linux with a web server and your web application installed. Every image starts from a base image, for example, Ubuntu, a base Linux image. You can create images yourself – images are created using a series of commands (called **instructions),** described in the Dockerfile. It is an ordered collection of **layers** - root filesystem changes stacked on top of one another. These changes can be running a command, adding a file or directory, creating environmental variables, and so on. Docker uses a filesystem called **AUFS,** which stands for **Augmented File System**. Pretty much every line of a Docker file (with some exceptions, which we are going to explain later) will create a new image and when you stack or augment them all on top of each other, you'll get your final Docker image. This is essentially a way of caching. For example, if you change only one line of your Docker file, Docker will not rebuild the entire image set. The Docker file will be sequentially when you start the process of building of an image. Docker will execute the instructions one by one, and return a final image. Each instruction creates a new layer in the image. We will cover the process in `Chapter 6`, *Creating Images*.

Docker images are highly portable across hosts – an image can be run in a Docker container on any host that runs Docker. It's important to know that Docker uses an image to run your code, not the Dockerfile. The Dockerfile is used to create the image when you run the `build` command – we will also get back to it in `Chapter 6`, *Creating* Images. Also, if you publish your image to the Docker Hub, you publish a resulting image, not a source Dockerfile. We will describe the process later in this book, in `Chapter 8`, *Publishing Images*.

The local images you have on your machine can be listed by running the `docker images` command:

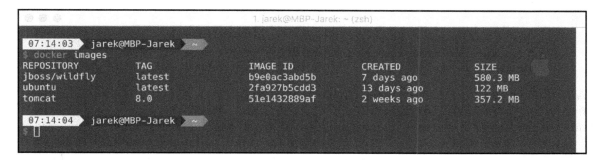

The images command will display a table with the following columns:

- `REPOSITORY` : This is the name of the repository. We will explain it in detail at the end of this chapter.
- `TAG` : It's similar to Git or other version control systems tag. It represents a specific set point in the repositories' commit history. You can have multiple tags when building the image. There's even a special tag called latest, which represents the latest version. The full form of a tag is `[REGISTRYHOST/][USERNAME/]NAME[:TAG]`, but the TAG column is just the `[:TAG]` part of the full tag. We will cover tagging in detail later in `Chapter 6`, *Creating Images*.
- `IMAGE ID` : This is the identifier for the image (actually it's the first 12 characters of the true identifier for an image). You may use it to refer to a specific image when executing image commands, but you can also use the image's name.
- `CREATED` : The date represents the time the repository was created. You can use it to verify how fresh the build of the image is.
- `SIZE` : This is the size of the image.

To remove all the images you have on your system, execute the following command:

```
docker rmi $(docker images -q)
```

Whenever you assign a tag that is already in use to a new image (for example, by building the image `myImage`, making a change in its Dockerfile, and then building `myImage` again), the old image will lose that tag but will still stay around, even if all of its tags are deleted. These older versions of your images are the untagged entries in the output of Docker images, and you can safely delete them with the following command:

```
$ docker rmi <IMAGE HASH>
```

To remove all un-tagged docker images, use the list of images and a filter:

```
$ docker rmi $(docker images -q -f
dangling=true)
```

Alternatively to creating your image from scratch, you can pick already prepared images from a hundreds available on the Internet. Also, you can publish an image in your private hub, so other people in your organization can pull it and reuse. We will cover the process of looking for images in `Chapter 5`, *Finding Images*. The downloaded images can be updated and extended freely, so downloading base image is a great way to get a serious speed boost when developing one by yourself. It's very common practice to download ready-to-run images, such as a webserver or database, for example, and build on top of it. You can have, for example, a base Apache image. You could use this as the base of all your web application images. This is possible due to the internal nature of an image – layers, which Docker images are composed from. We said a while ago that every instruction in the Dockerfile creates a new layer. Let's explain now what they are.

Layers

Each image consists of a series of layers that are stacked on one another. By using the union filesystem, Docker combines all these layers into a single image entity. The union filesystem allows transparent overlaying of files and directories of separate filesystems, giving a single, consistent filesystem as a result, as you can see in the following diagram:

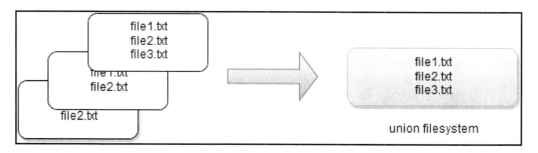

The contents and structure of directories that have the same path within these separate filesystems will be seen together in a single merged directory, within the new, virtual-like filesystem. In other words, the filesystem structure of the top layer will merge with the structure of the layer beneath. Files and directories that have the same path as in the previous layer will cover those beneath. Removing the upper layer will again reveal and expose the previous directory content. As we have mentioned earlier, layers are placed in a stack on top of one another. To maintain the order of layers, Docker utilizes the concept of layer IDs and pointers. Each layer contains the ID and a pointer to its parent layer. A layer without a pointer referencing the parent is the first layer in the stack, a base. You can see the relation in the following diagram:

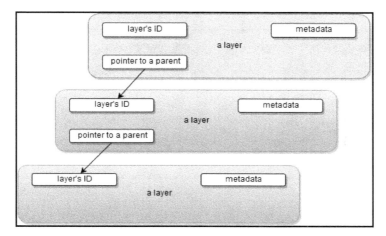

As you pull the image from Docker Hub, you actually can see the progress of each dependent layer being downloaded. Here's an example for the latest Ubuntu Linux:

```
1. root@02a5acae8ef0: / (docker)
11:15:36   jarek@MacBook-Pro-Jarek   ~
$ docker run -it ubuntu
Unable to find image 'ubuntu:latest' locally
latest: Pulling from library/ubuntu

5ba4f30e5bea: Pull complete
9d7d19c9dc56: Pull complete
ac6ad7efd0f9: Pull complete
e7491a747824: Pull complete
a3ed95caeb02: Pull complete
Digest: sha256:46fb5d001b88ad904c5c732b086b596b92cfb4a4840a3abd0e35dbb6870585e4
Status: Downloaded newer image for ubuntu:latest
root@02a5acae8ef0:/# []
```

Another advantage of using layers is the persistence of history. Layers can provide a history of how a specific image was built. Once all the layers are finished downloading, you can list the layers in the specific image using the `history` command:

```
$ docker history ubuntu
```

```
1. jarek@MacBook-Pro-Jarek: ~ (zsh)
11:26:32   jarek@MacBook-Pro-Jarek   ~
$ docker history ubuntu
IMAGE          CREATED        CREATED BY                                         SIZE       COMMENT
2fa927b5cdd3   7 days ago     /bin/sh -c #(nop) CMD ["/bin/bash"]                0 B
<missing>      7 days ago     /bin/sh -c sed -i 's/^#\s*\(deb.*universe\)$/      1.895 kB
<missing>      7 days ago     /bin/sh -c rm -rf /var/lib/apt/lists/*             0 B
<missing>      7 days ago     /bin/sh -c set -xe   && echo '#!/bin/sh' > /u      701 B
<missing>      7 days ago     /bin/sh -c #(nop) ADD file:025ef672711f22be39      122 MB

11:26:34   jarek@MacBook-Pro-Jarek   ~
$
```

Each line in the `history` command's output corresponds to a commit to a filesystem. The values in the SIZE column add up to the corresponding SIZE column for the image in docker image.

You can also see the graphical representation of the image using the ImageLayers web application available at `https://imagelayers.iron.io`:

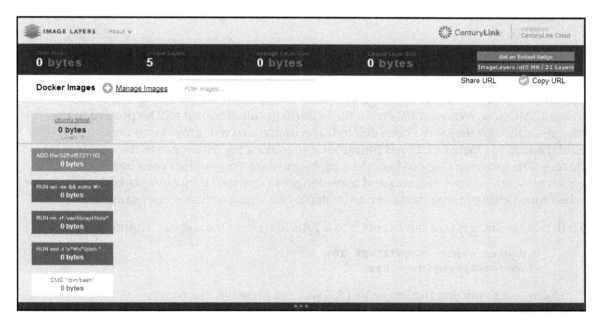

Layers have some interesting features. First, they are reusable. If two different images have a common part, let's say a Linux shell, for example, Docker tracks all of the pulled layers and will reuse the shell layer in both of the images. It's a safe operation; as you remember, layers are read-only. When downloading the second image, the layer will be reused and only the difference will be pulled from the Docker Hub. This saves time, bandwidth, and disk space of course, but it has another great advantage. If you modify your Docker image, for example, by bumping the version of your application, only the single layer gets modified. Instead of distributing the whole image, you push just the update, making the process simpler and faster. This is especially useful if you use Docker in your continuous deployment flow: pushing a Git branch will trigger building an image and then publishing the application for users. Due to the layers reuse feature, the whole process is a lot faster. Because of layers, Docker is lightweight in comparison to full virtual machines, which doesn't share anything. Because of the layer caching that Docker uses, when you pull an image (`https://docs.docker.com/reference/commandline/pull/`), you eventually don't have to download all of its filesystem. If you already have another image that has some of the layers of the image you pull, only the missing layers are actually downloaded. There is a word of warning, though, related to another feature of layers: apart from being reusable, layers are also additive.

Layers are additive – the image can get quite large as a result.

For example, if you create a large file in the container, make a commit (we will get to that in a while), then delete the file, and do another commit, this file will still be present in the layer history. Imagine this scenario: you pull the base Ubuntu image and install the Wildfly application server. Then you change your mind, uninstall Wildfly and install Tomcat instead. All those removed files from the Wildfly installation will still be present in the image – although they have been deleted. The image size will grow in no time. Understanding Docker's layered filesystem can make a big difference to the size of your images. The growing size can become a problem when you publish your images to a registry – it takes more requests and takes longer to transfer. Large images become an issue when thousands of containers need to be deployed across a cluster, for example.

To flatten the image, you can export it to a TAR file, using the `export` command:

```
$ docker export <CONTAINER ID> >
/home/docker/myImage.tar
```

 Exporting the image to TAR will not preserve its history.

The exported file can then be imported back, using the import command:

```
$ cat /home/docker/myImage.tar | docker
import - some-name:latest
```

If the free disk space is really an issue, you can pipe the output stream of export into the input stream of import:

```
$ docker export <CONTAINER ID> | docker
import - exampleimagelocal:new
```

Alternatively, you can use the `docker-squash` utility, available at GitHub `https://github.com/jwilder/docker-squash`, to make your images smaller. It will squash multiple Docker layers into one in order to create an image with fewer and smaller layers. Squashed images work the same as they were originally built, because this utility retains Dockerfile commands such as `PORT` or `ENV`. In addition, deleted files in later layers are actually removed from the image when squashed.

If necessary, you can also extract data files from the finished container with the `cp` (from copy) command:

```
$ docker cp <CONTAINER ID>:
/path/to/find/files /path/to/put/copy
```

Layers and images are closely related to each other. Docker deals with images and their layers with a few commands, and we have been using most of them already. Let's summarize them now:

Image-related command	Description
images	This lists the images
Build	This builds an image from a Dockerfile
history	This shows the history of an image
import	This creates a new filesystem image from the contents of a TAR archive
load	This loads an image from a TAR archive
rmi	This removes one or more images
Save	This saves an image's contents to a TAR archive
inspect	This returns low-level information on an image

Layers are a great feature in the container world. When used wisely, can be a great help when creating images. But, they also have a limitation. At present, the AUFS limit of 42 layers https://github.com/dotcloud/docker/issues/1171. This means that you should group similar commands where it is possible, which will result with just one single layer.

As we have said before, Docker images are stored as series of read-only layers. This means that once the container image has been created, it does not change. But having all the filesystem read-only would not have a lot of sense. What about modifying an image? Adding your software to a base web server image? Well, when we start a container, Docker actually takes the read-only image (with all its read-only layers) and adds a read/write layer on top of the layer's stack. Let's focus on containers now.

Containers

A running instance of an image is called a **container.** Docker launches them using the Docker images as read-only templates. To use a programming metaphor, if an image is a class, then a container is an instance of a class-a runtime object. Containers are lightweight and portable encapsulations of an environment in which to run applications. To turn an image into a container, the Docker engine takes the image, adds a read/write filesystem on top, and initializes various settings, including network ports, container name, ID, and resource limits (we will be talking about applying resource limits to a container in Chapter 7, *Running Containers*). To run a container, use the same command we used in the previous chapter when we tested our installation, docker run:

```
$ docker run [OPTIONS] IMAGE [COMMAND]
[ARG...]
```

 You can have many running containers of the same image.

There are a lot of run command options that can be used. Some of them include the network configuration, for example (we will explain Docker's networking in the next chapter); the -it (from interactive) option tells Docker to make the container interactive and to attach a terminal to its output and input. We will cover all of the options in detail in Chapter 7, *Running Containers*. Now, let's just focus on the idea of the container to better understand the whole picture. Let's try a simple command to start a new container using the latest version of Ubuntu. As a result of interactive run, once this container starts, you will get a bash prompt shell where you can execute Ubuntu's commands, like in a normal, ordinary shell:

```
$ docker run -it ubuntu:latest
/bin/bash
```

So what happens under the hood when we run this command?

The image, which is ubuntu:latest in our case, will be pulled down from a ubuntu repository, unless it's already available on your local machine.

The Docker engine takes the image and adds a read/write layer on top of the layer's stack, then initializes the image name, ID, and resource limits (such as CPU and memory). In this phase, Docker will also set up an IP address by finding and attaching an available IP address from a pool. The last step of the execution will be the actual command – passed as the last parameter: /bin/bash in our case – that starts a shell where you can log in. Docker will capture and provide the container output; it will be displayed in the console. You can now do things you would normally do when preparing an operating system to run your applications. This can be installing packages (via apt-get, for example), pulling source code with Git, downloading Node.js libraries using npm, and so on. All of this will modify the filesystem of the top, writable layer. If you then execute the commit command, a new image containing all of your changes will be created and ready to run later.

Sometimes we can tell Docker that we will not need a container after it is stopped. For this purpose, there is the -rm option available for the run command:

```
$ docker run -i -t -rm ubuntu:latest
/bin/bash
```

This will pull (of course, if it's not already present on your machine) and start the latest Ubuntu container and present us an interactive bash shell. As soon as we finish our work and stop the container, it will be deleted from the filesystem releasing some space on a drive.

To stop a container, use the docker stop command. The Docker stop has the following syntax:

```
$ docker stop [OPTIONS] <container
ID/name> [<container ID/name...]
```

There are not many options to the stop command; you can give the -t option to provide the time in seconds Docker should wait before stopping the container, with 10 seconds as the default value. For example, to stop the container with ID fa19b25b311e, simply execute the following command:

```
$ docker stop fa19b25b311e
```

A container when stopped will retain all settings and filesystem changes (in the top, read/write layer), but all processes will be stopped and you will lose anything in memory. This is what differentiates a stopped container from a Docker image. Sometimes you need to stop all of the running containers, so this command may come in handy:

```
docker stop $(docker ps -q)
```

To list all containers you have on your system – either running or stopped – execute the `ps` command:

```
$ docker ps -a
```

As a result, Docker client will list a table containing container IDs (a unique identifier you can use to refer to the container in other commands), creation date, the command used to start a container, status, exposed ports, and a name (assigned by you or the funny name Docker has picked for you):

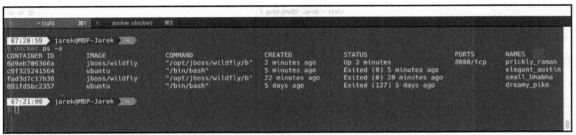

As you can see, the output will contain detailed information about the container status and uptime and a command used to start in the container.

To remove a container, you can just use the `rm` command. If you want to remove all stopped containers at once, you can use the list of containers (given by the `ps` command) and a filter:

```
$ docker rm -v $(docker ps -q -f
status=exited)
```

Saving changes to a container

Although an image is always read-only and immutable, we can actually make changes to a running container – the top layer of a container stack is always the read/write (writable) layer. This can be adding or modifying files, such as installing a software package, configuring the operation system, and so on.

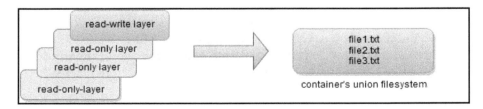

If you modify a file in the running container, the file will be copied out of the underlying read-only layer and into the top, read/write layer. Your changes will be applied only in the top layer, and the union filesystem will hide the underlying file. The original file will not be destroyed – it still exists in the underlying, read-only layer. If you delete the container, and relaunch the same image again, Docker will start a fresh container without any of the changes made in the previously running container.

In other words, your changes to the filesystem will not affect the base image. However, you can create a new image from a running container (and all its changes) using the commit command:

```
$ docker commit <container-id>
<image-name>
```

To save changes you have made to the container, you must commit them.

During runtime, if the process in a container makes changes to its filesystem, there will be of course a difference between the current container filesystem and the filesystem of the image from which the container was created. If you run the `docker commit` command, this difference becomes a new read-only image, from which you can create new containers. Otherwise, if you remove the container, this difference will disappear. You can make updates to a container, but a series of updates will engender a series of new container images, so system rollbacks are easy. Take a look at what happens after you do a commit:

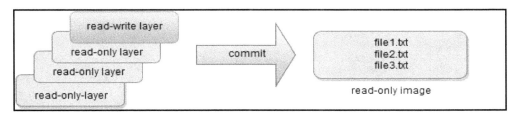

Let's see an example. First, we pull a base image called busybox. Busybox combines tiny versions of many common UNIX utilities into a single small executable. It provides replacements for most of the utilities you usually find in GNU, such as file utilities, shell tools, and so on:

```
$ docker pull busybox
```

Now, we make changes to a container of this image; in this case, we make a new folder:

```
$ docker run busybox mkdir /home/test
```

At the moment, we can get a `busybox` container ID using the command:

```
$ docker ps -a
```

Let's commit this changed container – this will create a new image called `busybox_modfied`:

```
$ docker commit <CONTAINER ID>
busybox_modified
```

In response to the successful commit, Docker will just output the full ID of newly generated images.

To avoid data corruption or inconsistency, Docker will pause a container you are committing changes to. Although it's not recommended to do so, you have an option to disable this behavior, setting the `--pause` option to `false`.

If we list the images we have now, both `busybox` and `busybox_modified` should be present on the list. To see them, execute the `images` command:

```
$ docker images -a
```

As you can see, the new `busybox_modified` is present on the list of images available locally:

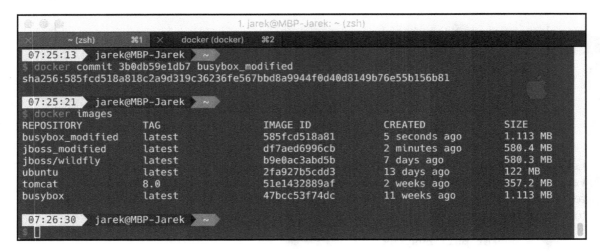

To see the difference between both images, we can use the following check for folders:

```
$ docker run busybox [ -d /home/test ]
&& echo 'Directory found' || echo
'Directory not found'
$ docker run busybox_modified [ -d
/home/test ] && echo 'Directory found'
|| echo 'Directory not found'
```

Now we have two different images (busybox and busybox_modified) and we have a container made from busybox that also contains the change (the new folder, /home/test). The commit command takes a container's top-level read/write layer and turns it into a read-only layer. In effect, the container (no matter if it's running or stopped) becomes new, read-only, immutable image.

When the container is deleted the writable layer is also deleted.

Creating images by altering the top writable layer in the container is useful when debugging and experimenting, but it's usually better to use Dockerfile to manage your images in a documented and maintainable way. We will do it in Chapter 6, *Creating Images*.

 A container is a stateful instantiation of an image.

We have been using a couple of container-related commands in this section, let's summarize them in a table:

Container-related command	Description
attach	This is used to attach to a running container
commit	This is used to build an image from a Dockerfile
cp	This shows the history of an image
create	This creates a new filesystem image from the contents of a TAR archive
diff	This loads an image from a TAR archive
exec	This removes one or more images
inspect	This saves an image's contents to a TAR archive
kill	This returns low-level information on an image

start / stop / restart / pause / unpause	This manages the container's run status
logs	This fetches the logs of a container
port	This lists the port mappings or a specific mapping for the container
rename	This is used to rename a container
run	This is used to run a command in a new container
stats	This is used to display a live stream of container(s) resource usage statistics
top	This is used to display the running processes of a container
Update	This is used to update the configuration of one or more containers
Wait	This is used to block until a container stops, then print its exit code

We have now learned about the build (images) and run (containers) pieces of our containerization world. We still are missing the last element – the distribution component. The distribution component of Docker consists of Docker registry, index, and repository. Let's focus on them now to have a complete picture.

Docker registry, repository and index

Docker utilizes a hierarchical system for storing images, as shown in the following diagram:

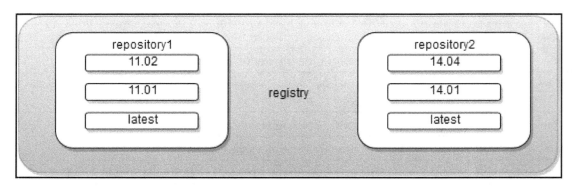

The first component in this system is the registry. The images you build will be stored in a remote registry for others to use. Docker registry is a service (an application, in fact) that stores your Docker images. Docker Hub is an example of the publicly available registry – it's free and serves a huge, constantly growing collection of existing images. We are going to cover Docker Hub in detail in Chapter 5, *Finding Images*. There are, of course, other registries available on the Internet, such as Artifactory (https://www.jfrog.com/artifactory), Google Container Registry (https://cloud.google.com/container-registry), and Quay (https://quay.io).

The **repository**, on the other hand, is a collection (namespace) of related images, usually providing different versions of the same application or service. In other words, it is a collection of different docker images with the same name and different tags. If your app is named "hello-world" and your username (or namespace) for the Registry is developingWithDocker, then your image will be placed in the developingWithDocker/hello-world repository. You can tag an image, and store multiple versions of that image with different IDs in a single named repository, access different tagged versions of an image with a special syntax, such as username/image_name:tag. A Docker repository is identified by a URI and can either be public or private. The URI looks like:

```
{registryAddress}/{namespace}/{repositoryName}:{tag}
```

The Docker Hub is the default registry and Docker will pull images from the Docker Hub if you do not specify a registry address.

The registry address can be omitted for repositories hosted with Docker Hub.

We have mentioned tags earlier in this chapter – we will get back to them in detail in Chapter 6, *Creating Images*. A registry typically hosts multiple Docker repositories.

The difference between Registry and repository can be confusing at the beginning, so let's describe what will happen if you execute the following command:

```
$ docker pull ubuntu:14.04
```

The command downloads the image tagged `14.04` within the `ubuntu` repository from the Docker Hub registry. The Ubuntu repository doesn't use a username, so the namespace part is omitted in this example.

Let's summarize the repository-related commands in a table:

Repository-related command	Description
login	This is used to log in to a Docker registry
logout	This is used to log out from a Docker registry
pull	This is used to pull an image or a repository from a registry
push	This is used to push an image or a repository to a registry
search	This is used to search the Docker Hub for images

Although the Docker Hub is public, you get one private repository for free with your Docker Hub user account, but it's not usable for organizations you're a member of. If you need more accounts, you can upgrade your Docker Hub plan, which will not be free of charge. There are a couple of payment plans based on the number of private repositories you need. We will cover the Docker Hub in detail in `Chapter 5`, *Finding Images,* and `Chapter 8`, *Publishing Images.*

Private registries, on the other hand, can be set up just for you or other users in your organization, in your company's own network.

 You can create the private registry behind your company's firewall.

To run your totally private registry, you can use the Docker Hub itself. It's an open source application, and is also available as a Docker image. The simplest case is just running the following command:

```
$ docker run -d -p 5000:5000 --name
registry registry:2
```

As a result, you will start a private registry on your own machine.

The last component you should be aware of is an Index. An Index manages search and tagging but also user accounts and permissions. In fact, the registry delegates authentication to the index. When executing remote commands such as push or pull, the index first will look at the name of the image and then check to see if it has a corresponding repository. If so, the index verifies if you are allowed to access or modify the image. If you are, the operation is approved and the registry takes or sends the image.

Summary

Let's summarize what we have learned so far. We already know that the Dockerfile is the source code of the Image. It contains ordered instructions on how to build an image. An image is a specific state of a filesystem: a read-only, frozen immutable snapshot of a live container. It's composed of layers representing changes in the filesystem at various points in time; layers are a bit like the commit history of a Git repository. Containers, on the other hand are runtime instances of an image. They can have state (for example, running or stopped). You can make changes to the filesystem on a container and commit them to make them persisted, but only changes in the filesystem can be committed – memory changes will be lost. Commit always creates a new image. We also mentioned the concept of a registry, which holds a collection of named repositories, which themselves are a collection of images tracked by their IDs. A registry is like a Git repository: you can push and pull containers. We are going to cover repositories in detail in Chapter 5, *Finding Images*.

After reading this chapter you should have an understanding the nature of images with their layers and containers. But Docker provides another way of extending and opening containers to the external world: networking and persistent storage. We are going to cover this subject in the next chapter.

4
Networking and Persistent Storage

In the previous chapter, we learned about images and containers and a way to modify them. For all practical purposes, the service running inside a container needs to be exposed to the outside world. The Docker tool chain provides a very powerful network interface that enables you to expose as well as control network connectivity as per your requirement. In this chapter, we will dive deep into the docker networking approach. The persistent storage will be useful for storing data, because, as you remember from the previous chapters, Docker filesystems are temporary, so to speak. If you stop the running container, all your changes will be lost: any deleted files will be back, and any changes in the existing files you have made will not be present. In this chapter, we are going to cover the following topics:

- Docker networking, including network types such as host, bridge, or overlay
- Exposing and mapping ports
- Linking containers
- Creating Docker volumes

Let's begin with a networking overview.

Docker networking

Docker uses the concept of the **Container Network Model** (**CNM**). In essence, CNM allows you to create small, segmented networks for groups of containers to communicate over. Let's explain the model using the following diagram:

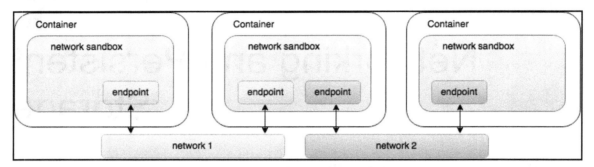

There are three entities present in the CNM:

- **sandbox:** This is an isolated environment holding the networking configuration for a container.
- **endpoint**: This is a network interface that can be used for communication over a specific network. Endpoints join to exactly one network. Multiple endpoints can exist within a single network sandbox.
- **network**: It's a group of endpoints that are able to communicate with each other. You could create, for example, two separate networks, and they will be completely isolated. Network can be identified by their names (such as **backend** and **frontend)** or IDs (generated automatically by Docker during the network creation).

Docker networking model also introduces the concept of network drivers. By default, two network drivers are provided by Docker: the `bridge` and the `overlay` driver. We will get back to it in a moment.

All containers on the same network can communicate with each other freely. An endpoint provides network connectivity for a sandbox – if you need to join a container to multiple networks, there should be multiple endpoints per container. This networking model is highly configurable (and allowing quite complex networking configurations), but also quite easy to set up using just the defaults. In fact, Docker creates some default networks for us out of the box.

The `docker` command that we will be using throughout this chapter to deal with networking is the `network` command. As you remember from the previous chapter, the concise help is always available from the shell (or command line) – let's look at the output of the `docker network help` command:

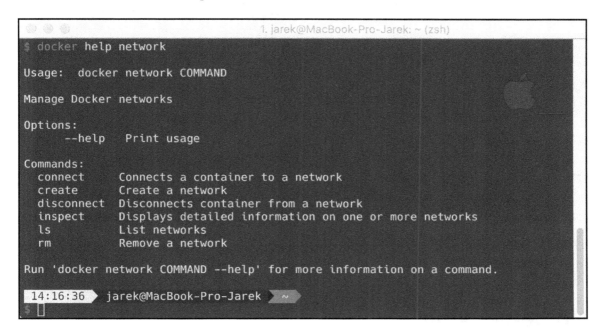

```
$ docker help network

Usage:  docker network COMMAND

Manage Docker networks

Options:
      --help    Print usage

Commands:
  connect       Connects a container to a network
  create        Create a network
  disconnect    Disconnects container from a network
  inspect       Displays detailed information on one or more networks
  ls            List networks
  rm            Remove a network

Run 'docker network COMMAND --help' for more information on a command.

 14:16:36   jarek@MacBook-Pro-Jarek   ~
$
```

There are not many commands related to networking, but they are quite useful. Let's begin with explaining the default networks.

Default networks

When you install Docker, three default networks will be automatically created – you can list them using the `network ls` command, as follows:

```
$ docker network ls
```

Docker will output the list of available networks, including their ID, network name, driver (we will cover drivers in a while), and a scope, as you can see in the following screenshot:

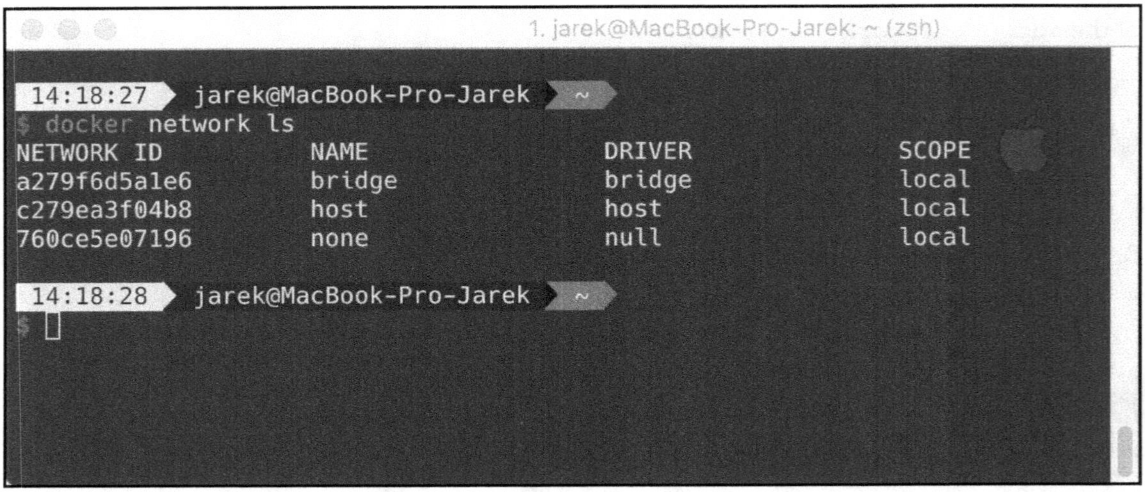

```
                              1. jarek@MacBook-Pro-Jarek: ~ (zsh)

 14:18:27    jarek@MacBook-Pro-Jarek    ~
$ docker network ls
NETWORK ID          NAME                DRIVER              SCOPE
a279f6d5a1e6        bridge              bridge              local
c279ea3f04b8        host                host                local
760ce5e07196        none                null                local

 14:18:28    jarek@MacBook-Pro-Jarek    ~
$
```

We have three networks installed by default: host, none, and bridge. Let's discuss them in more detail, starting with the simplest one, none.

No networking

To cut the long story short, none mode does not configure networking at all. The DRIVER column listed earlier contains null, which means that there is no driver being used by this network. It's useful when you don't need your container to have network access.

Let's run the simple example by running the busybox image without the network:

```
1. jarek@MacBook-Pro-Jarek: ~ (zsh)
14:21:10  jarek@MacBook-Pro-Jarek   ~
$ docker run --net=none busybox
Unable to find image 'busybox:latest' locally
latest: Pulling from library/busybox

8ddc19f16526: Pull complete
Digest: sha256:a59906e33509d14c036c8678d687bd4eec81ed7c4b8ce907b888c607f6a1e0e6
Status: Downloaded newer image for busybox:latest

14:21:35  jarek@MacBook-Pro-Jarek   ~
$
```

The container's networking details, such as the IP address, for example, can use the `docker inspect` command and then filter the output using `grep`. To do this, execute the following:

```
$ docker inspect <container ID or name> | grep IPAddress
```

If we now inspect the container that was started with the `--net=none` option, we will see that the new container was not assigned an IP address assigned:

```
1. jarek@MacBook-Pro-Jarek: ~ (zsh)
 docker (docker)  ⌘1      ~ (zsh)   ⌘2

14:30:22  jarek@MacBook-Pro-Jarek   ~
$ docker inspect 85fdf39db93d | grep IPAddress
            "SecondaryIPAddresses": null,
            "IPAddress": "",
                "IPAddress": "",

14:30:24  jarek@MacBook-Pro-Jarek   ~
$
```

Host network

If you start your container with the `--net=host` option, then the container will use the host network. It's a network created by default and it is using the `host` driver. It's as fast as the normal networking: there is no bridge, no translation, nothing. That's why it can be useful when you need to get the best network performance. In this mode, container shares the networking namespace of the host (your local machine, for example), directly exposing it to the outside world. In the case of `--net=host`, the container can be accessed through the host's IP address. This also means that you need not use port mapping to reach services inside the container. However, you need to be aware that this can be dangerous. If you have an application running as root and it has vulnerabilities, there will be a risk of security breach – someone can get the remote control of the host network via the Docker container.

Bridged network

We will focus a little bit more on the `bridge` network because this will be probably the most frequently used one. The `bridge` network is kind of special – it's present on all Docker hosts. You can see it as part of a host's network stack. You can see it by using the `ifconfig` command on your Mac or Linux machine, for example:

```
1. jarek@MacBook-Pro-Jarek: ~ (zsh)
$ ifconfig bridge0
bridge0: flags=8863<UP,BROADCAST,SMART,RUNNING,SIMPLEX,MULTICAST> mtu 1500
        options=63<RXCSUM,TXCSUM,TSO4,TSO6>
        ether 2a:cf:e9:31:2c:00
        Configuration:
                id 0:0:0:0:0:0 priority 0 hellotime 0 fwddelay 0
                maxage 0 holdcnt 0 proto stp maxaddr 100 timeout 1200
                root id 0:0:0:0:0:0 priority 0 ifcost 0 port 0
                ipfilter disabled flags 0x2
        member: en1 flags=3<LEARNING,DISCOVER>
                ifmaxaddr 0 port 5 priority 0 path cost 0
        member: en2 flags=3<LEARNING,DISCOVER>
                ifmaxaddr 0 port 6 priority 0 path cost 0
        Address cache:
        nd6 options=1<PERFORMNUD>
        media: <unknown type>
        status: inactive

14:32:59  jarek@MacBook-Pro-Jarek  ~
$
```

It's also the default network in Docker. When the Docker service daemon starts, it configures a virtual bridge named `docker0`. Unless you specify a network with the `docker run --net=<NETWORK>` option, the Docker daemon will connect the container to the `bridge` network by default. Also, if you create a new container, it will be connected to the `bridge` network. Docker will find a free IP address from the range available on the bridge and will configure the container's `eth0` interface with that IP address. From now on, if the new container wants to, for example, connect to the Internet, it will use the bridge – the host's own IP address will be used as the gateway. This bridge will automatically forward packets between any other network interfaces that are attached to it and also allow containers to communicate with the host machine as well as with the containers on the same host.

 By default, Docker containers can make connections to the outside world, they connect via the docker0 interface, but the outside world cannot connect to containers.

The `docker network inspect` command that we saw earlier shows all the connected containers and their network resources on a given network. Containers in this default network are able to communicate with each other using IP addresses.

Sometimes, the default networks created by Docker are not enough. Luckily, Docker gives us a possibility to create our own custom network. Let's create a custom network.

Creating a network

As you can see from the `network help` command, there's a `create` command. Run from the shell or command line:

```
$ docker network create backend
```

This is the simplest form of the command, and yet it will be used probably the most often. It takes a default driver (we haven't used any options to specify a driver – we will cover network types and drivers in a while). As the output, Docker will print out the network ID. You can use this ID later when referring to this network when connecting containers to it or inspecting the network's properties.

The last parameter of the command is the network's name – which is a lot more convenient and easier to remember than the ID.

The network name in our case is `backend`. The network creates commands that take in more parameters, as shown in the following table:

Option	Description
`-d, --driver="bridge"`	This is the driver that is used to manage the network
`--aux-address=map[]`	Auxiliary ipv4 or ipv6 addresses are used by the network driver
`--gateway=[]`	ipv4 or ipv6 gateway is used for the master subnet
`--ip-range=[]`	This is used to allocate container IP from a subrange
`--ipam-driver=default`	This is the IP address management driver
`-o, --opt=map[]`	This sets the driver's specific options
`--subnet=[]`	This is the subnet in CIDR format that represents a network segment

One of the most important parameters is the driver with the value `bridge` drivers that let you specify the network type. Docker has a couple of drivers available by default. We are going to cover them in detail in a short while, but first, let's connect a container to the network.

Running a container in a network

After you create the network, you can launch containers on it using the `docker run --net=<NETWORK>` option, where `<NETWORK>` is the name of one of the default networks or the one you have created yourself, for example:

```
docker run -it --net=bridge ubuntu
```

If you don't want to explicitly state what network a container should start with, but just want to inform Docker that you would like the container to connect to the same network that the other container uses, execute the run command with a `--net` option with the `container:` prefix, specifying other container's ID or name. So, for example, execute the following commands:

```
docker run -it --name=myUbuntu --net=bridge ubuntu
docker run -it --net=container:myUbuntu busybox
```

This will make your `busybox` container run on the same network that the Ubuntu container is running on, no matter what network it is. The containers you launch into the same network must be run on the same Docker host. Each container in the network can immediately communicate with other containers in the network.

However, the network itself isolates the containers from external networks, as shown in the following diagram:

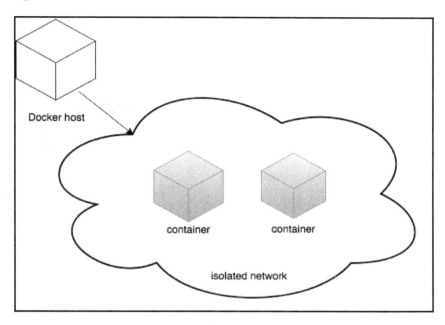

Let's run a container on networks:

1. Let's connect two containers to the network to see if it works. First, we are going to create a network:

   ```
   docker network create testNetwork
   ```

2. Next, let's create the first container, which will be busybox, and connect it to testNetwork:

   ```
   docker run -it --name=container1 --net=testNetwork busybox
   ```

3. Now, if we run the second `busybox` container and connect it to `testNetwork`, using the same `--net=testNetwork`, we can see that both containers can see each other they run on the same network and the `ping` command actually responds:

docker run –it --name=container2 --net=testNetwork busybox

```
C:\Windows\system32\cmd.exe - docker run -it --name=container2 --net=testNetwork busybox            —    □    ×
Microsoft Windows [Version 10.0.14393]
(c) 2016 Microsoft Corporation. Wszelkie prawa zastrzeżone.

C:\Users\jarek>docker run -it --name=container2 --net=testNetwork busybox
/ # ping container1
PING container1 (172.19.0.2): 56 data bytes
64 bytes from 172.19.0.2: seq=0 ttl=64 time=0.056 ms
64 bytes from 172.19.0.2: seq=1 ttl=64 time=0.077 ms
64 bytes from 172.19.0.2: seq=2 ttl=64 time=0.068 ms
64 bytes from 172.19.0.2: seq=3 ttl=64 time=0.063 ms
64 bytes from 172.19.0.2: seq=4 ttl=64 time=0.040 ms
64 bytes from 172.19.0.2: seq=5 ttl=64 time=0.090 ms
64 bytes from 172.19.0.2: seq=6 ttl=64 time=0.118 ms
64 bytes from 172.19.0.2: seq=7 ttl=64 time=0.128 ms
64 bytes from 172.19.0.2: seq=8 ttl=64 time=0.061 ms
64 bytes from 172.19.0.2: seq=9 ttl=64 time=0.062 ms
64 bytes from 172.19.0.2: seq=10 ttl=64 time=0.084 ms
64 bytes from 172.19.0.2: seq=11 ttl=64 time=0.064 ms
64 bytes from 172.19.0.2: seq=12 ttl=64 time=0.051 ms
^C
--- container1 ping statistics ---
13 packets transmitted, 13 packets received, 0% packet loss
round-trip min/avg/max = 0.040/0.074/0.128 ms
/ #
```

4. So we have successfully attached the second container to `testNetwork` (using the default `bridge` driver).

5. Now let's take a look at the network details. To do this, we will use the `network inspect` command:

docker network inspect testNetwork

Docker will output a comprehensive report about the network:

```
C:\Windows\system32\cmd.exe                                                    —   □   ×

C:\Users\jarek>docker network inspect testNetwork
[
    {
        "Name": "testNetwork",
        "Id": "eb66073cd1218fb090de281789c6475df57907c58576df27e77fbeae6b60a229",
        "Scope": "local",
        "Driver": "bridge",
        "EnableIPv6": false,
        "IPAM": {
            "Driver": "default",
            "Options": {},
            "Config": [
                {
                    "Subnet": "172.19.0.0/16",
                    "Gateway": "172.19.0.1/16"
                }
            ]
        },
        "Internal": false,
        "Containers": {
            "1268ce631760fc548304cc1fab40c144784bd3ea73aeae4f513431e4d6730f15": {
                "Name": "container1",
                "EndpointID": "76aa5ecc75a3c4a53f0cdd95a88d75ca2b64050b8b217f750efef26d518c6390",
                "MacAddress": "02:42:ac:13:00:02",
                "IPv4Address": "172.19.0.2/16",
                "IPv6Address": ""
            },
            "46fbb4b5c56b5a52d83b71dd8f6ae13498583450e39526150f69588d15212715": {
                "Name": "container2",
                "EndpointID": "d36a30bb8e155cda5a478ff2d58bf9e3b33e06dfbbcbeceb24689183922343c9",
                "MacAddress": "02:42:ac:13:00:03",
                "IPv4Address": "172.19.0.3/16",
                "IPv6Address": ""
            }
        },
        "Options": {},
        "Labels": {}
    }
]
```

As you can see, there are a lot of interesting details in this report, such as the driver being used and a list of containers currently connected to this network.

Just as the container can be connected to a network, it can also be disconnected and the corresponding network interface will be removed. The syntax of the `network disconnect` command is as follows:

```
docker network disconnect <network ID or name> <container Id or name>
```

For example, to disconnect our `container1` from `testNetwork`, we need to execute the following command:

```
docker network disconnect testNetwork container1
```

The intention of the possibility to create separate networks is to segregate services so that the only things on a network are the ones that need to talk to each other. In practice, you will probably have a lot of networks with small numbers of containers connected to them. Networks are all isolated from each other.

If two containers are not on the same network, they cannot talk directly.

A typical example would be a load balancer, a web application frontend, a web application backend, and finally, a database.

You may want that your containers running on separate Docker hosts to communicate over the network someday. In this case, the multi-host networking feature of Docker comes in handy.

Creating multi-host networking

So far, we've been learning about the `bridge` network driver, which has a local scope, meaning bridge networks are local to the Docker host. In addition to basic network drivers (`null`, `bridge`, and `host`), Docker also provides the `overlay` network driver. It has a global, scope meaning that `overlay` networks can exist across multiple Docker hosts. You can use the `overlay` network to connect to multiple hosts. Those Docker hosts can exist in different datacenters, or even different cloud providers. When creating multi-host networks in Docker, you have two options. The first one is to have Docker Engine running in swarm mode. Swarm mode has been introduced in Docker version 1.12 – if you have Docker for Mac or Docker for Windows (as opposite to Docker Toolbox), you can enable swarm mode. In other cases, when you are running the older version of Docker, you will also be able to create multi-host networking, but you will need a key-value store configured. Let's begin with swarm mode, and then we will cover the key-value store setup.

Swarm mode

To explain what swarm mode is, first we'll need to understand some of the terms behind this feature. Swarm itself is a cluster of running Docker Engines. A node is the single instance of Docker Engine that belongs to a cluster. There is a requirement, however, that all Docker hosts that are going to participate in a swarm need to have the following ports open:

- TCP port 2377 (for communication related to swarm management)
- TCP and UDP port 7946 (for nodes to communicate)
- TCP and UDP port 4789 (for overlay network traffic that we are creating now)

Having these ports open, we can initialize our Docker swarm. Swarm mode is disabled by default; you can enable it using the `docker swarm init` command, as shown in the following screenshot:

```
C:\Windows\system32\cmd.exe                                              —   □   ×

C:\Users\jarek>docker swarm init
Swarm initialized: current node (5ehrihvpd6y9hqulqsjyav841) is now a manager.

To add a worker to this swarm, run the following command:

    docker swarm join \
    --token SWMTKN-1-0vpwtxueqqr9ufx24zs1fw7zqou38p8w5bwqodoipgbm2scrdv-9owikcgrpuz4izuwy5ghni3xc \
    10.0.75.2:2377

To add a manager to this swarm, run 'docker swarm join-token manager' and follow the instructions.

C:\Users\jarek>
```

The first Docker Engine you execute this command on becomes a swarm manager – it will coordinate the rest of the nodes participating in the cluster.

As you can see in the preceding screenshot, running `docker swarm init` for the first time gives a special output: a command to run on the additional Docker hosts that you would like to participate in newly created swarm. It will be this one in our example:

```
docker swarm join
--token SWMTKN-1-
0vpwtxueqqr9ufx24zs1fw7zqou38p8w5bwqodoipgbm2scrdv-
9owikcgrpuz4izuwy5ghni3xc \
    10.0.75.2:2377
```

Of course, you will want to make sure that other machines can access manager's IP address. If you run the preceding command on other machines, they will join the cluster. If you now run the `docker info` command, you can see the current state of the swarm. You will get information about the state of the swarm (it's `active`), the current host's node identifier, and a number of nodes participating in the swarm. To see a detailed list of nodes in the swarm, you can execute the following command:

```
docker node ls
```

The output will contain the list of nodes with their hostnames, availability status, and a manager status. Having our little swarm up and running, we can create an overlay network to enable to hosts participating in a swarm to communicate with each other. This will be the same `network create` command we already know; this time, however, we are going to use the overlay driver:

```
docker network create --driver overlay mynet
```

If you now list the networks, you will see `mynet` as an overlay network with a swarm scope, as shown in the following screenshot:

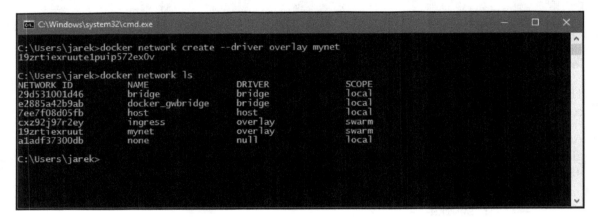

If you are unable to run Docker in the latest version (supporting swarm mode), you can also create multi-host networking. To do this, you will need a key-value store. Let's set it up now.

Key-value store overlay networking

There is one requirement. In order to create an overlay network, you need to have a key-value store configured:

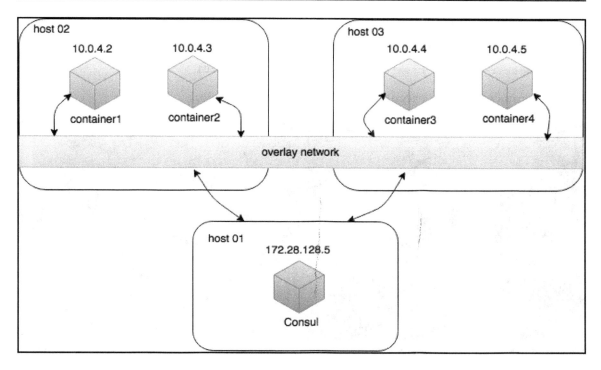

Docker (through `libkv` – a distributed key-value store abstraction library) supports different key-value stores. For overlay networking, you can use stores such as Consul, Etcd, Zookeeper (distributed store), and BoltDB (local store). We will be using Consul (`https://www.consul.io`) in our example.

Docker overlay networking can seem a bit complicated at first, but it's quite easy to understand in the practical example. Let's create an overlay network. We will need a couple of separate Docker hosts to test it. We are going to do this on Windows machine this time, but the procedure is the same on Mac and Linux. As you may remember from `Chapter 2`, *Installing Docker*, if you need to create additional hosts on Linux OS, you need to install a `docker-machine` first – it's not included by default.

To simulate separate hosts, we will begin by creating a new host using the `docker-machine create` command:

docker-machine create --driver=virtualbox host01

As the command is being executed, we get the following result:

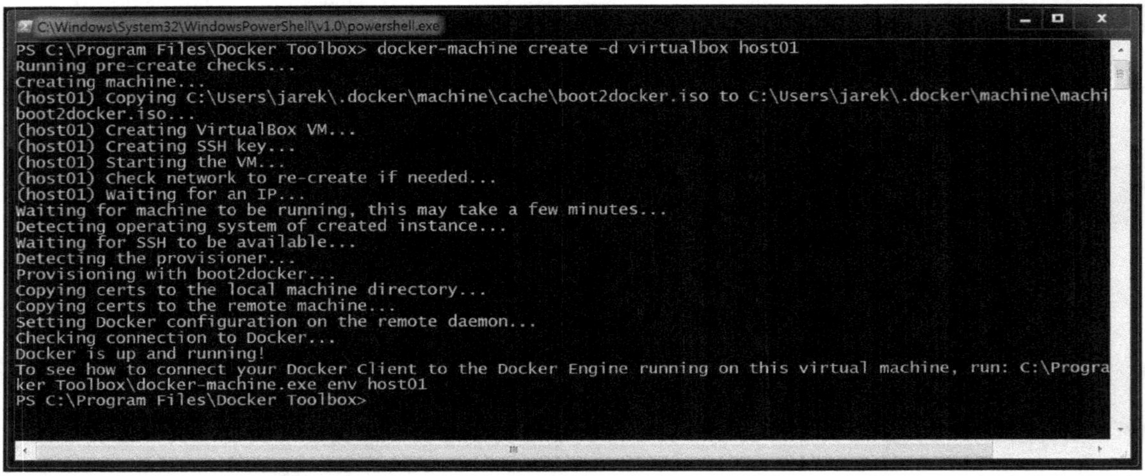

Now we have the docker host running, let's install Consul on the host. It will play the role of a service discovery server for us and will enable our hosts to share the network and communicate. Note that we are going to run it as a daemon and map the port number 8500 on Consul (we will get back to exposing and publishing ports in a while, later in this chapter). Also, as you can see, we need to prefix the command with `config host01`, because we have now four (including the default) Docker hosts running and we need to instruct Docker's Engine on which we are going to run the container:

```
docker $(docker-machine config host01) run -d -p "8500:8500" -h
"consul" progrium/consul --server -bootstrap
```

```
C:\Windows\System32\WindowsPowerShell\v1.0\powershell.exe
PS C:\Program Files\Docker Toolbox> docker $(docker-machine config host01) run -d -p "8500:8500" -h "consul"
nsul -server -bootstrap
Unable to find image 'progrium/consul:latest' locally
latest: Pulling from progrium/consul

c862d82a67a2: Pull complete
0e7f3c08384e: Pull complete
0e221e32327a: Pull complete
09a952464e47: Pull complete
60a1b927414d: Pull complete
4c9f46b5ccce: Pull complete
417d86672aa4: Pull complete
b0d47ad24447: Pull complete
fd5300bd53f0: Pull complete
a3ed95caeb02: Pull complete
d023b445076e: Pull complete
ba8851f89e33: Pull complete
5d1cefca2a28: Pull complete
Digest: sha256:8cc8023462905929df9a79ff67ee435a36848ce7a10f18d6d0faba9306b97274
Status: Downloaded newer image for progrium/consul:latest
f182ac98947d8d08120c3f43301fd62e6ca076ca0967304626e7916ecbe2f969
PS C:\Program Files\Docker Toolbox>
```

With Consul running, let's create two additional Docker hosts, which we are actually going to connect to the same multi-host, overlay network. Note that this time we are giving special instructions to Docker's Engine, saying that we want them to use the cluster store with Consul protocol, using the port that we mapped earlier, 8500:

```
docker-machine create -d virtualbox  --engine-opt="cluster-
store=consul://$(docker-machine ip host01):8500" --engine-
opt="cluster-advertise=eth1:0" host02
```

```
C:\Windows\System32\WindowsPowerShell\v1.0\powershell.exe
PS C:\Program Files\Docker Toolbox> docker-machine create -d virtualbox  --engine-opt="cluster-store=consul://
achine ip host01):8500" --engine-opt="cluster-advertise=eth1:0" host02
Running pre-create checks...
Creating machine...
(host02) Copying C:\Users\jarek\.docker\machine\cache\boot2docker.iso to C:\Users\jarek\.docker\machine\machi
boot2docker.iso...
(host02) Creating VirtualBox VM...
(host02) Creating SSH key...
(host02) Starting the VM...
(host02) Check network to re-create if needed...
(host02) Waiting for an IP...
Waiting for machine to be running, this may take a few minutes...
Detecting operating system of created instance...
Waiting for SSH to be available...
Detecting the provisioner...
Provisioning with boot2docker...
Copying certs to the local machine directory...
Copying certs to the remote machine...
Setting Docker configuration on the remote daemon...
Checking connection to Docker...
Docker is up and running!
To see how to connect your Docker Client to the Docker Engine running on this virtual machine, run: C:\Progra
ker Toolbox\docker-machine.exe env host02
PS C:\Program Files\Docker Toolbox>
```

Next is the third and the last host. Again, the same instructions for the engine are given. Use a cluster store with the Consul protocol through port number 8500:

```
docker-machine create -d virtualbox  --engine-opt="cluster-
store=consul://$(docker-machine ip host01):8500" --engine-
opt="cluster-advertise=eth1:0" host03
```

Let's summarize now: we have three different Docker hosts running on our local machine. The first one is running a Consul container, and the next ones are aware of the Consul host listening on port 8500. Let's list these hosts then using the machine's ls command:

```
C:\Windows\System32\WindowsPowerShell\v1.0\powershell.exe
PS C:\Program Files\Docker Toolbox> docker-machine ls
NAME      ACTIVE   DRIVER       STATE     URL                          SWARM   DOCKER   ERRORS
default   *        virtualbox   Running   tcp://192.168.99.100:2376            v1.11.1
host01    -        virtualbox   Running   tcp://192.168.99.102:2376            v1.11.2
host02    -        virtualbox   Running   tcp://192.168.99.104:2376            v1.11.2
host03    -        virtualbox   Running   tcp://192.168.99.105:2376            v1.11.2
PS C:\Program Files\Docker Toolbox>
```

So far so good. We have four hosts ready, each with a different IP address. Now let's get back to the point and create an overlay network on our second host (host02). We do this using the network create command, this time using the overlay driver. The name of our network will be myOverlayNetwork:

```
docker $(docker-machine config host02) network create -d overlay
myOverlayNetwork
```

If we now list the networks available on the second host, we will see that overlay network named myOverlayNetwork is present on the list. We can list the networks using the network ls command, again prefixing the command with config host02 to instruct Docker that we want the list of networks from the host02 host:

```
docker $(docker-machine config host02) network ls
```

If you execute the same command, but with the third host (host03), surprisingly, myOverlayNetwork will also be available, even if we haven't created it explicitly for host03. This is where Consul comes in. As you remember, during the creation of the hosts, we instructed the Docker Engine to use Consul listening on port 8500. As a result, our host02 and host03 share the same overlay network.

List the network on host03, to find out that `myOverlayNetwork` is also active on the third host:

```
docker $(docker-machine config host03) network ls
```

```
C:\Windows\System32\WindowsPowerShell\v1.0\powershell.exe
PS C:\Program Files\Docker Toolbox> docker $(docker-machine config host03) network ls
NETWORK ID          NAME                DRIVER
3d5d9dea7278        bridge              bridge
1681fe4fc49a        host                host
fe730cba550b        myOverlayNetwork    overlay
3054b9dfca38        none                null
PS C:\Program Files\Docker Toolbox>
```

Now, let's find out whether it's actually working. This will be a rather simple test – we are going to run an nginx web server container in host02 and will try to see if it's visible from host03. To do this, execute the command on host02. Note that we are using `--net=myOverlayNetwork` to instruct Docker that we want to connect nginx to the overlay network we have just created:

```
docker $(docker-machine config host02) run -itd --name=nginx
--net=myOverlayNetwork nginx
```

To test the multi-host network, we will fetch the default nginx index page from `host03`. Let's install busybox, which contains the `wget` command (a command used to get the resource from the Web). Again, we are connecting the `busybox` container to the same overlay network:

```
docker $(docker-machine config host03) run -it --net=myOverlayNetwork
busybox
```

And then run the `wget` command to fetch a web page from the nginx server running on a different host:

```
wget -O- http://nginx
```

```
C:\Windows\System32\WindowsPowerShell\v1.0\powershell.exe                    _ □ x
/ # wget -O- http://nginx
Connecting to nginx (10.0.0.2:80)
<!DOCTYPE html>
<html>
<head>
<title>Welcome to nginx!</title>
<style>
    body {
        width: 35em;
        margin: 0 auto;
        font-family: Tahoma, Verdana, Arial, sans-serif;
    }
</style>
</head>
<body>
<h1>Welcome to nginx!</h1>
<p>If you see this page, the nginx web server is successfully installed and
working. Further configuration is required.</p>

<p>For online documentation and support please refer to
<a href="http://nginx.org/">nginx.org</a>.<br/>
Commercial support is available at
<a href="http://nginx.com/">nginx.com</a>.</p>

<p><em>Thank you for using nginx.</em></p>
</body>
</html>
                         100%  |*******************************************************|    612   0:00:00 ETA
/ #
```

The `wget` command will output the downloaded index page of nginx to the console: that's it – we have created a multi-host container network, using three separate machines. The first one was running the Consul server and enabling the remaining two hosts to find themselves and communicate. Just like with the `bridge` networks, you should use these overlay networks with small groups of containers that actually need to communicate with each other.

When creating a multi-host network, we opened a port on the Consul server. Exposing and publishing network ports is a great way to make the container be able to communicate with the other containers and the external world. Let's look at exposing and mapping ports in more detail.

Exposing and mapping ports

It's a common scenario that you will want your containerized application to accept incoming connections, either from other containers or from outside of Docker. It can be the application server listening on port 80 or the database accepting incoming requests. You can expose a port in two ways, either in the Dockerfile with the EXPCSE instruction (we will do it in the chapter about creating images later) or in the run command using the --expose option. These are equivalent commands, though --expose will accept a range of ports as an argument (for example, --expose=1000-2000).

You can also explicitly bind a port (or group of ports) from the container to the host using the -p flag. This configuration depends on the host, so there is no equivalent instruction allowed us in the Dockerfile. Dockerfiles need to be host independent and portable.

 You can bind a port using -p at runtime only.

So, what's the difference between --expose and -p ? Well, --expose will expose a port at runtime, but will not create any mapping to the host.

 If you EXPOSE a port, the service in the container is not accessible from outside Docker, but from inside other Docker containers. So this is good for intercontainer communication.

The EXPOSE instruction exposes ports for use within links, which we are going to explain in a while.

The -p option, on the other hand, is like publish – it will create a port mapping rule, mapping a port on the container with the port on the host system. If no port on the host is specified, Docker will automatically allocate one. Note that if you execute -p, but do not execute EXPOSE, Docker does an implicit EXPOSE. This is because if a port is open to the public, it is automatically also open to other Docker containers.

It seems that there should be another option, allowing to map ports exposed in an image (that is in the Dockerfile) automatically during the startup of the container. And here it is: the -P option (capital P this time) will map a dynamically allocated host port to all container ports that have been exposed by the Dockerfile by the EXPOSE instruction. Let's briefly summarize the options in a table:

Instruction	Meaning
EXPOSE	This signals that there is a service available on the specified port. This is used in the Dockerfile that makes exposed ports open for other containers.
--expose	This is similar to EXPOSE, but is used at runtime.
-p	This specifies a port mapping rule, mapping the port on the container with the port on the host machine. This makes a port open from outside of Docker.
-P	This map is the dynamically allocated port on the host machine to all ports exposed using EXPOSE or --expose.

Note that we will start nginx as a daemon, Docker will respond with the container ID for future reference, so you can stop the container using kill or show its details by using the inspect command). If we execute a ps command now, to list of active and running containers, in the PORTS column we will get the port mapping that took place. In our case, Docker mapped nginx's exposed port number 80 to port number 32773 on the host machine and exposed port number 443 to port number 32772 on the host machine:

```
docker run --name nginx -d -P nginx
```

The quickest way of determining the current port mapping is just the `ps` command (as you remember from the previous chapters, it's being used to see the list of running containers).

The `-p` option, on the other hand, gives us more control. In this case, Docker will not automatically pick any port – it's up to you what ports on the host should be mapped to the container's ports. The syntax of the `-p` option is quite straightforward: you just enter the container exposed port number, a colon, and then a port you would like to be mapped on the host machine:

```
docker run -p <containerPort>:<hostPort> <image ID or name>
```

If you need to, you can also expose a whole range of ports to other containers using either the `EXPOSE` instruction in a Dockerfile (`EXPOSE 7000-8000`, for example) or the `run` command:

```
docker run --expose=7000-8000 <container ID or name>
```

Of course you can then publish a range of ports to the host machine via Docker's `run` (`https://docs.docker.com/engine/reference/commandline/cli/`) command:

```
docker run -p 7000-8000:7000-8000 <container ID or name>
```

Ok, let's stop our nginx using the `stop` command and start another container, this time mapping the container port `80` (which is exposed in the Dockerfile) to our host machine port number `8080`:

```
docker run --name nginx -d -p 8080:80 nginx
```

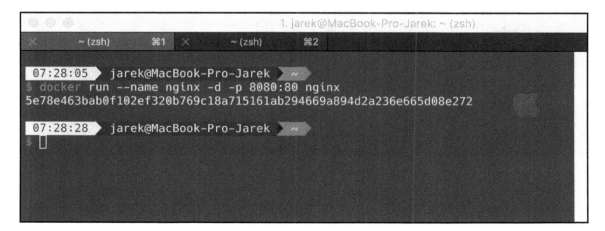

When started, you can access the default nginx welcome page at your host machine local address and mapped port `8080` by using the link `http://localhost:8080`.

As an alternative to the `ps` command, you can execute the `port` command, using the container ID as a parameter (the ID that Docker has given back during the container startup) to determine what ports have been mapped. The following is the port in my case:

```
docker port
e1926dc061c5125b5aa3fd2685bcda4cf26ee99def4b2a1ae5e53721b88231c1
```

As a result, Docker will output the mapping, saying that port number 80 from the container has been mapped to the port number `8080` on the host machine:

You can also see information about exposed (and mapped, if any) ports using the inspect command:

```
docker inspect
e1926dc061c5125b5aa3fd2685bcda4cf26ee99def4b2a1ae5e53721b88231c1
```

If you scroll to the Ports section, you will find the list of ports that have been exposed by the image (this will be TCP 443 and TCP 80 in the case of nginx) and a corresponding mapped port on the host machine, if you decided to run the container with the -p or -P option:

```
1. jarek@MacBook-Pro-Jarek: ~ (zsh)
        ~ (zsh)      ⌘1    ×        ~ (zsh)      ⌘2
      "Ports": {
          "443/tcp": null,
          "80/tcp": [
              {
                  "HostIp": "0.0.0.0",
                  "HostPort": "8080"
              }
          ]
      },
      "SandboxKey": "/var/run/docker/netns/09ac7557fd6d",
      "SecondaryIPAddresses": null,
      "SecondaryIPv6Addresses": null,
      "EndpointID": "5bf09c7d467c08b70754990ad5583d210ab374a6d45aeeba4e50679c4b2c4aa7",
```

Note that the nginx image has two ports exposed, but we have mapped only one of them, port number 80. You can either run the container with the -P option to map all of the exposed ports automatically (to a random high port within the port range on your Docker host) or you can have multiple -p options to map each one of them individually. If there's a need to, you can even map multiple host machine ports to a single exposed port in the container like this:

```
docker run --name nginx -d -p 8080:80 -p 8081:80 nginx
```

The -p flag can be used multiple times to configure multiple ports.

Mapping ports is a wonderful feature. It gives you the flexible configuration possibilities to open your containers to the external world. In fact, it's indispensable if you want your containerized web server, database, or messaging server to be able to talk to others.

Docker networking is quite a new feature. Yet there is another feature of Docker that may come in handy: links between containers. Let's get to know them.

Linking containers

Docker contains a mechanism that allows linking multiple containers together. Linked containers send connection information from one container to another. When creating a link, the information about a source container is being sent to a target container. A good example for such use case can be linking a web application container to the database container. After linking, the database container will expose some information to the web application container (such as the database name, the URL to connect to, the username, and the password). To link containers together, we use the `--link` option in the run command. If we link one container to another, two things will happen under the hood. First, Docker will update the linked container's `/etc/hosts` file automatically to reference to the container we are linking to.

Let's try it for the example. First, let's run the MySQL container on the `bridge` network:

```
testDir — docker run --name mysql -e MYSQL_ROOT_PASSWORD=my-secret-pw -it mysql — docker — docker run --name my...

12:08:00    jarek@MacBook-Pro-Jarek    ~/testDir
$ docker run --name mysql -e MYSQL_ROOT_PASSWORD=my-secret-pw -it mysql
Initializing database
2016-06-25T10:08:04.116398Z 0 [Warning] InnoDB: New log files created, LSN=45790
2016-06-25T10:08:04.296852Z 0 [Warning] InnoDB: Creating foreign key constraint system tables.
2016-06-25T10:08:04.388183Z 0 [Warning] No existing UUID has been found, so we assume that this is the f
irst time that this server has been started. Generating a new UUID: b4dad3cb-3abc-11e6-bf05-0242ac110002
.
2016-06-25T10:08:04.396725Z 0 [Warning] Gtid table is not ready to be used. Table 'mysql.gtid_executed'
cannot be opened.
2016-06-25T10:08:04.397829Z 1 [Warning] root@localhost is created with an empty password ! Please consid
er switching off the --initialize-insecure option.
2016-06-25T10:08:06.594555Z 1 [Warning] 'user' entry 'root@localhost' ignored in --skip-name-resolve mod
```

Next, let's run the second container, again the latest Ubuntu, but this time linking it with the MySQL container:

```
docker run -it --name=ubuntu --link mysql:mysql ubuntu
```

Notice that the MySQL container has to be running.

You can link only to the running container.

You can notice that Docker automatically adjusted the /etc/hosts file of the Ubuntu container, inserting an entry for the MySQL instance:

```
12:20:10   jarek@MacBook-Pro-Jarek   ~
$ docker run -it --name=ubuntu --link mysql:mysql ubuntu
root@60886fca65fb:/# more /etc/hosts
127.0.0.1        localhost
::1      localhost ip6-localhost ip6-loopback
fe00::0 ip6-localnet
ff00::0 ip6-mcastprefix
ff02::1 ip6-allnodes
ff02::2 ip6-allrouters
172.17.0.2       mysql 5d22b0ea87d4
172.17.0.3       60886fca65fb
root@60886fca65fb:/#
```

The /etc/hosts linking is persistent – if you restart the source container and it will be given a new IP address, the linked container's /etc/hosts files will be automatically updated with the source container's new IP address.

The second important thing that will happen when creating a link, is the transfer of some exposed environment variables from the container we are linking to. Take a look at our linked Ubuntu container; it magically knows a lot about the location and setup of the linked MySQL database, all thanks to the --link option (and of course, thanks to the properly defined MySQL image, exposing this information):

```
root@60886fca65fb:/# env | grep MYSQL
MYSQL_ENV_MYSQL_ROOT_PASSWORD=my-secret-pw
MYSQL_ENV_GOSU_VERSION=1.7
MYSQL_PORT_3306_TCP_PORT=3306
MYSQL_PORT_3306_TCP=tcp://172.17.0.2:3306
MYSQL_ENV_MYSQL_VERSION=5.7.13-1debian8
MYSQL_ENV_no_proxy=*.local, 169.254/16
MYSQL_NAME=/ubuntu/mysql
MYSQL_PORT_3306_TCP_PROTO=tcp
MYSQL_PORT_3306_TCP_ADDR=172.17.0.2
MYSQL_ENV_MYSQL_MAJOR=5.7
MYSQL_PORT=tcp://172.17.0.2:3306
root@60886fca65fb:/#
```

Each variable is prefixed by the uppercase alias, taken from the `--link` command, which is MYSQL in our case. The exposed environment variables can come from a couple of places:

- The `--env` (`-e` for short) and `--env-file` options on the `docker run` command when starting the source container.

- The `ENV` Dockerfile command – we will learn how to do it in the upcoming chapters.
- Each port exposed by the source container. Docker will generate three environment variables for each open port in the source container: one for the address, one for the port number, and one for the protocol.
- Unlike host entries, IP addresses stored as the environment variables are not automatically updated if the source container is restarted.

 You can link multiple containers to a single source. For example, you can have multiple web containers attached to your single database container.

Within a user-defined `bridge` network, linking is not supported. It works only on the bridge network created by default. If you need your containers to communicate on your created `bridge` network, you can expose and publish container ports on containers in this network. This is useful if you want to make a portion of the `bridge` network available to an outside network.

Docker's linking feature is a great way for source container to provide information about itself to a recipient container. In fact, this is internal to Docker and doesn't require exposing any network ports. That's a big benefit of linking: we don't need to expose the source container to the network.

The possibilities of configuring even complex network configuration are very broad in Docker. Containers can be a part of as many networks as you need. They can be a part of local `bridge` networks and overlay networks at the same time. If that's not enough, you can use external plugins to provide other networking options. Let's present this briefly.

Networking plugins

Docker Engine network plugins extend Docker to support a wide range of networking technologies, such as VXLAN, IPVLAN, MACVLAN, or something completely different. Network driver plugins are supported via the `LibNetwork` project. Some of the existing network plugins include, for example, a Weave Network Plugin – a network plugin that creates a virtual network that connects your Docker containers – across multiple hosts or clouds and enables automatic discovery of applications. Weave networks are resilient, partition tolerant, secure, and work in partially connected networks, and other adverse environments – all configured with delightful simplicity.

Networking possibilities are almost endless in Docker. It's hard to imagine a scenario that would be impossible to set up in Docker – by either using bridge or overlay networks. If the default set of drivers is not enough – you can always try to find a specific driver on the Internet – or develop it yourself. Let's focus now on another very important aspect of Docker container's extensibility- volumes.

Docker volumes

As you remember from the previous chapter, Docker filesystems are kind of temporary by default. If you start up a Docker image (that is, run the container) you'll end up with a read/write layer on top of the layer's stack. You can create, modify, and delete files as you wish, but if you stop the container and start it up again, all your changes will be lost: any files you previously deleted will now be back, and any new files or edits you made won't be present. Of course, you can commit the changes back into the image to have them persisted. This is a great feature if you want to create a complete setup of your application in the image, altogether with all its environment variable. But this is not very convenient when it comes to storing and retrieving data. At best we should separate out the container lifecycle from the data. Ideally, you would probably want to keep these separate so that the data generated (or being used) by your application is not destroyed or tied to the container lifecycle and can thus be reused. The perfect example is a web server: the Docker image contains web server software, configured and ready to use. But the data the server will be using (your web pages) should be separated from the image, so you can change it anytime without modifying an image. And vice versa – you can, let's say, upgrade the web server software to a new version or tweak its configuration without modifying a data it will be serving. This is done via volumes, which we will focus on in this part of the chapter. Volumes are not a part of the Union File System, so the write operations are instant and as fast as possible, so there is no need to commit any changes.

> Volumes live outside of the Union File System and exist as normal directories and files on the host filesystem.

Let's begin by creating a volume.

Creating a volume

In Docker, you have basically three options to create volumes:

- Creating a nameless volume by simply mapping volume to host directory (by using the -v argument for the docker run command)
- Creating a Docker container image only for data (and then using the --volumes-from for docker run command)
- Creating a Docker named volume explicitly (using the docker volume create command)

Let's discuss them one by one, starting with the -v option for the docker run command. We will begin by running the latest Ubuntu and create a volume for our data:

```
docker run -it -v /Users/jarek/testDir/:/data ubuntu
```

The parameters in the -v option are the directory on the host (your own operating system) – it is /Users/jarek/testDir in my example—a colon, and a path at which it will be available for the container: /data in my case. As you can see, it's a volume without a name – just a mapping. This way, during the startup of the container, Docker has created a volume, which is a kind of mapped directory. It will be available for the container and also available from the host operating system. Any files already existing in the mapped directory (/Users/jarek/testDir in our case) will be available inside the container – they will not be deleted during the mapping. Because you have not specified a name for the volume, Docker will create a name for you. It will not be as funny as a container name we have seen before, but is unique enough to identify a volume using it. Let's check if the volume is here using the volume ls command:

The `volume ls` command can take some filter parameters, which can be quite useful. For example, you can list volumes that are not being used by any container:

```
docker volume ls -f dangling=true
```

Alternatively, list volumes are being created with a specific driver (we are going to cover drivers in a short while):

```
docker volume ls -f driver=local
```

The `name` filter matches on all or part of a volume's name, for example, the following command:

```
docker volume ls -f name=da
```

This will give you the list of all volumes containing `da` in their name:

Apart from mapping a volume to a known host directory, you can also create a volume that will not be mapped explicitly with a path on the host—just enter the path at which it will be available for the container, without a colon. If the container's base image contains data at the specified mount point, that data will be copied into the new volume upon volume initialization. (This does not apply when specifying a host directory explicitly, `http s://docs.docker.com/engine/tutorials/dockervolumes/`.) The idea behind it is that you should not care about the location of the volume on the host system, this way making the image portable between different hosts.

Consider the following command as an example:

```
docker run -it -v /data2 ubuntu
```

This time, Docker will create volume and map it to a internal path of the Docker setup on the host machine (it will be `/var/lib/docker/volumes` on the Macintosh).

If you are wondering what that host path is, inspect the volume using the volume inspect command. First, you will need to find out which is the volume associated with the container. You can do it by executing the `docker inspect` command on your container. The volume ID will be listed in the `inspect` command output.

With the volume name, you can just run `docker volume inspect <volumeName>`, which will be the following in my case:

```
docker volume inspect
3840cf476f0db530a9e62d5251975156eb5418bd9ba75e7435eb427ece46fc22
```

```
07:30:43   jarek@MacBook-Pro-Jarek   ~
$ docker volume inspect 3840cf476f0db530a9e62d5251975156eb5418bd9ba75e7435eb427ece46fc22
[
    {
        "Name": "3840cf476f0db530a9e62d5251975156eb5418bd9ba75e7435eb427ece46fc22",
        "Driver": "local",
        "Mountpoint": "/var/lib/docker/volumes/3840cf476f0db530a9e62d5251975156eb5418bd9ba75e743
5eb427ece46fc22/_data",
        "Labels": null,
        "Scope": "local"
    }
]

07:30:45   jarek@MacBook-Pro-Jarek   ~
$
```

The output of the command briefly shows the details of the volume – its name, the driver being used (we will get to it shortly), a mount point in the host system, assigned labels, and a scope. As you can see, in my case, Docker assigned a mount point for this volume somewhere in /var/lib/docker/volumes. You are not limited to just one volume per container. That would be a serious limitation.

 You can use the -v multiple times to mount multiple data volumes.

The -v option can be used not only for directories, but for single files as well. This can be very useful if you want to have configuration files available in your container. The best example for it is the example from the official Docker documentation:

```
docker run -it -v ~/.bash_history:/root/.bash_history ubuntu
```

Executing the preceding command will make you having the same bash history between your local machine and a started Ubuntu container. And best of all, if you exit the container, the bash history on your own local machine will contain the bash commands you have been executing inside the container.

Mapping a single file from a host allows exposing a configuration for your containers.

The trick for sharing the data between containers is to use the --volumes-from option when executing the docker run command. This way if one of your containers has volumes mounted already, you can instruct Docker to use the same volumes when starting another container. Consider the following example:

```
docker run -it --name myUbuntu -v /data ubuntu
```

This will start Ubuntu with volume mounted as /data. Start another container using the following command:

```
docker run -it --name myBusyBox --volumes-from myUbuntu busybox
```

Here, your Ubuntu and busybox containers will share the same volume and thus, the same data. You can use multiple --volumes-from options to combine data volumes from several containers. Also, chaining is possible – you can mount chained --volumes_from in a group of containers.

The common practice when working with Docker is to create data-only containers. The only purpose of data-only containers is to carry on the volume. For any other containers that you then want to connect to this data volume container, use the Docker's `---volumes-from` option to grab the volume from this container and apply them to the current container. Let's consider the following example:

```
$ docker create -v ~/docker-nginx/html:/usr/share/nginx/html --name
myWebSiteData nginx
```

By executing the preceding command, we are creating a container with the name `myWebSiteData`. Its only purpose will be to have a `/usr/share/nginx/html` volume attached and mapped to `~/docker-nginx/html` in your home directory. You may ask what image should you pick as a base for the data-only container. Well, it doesn't matter that much – we are not going to run this container anyway, so it will not be wasting resources such as CPU or RAM. You may use the same image for the data container as for the container with the application you are going to run. You don't leave data containers running, so it won't consume resources. Using the same image can be important for several reasons:

- It will take up less space as you already have the image layer cached (as you remember from Chapter 3, *Understanding Images and Containers*, Docker caches and shares the same layers between images)
- The image could be used to fill the volume with some initial data, such as default configuration files, for example
- The permissions and ownership will be correct

With our data-only container ready, we can use it to provide a volume for another container (with our application, for example), using the `--volumes-from` option for the `docker run` command, just like we did previously, when dealing with nameless volumes.

Let's say we want to run `nginx` with the volume referenced in our data-only `myWebsiteData` container:

```
$ docker run --name docker-nginx -p 80:80 -d --volumes-from
myWebsiteData nginx
```

Of course, the data-only container can be shared among other containers – in our case, you can run as many `nginx` containers as you like – as long as you enter the same `--volumes-from` option, they will share the same data.

Apart from creating a volume when starting a container or using data-only containers, there is a command that allows creating the volume before starting any containers. It's the last option on our list: the possibility to create Docker volumes explicitly, using the `docker volume create` command.

We will use it now, and this time, we will aslo provide a more friendly name for our volume. To create a volume, execute the volume create command:

```
docker volume create --name data
```

Again, the new data volume will be available when you list volumes using the `volume ls` command. To mount a volume in a container during its startup, use the same `-v` option when starting a container:

```
docker run -it -v data:/data ubuntu
```

The data volume will then be available for your container in `/data`. It's also possible to run another container with the same volume mounted.

> Volumes can be shared between containers – just run them with mapping the same volume.

When it comes to creating your own images using Dockerfile, the VOLUME instruction comes in handy. Actually, we will be using it later in the book, when creating images from a Dockerfile.

It creates a mount point with the specified name and marks it as holding externally mounted volumes from native host or other containers. Creating volumes using the VOLUME instruction has one important difference to using option during the container startup: you cannot specify a host directory when using the VOLUME instruction. Dockerfiles are meant to be portable and shared. The host directory volume is 100% host dependent and will break on any other machine, which is a little bit off the Docker idea. Because of this, it is only possible to use portable instructions within a Dockerfile. A benefit of using shared volumes is that they are host-independent. This means that a volume can be made available on any host that a container is started on as long as it has access to the shared storage and has the plugin (driver) installed.

> If you need to specify a host directory when creating a volume, you need to specify it at runtime.

Removing a volume

The same as with creating volumes, there are two ways of removing a volume from Docker. One way is to remove a volume by referencing a container's name and executing the `rm -v` command:

```
docker rm -v <containerName>
```

```
                                testDir — jarek@MacBook-Pro-Jarek — ~/testDir — -zsh — 104×14

  10:01:40    jarek@MacBook-Pro-Jarek    ~/testDir
$ docker rm -v myUbuntu
myUbuntu

  10:01:49    jarek@MacBook-Pro-Jarek    ~/testDir
$
```

Docker will not warn you when removing a container without providing the `-v` option to delete its volumes. As a result, you will have dangling volumes – volumes that are no longer referenced by a container.

You can also remove the volume using the `volume rm` command:

```
docker volume rm <volumeName>
```

If the volume happens to being used by the container, Docker Engine will not allow deleting it and will give you a warning message:

```
                                testDir — jarek@MacBook-Pro-Jarek — -zsh — 104×14
              ~/testDir                                              docker                        +
$ docker volume ls
DRIVER              VOLUME NAME
local               1ca9f29df4108d197b5f5c44d674b55bef478dc0d14650433bff3cf70bb31c7b
local               3840cf476f0db530a9e62d5251975156eb5418bd9ba75e7435eb427ece46fc22
local               data

  09:14:23    jarek@MacBook-Pro-Jarek    ~/testDir
$ docker volume rm data
Error response from daemon: Unable to remove volume, volume still in use: remove data: volume is in use
- [814f8e086a25d26acbda076166b2e11f3afaee074c7e712412b69de6782a1e4b, 6e3fbaf59463e67702ea55ffdc4d673e892
4d3a177f8b04c7837366e7538444f]

  09:14:29    x   jarek@MacBook-Pro-Jarek    ~/testDir
$
```

The handy shortcut to remove all volumes not being referenced by any container is using a `dangling=true` filter from the `volume ls` command:

```
docker volume rm $(docker volume ls -qf dangling=true)
```

As you can see, creating, sharing, and removing volumes in Docker is not that tricky. It's very flexible and allows creating a setup you will need for your applications. But there's more to this flexibility. When creating a volume, you can specify a `--driver` option (or `-d` for short), which may be useful if you need to map some external, not-so-standard storage. The volumes we have created so far were using the `local` filesystem driver (the files were being stored on the local drive of the host system) – you can see the driver name when inspecting a volume using the `volume inspect` command. There are other options though, let's look at them now;

Volume drivers

The same as with network driver plugins, the volume plugins extend the capabilities of the Docker Engine and enable integration with other types of storage. There are tons of ready-to-use plugins available for free on the Internet; you can find a list on Docker's GitHub page. Some of them include the following:

- **Docker Volume Driver for Azure File Storage**: This is a Docker Volume Driver that uses Azure File Storage to mount file shares on the cloud to Docker containers as volumes. It uses network file sharing by utilizing the SMB (Server Message Block) and CIFS (Common Internet File System) protocols capabilities of Azure File Storage. You can create Docker containers that can migrate from one host to another seamlessly or share volumes among multiple containers running on different hosts.

- **IPFS:** The abbreviation stands from **InterPlanetary File System**. It's an open source volume plugin that allows using an IPFS filesystem as a volume. IPFS is a very interesting and promising storage system – it makes, possible to distribute high volumes of data with high efficiency. It provides deduplication, high performance, and clustered persistence, provides secure P2P content delivery, fast performance, and decentralized archiving. IPFS provides resilient access to data, independent of low latency or connectivity to the backbone.

- **Keywhiz:** This driver can be used to make your container talk to a remote Keywhiz server. Keywhiz is a system for managing and distributing secret data, such as TLS certificates/keys, GPG keys, API tokens, and database credentials. Instead of putting this data in config files or copying files (which is likely to be leaked or difficult to track), Keywhiz makes managing it easier and more secure: Keywhiz servers in a cluster centrally store secrets encrypted in a database. Clients use mutually authenticated TLS (mTLS) to retrieve secrets they have access to.

As you can see from the preceding examples, they are quite interesting, sometimes even exotic. Because of the extendable nature of Docker and its plugin architecture, you can create very flexible setups. But third-party drivers do not always introduce completely new storage types, sometimes they just extend the existing drivers. An example of that is `Local Persist Plugin`, a volume plugin that extends the default local driver's functionality by allowing you to specify a mount point anywhere on the host, which enables the files to always persist, even if the volume is removed via Docker's `volume rm` command.

If you need a volume plugin that is not yet available, you can just write your own – the process is very well documented on Docker's GitHub page, together with extensible examples.

Summary

We've now covered how to open our containers to the external world – we can use networking and mounted volumes to be able to share data between containers and other hosts. Let's summarize what we have learned so far in this chapter. We know that containers from the same Docker host see each other automatically on the default `bridge` network, only if the container is bound to default bridge. We can make containers running on different hosts to communicate with each other. To do this, we need a multi-host `overlay` network. You will need Docker version 1.12 or later running in swarm mode, or alternatively, a key-value storage running. If the drivers provided by Docker are not enough, we can use the network plugins to further extend the networking data exchange. We went through the volume creation process and know that volumes persist data even through container restarts; we also know that changes to files on the volume are made directly, but they will not be included when you update an image.

Volumes allow sharing data between the host filesystem and the Docker container, or between other Docker containers, and they persist even if the container itself is deleted. We can use the volume drivers to further extend the file exchange possibilities.

In the next chapter, we will focus on the Docker hub. We will learn how to find images that will be our foundation for the next chapters, where we will actually create our images using Dockerfiles.

5
Finding Images

In previous chapters, we have learned how to install Docker and we got familiar with the Docker architecture, networking, and persistent storage features. We have mentioned about working with the Docker Hub and remote repositories a little in `Chapter 3`, *Understanding Images and Containers*, but this time we will go into more details.

This chapter will cover the following topics:

- The Docker Hub
- Image tags
- Searching for images using the web interface and a command line
- Docker Hub REST API

Before we actually build our own images in the next chapter, we are going to focus on working with Docker Hub first-creating an account, authenticating, looking for images, and pulling them. We will go into more details of version and tags, explaining one of the most misunderstood Docker tags, `latest`. This chapter will also present the REST API of Docker Hub, which may come in handy if you plan to use Docker Hub programmatically—from your own applications or integration flow.

This time also we will create an account on the Docker Hub—it will be mandatory when we publish our images to the world.

The Docker Hub

The main functionality of the Docker registry is to find a certain image based on a description. The registry handles Docker Images in repositories. It's important to understand the difference between registry and repository. Docker registry is a service that is storing your Docker Images, and repository is a collection of different docker images with the same name, which have different tags (we will get back to tags in a while). Like the git counterpart, a Docker repository is identified by a URI and can either be public or private.

The most recognized hosted version of a Docker registry is the Docker Hub. It comes with a nice and usable UI. The Docker Hub is a software-as-a service (SaaS) platform for sharing and managing Docker images. In other words, it's a cloud-based registry service capable of hosting and distributing images. Images are being kept either in public or private repositories. Currently, the Hub serves hundreds of thousands public repositories and the number grows every day. Almost one third of these public repositories are using automated builds, which means that the images are being built by the Hub itself using a published Dockerfile. The rest of the repositories contain images that have been uploaded manually via a `docker push` command. Docker Hub is available at `https://hub.docker.com/`.

 Docker Hub is the default registry. If you do not provide registry host name using registry-related commands such as `login`, `pull`, or `push`, Docker will use the Docker Hub.

A registry offers operations such as pushing (uploading an image into a repository) and pulling (downloading an image from a repository). Docker registry has also another important role to play, the index. The index maintains information about user accounts, checksums of the images, and public namespaces. In fact, the Docker Hub is a centralized index for public repositories.

The Docker Hub is a public service and you get one private repository for free if your register your account. If you need more private repositories you can upgrade your Docker Hub plan, which will not be free of charge.

Docker Hub is not just a registry and index-a place to search, store or get images from-it's rather an umbrella project; it allows linking to code repositories (such as GitHub or BitBucket), create automated builds of your images, and test them. Docker Hub allows also linking to the Docker Cloud so you can deploy images to your own hosts. All these aspects will be useful when creating your image workflow automation throughout the development pipeline. We will cover these development-related features such as publishing and creating automated builds in detail in `Chapter 8`, *Publishing Images*.

Apart from managing single user accounts and authentication, the Docker hub also manages organizations. By creating an organization, you can easily give your coworkers access to shared image repositories and let Docker Hub manage the team collaboration and change management.

Let's summarize the Docker Hub features:

- **Accounts**: This helps in user management and authentication.
- **Organizations**: This is used to create work groups to manage access to image repositories.
- **Image repositories**: This is used to search, `pull`, `push`, and `manage` images from either community, official, or private image repositories.
- **Automated builds and web hooks**: This is used to automatically trigger the image build process when changes to a source code are being made. Web hooks are a part of automated builds and let you execute different actions after pushing the image to a repository.
- **Integration source code repositories**: This is used to link your GitHub and/or Bitbucket source code repositories to create a development workflow.
- **REST API**: Almost every feature available through the Docker Hub's web interface is also available as a well-documented REST endpoint you can use to deal with Docker Hub programmatically.

The Docker Hub account (it's called Docker ID) is not mandatory for searching and pulling images. In fact, as you remember, we have pulled a lot of `hello-world`, `nginx`, and `ubuntu` images to demonstrate the Docker's architecture in the previous chapters, not having the proper Docker ID registered.

Docker Hub account is not mandatory for searching and pulling images from the Docker Hub—you can download images without signing in or even having an account.

However, in order to publish images, post your comments, or to star a repository, you will need a Docker ID. By leaving comments, you can interact with other members of the Docker community and maintainers of the specific images.

Like in any matured community, your comments should be precise and meaningful. If you find any comments that are not appropriate, you can flag them for examination.

Starring a repository serves the same purpose as stars on the GitHub—it's a way to show that you like a repository. Stars function also has an easy way of bookmarking your favorite repositories. As of the time of writing this book, the `ubuntu` repository was the most starred one. Let's begin with account creation.

Docker Hub account

In order to get your Docker ID, head to `http://hub.docker.com`and scroll to the **Sign Up** part. You will need to provide a username (it will become a namespace for images you will publish), password, and valid e-mail address, as shown in the following screenshot:

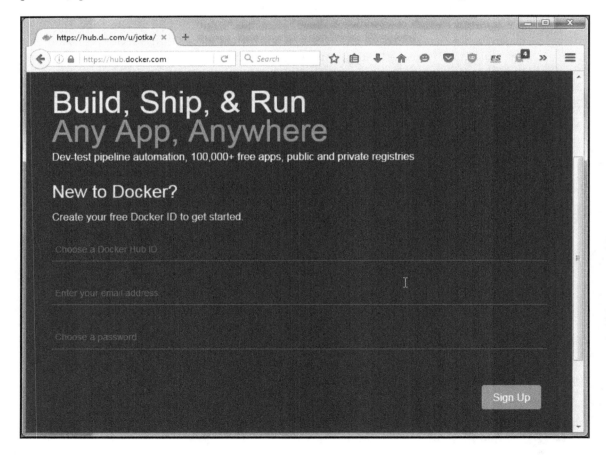

A valid e-mail address is required to register because the activation e-mail will be sent to this address.

> If you can't find the validation e-mail, check the `Spam` folder and exclude `docker.com` from bad senders. If you still cannot find it, go to `https://hub.docker.com/login/` and perform the same procedure as for the password reset the activation link will be sent again.

From there, you can log in using your Docker ID. When you first log into your new account, you will land on the Docker Dashboard, a page with tabbed interface, as shown in the following screenshot:

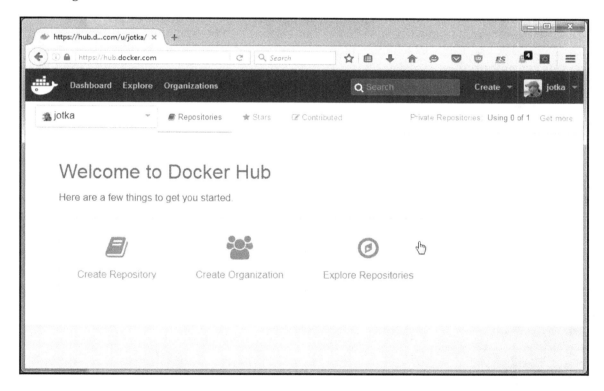

The first tab holds a list of your repositories; it will contain nothing for the fresh account and provide some quick shortcuts for creating a repository, organization, or exploring repositories. Note that you can also search for images using the `search` field in the header of the site, it's always at hand. The second tab serves the purpose of your bookmarks viewer-it lists the repositories you have starred.

The Dashboard also presents a link to the account settings page, where you can set your default repository visibility (it's `public` by default, you can change it to `private`). From here, you can also set your personal details such as name, location, web page address, or add additional e-mail address linked with your Docker ID (only can be primary). Those e-mail addresses will be used for all announcements and communication from Docker. The **Settings** page allows also converting your personal (User) account into the Organization account. Let's clarify what an Organization account is.

Organization account and teams

Organizations and groups allow you to collaborate across your organization or team. You can add new organizations and see what organizations you belong to in the account's `Settings` tab. You can also see them below your username on your repositories page and in your account profile.

If you switch your Dashboard to the organization you belong to, it will differ slightly from the personal user dashboard, as shown in the following screenshot:

The main difference is the presence of the `Teams` tab, where you can define teams within your organization. Docker Hub will automatically create the `Owners` team. The `Owners` team is kind of special—you need to be a member of the organization's `Owners` team to create a new repository, a new automated build and also a new team within this organization. If you belong to the `Owner` team, you can assign access right in the `Collaborators` section of the repository view. This can be read access (allowing you to view, search, and pull a private repository in the same way as they can a public repository), write access (allowing you to `push` an image), or admin access (allowing you to modify the repositories properties such as description, collaborators rights, public or private visibility, or delete the repository). You can add or invite users to any of the organization's teams, by selecting the team and entering a username (for current Docker Hub users) or e-mail address, if they are not yet registered:

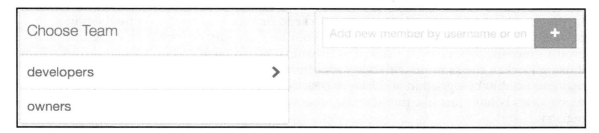

In result, the invited users will receive an e-mail with an invitation to join the team.

Collaborators

The Docker Hub introduces a term collaborator. A collaborator is simply another Docker Hub user, who you can give access to your repository, either public or private. You do it in the repository's **Settings** page, in the **Collaborators** tab, as shown in the following screenshot:

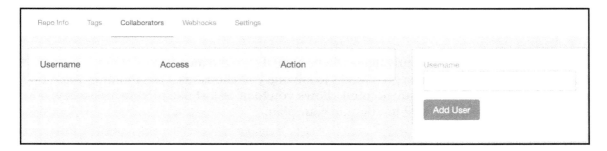

Collaborators are not allowed to perform any administrative tasks such as deleting the repository or changing its status from private to public. They can, however, use your repository by executing `docker push` and `docker pull` commands. If you need more specific and detailed access rights setup for your repositories, consider using organization and teams provided by Docker Hub.

> It is worth noting, that a collaborator cannot add other collaborators. Only you, as the owner of the repository has administrative access.

Private Repositories

If you want to store images that you want to keep private, you need to store them in a private repository. It will be visible only to your own account or within an organization or group. Once the repository is marked as private, you can push and pull images to and from it using Docker, the same as with other repositories that are public. The only difference is that you need to be signed in and have access to work with a private repository. Private repositories behave just like public ones; however, they will not be listed on the public registry.

In the repository's `Settings` page, you can switch its visibility, to be either `public` or `private`, as shown in the following screenshot:

Visibility Settings

Make this Repository Private   Make Private

Private repositories are only available to you or members of your organization.
You are using 0 of 1 private repositories.

If you make your repository private, it will be available to the members of your organization and you can also give access to anyone you choose as a collaborator. As you remember, the free Docker Hub account allows you to have just one private repository, if you want more, you will need to upgrade your plan.

Logging into Docker Hub

You can of course login into your account using the Docker Hub page, but a more common action would be to log in using the shell or command line. Let's log into the Docker Hub registry using our account:

```
docker login --username myUser --password 123
```

By default, Docker assumes the registry you are logging into will be Docker Hub. To log into a different registry, provide a registry's hostname as the last parameter of the `login` command:

```
docker login --username myUser --password 123 localhost:8080
```

Let's log into the Docker Hub, on a Mac this time:

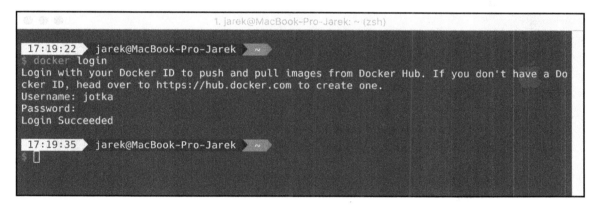

If you are authenticated correctly, the Docker will respond briefly, saying that we're ready to pull images from the registry:

```
Login Succeeded
```

After you login, an interesting thing will happen behind the scenes. Since communicating with a registry to pull, push, and look for images is very common when working with Docker, your credentials will be stored for future use. This way you can automate things. Docker will get the credentials from the local storage and use it on your behalf when you request things such as pulling or pushing an image. By default, Docker will use just a plain text file named `.docker/config.json` written in your home directory (or profile folder on MS Windows):

```
1. jarek@MacBook-Pro-Jarek: ~ (zsh)

17:20:13    jarek@MacBook-Pro-Jarek    ~
$ more .docker/config.json
{
        "auths": {
                "https://index.docker.io/v1/": {
                        "auth": "■■■■■■■■■■■■■■■■■■■■■■■"
                }
        }
}

17:20:21    jarek@MacBook-Pro-Jarek    ~
$ []
```

The structure of this file supports multiple registries at once. In our case, we just have one entry for the default, official Docker index (`index.docker.io`), but we could have more if we need it. From now on, when the registry needs authentication (for example, when doing a `push` command), Docker will pick your credentials from the `config.json` file. Of course, the registry you going to work with must match the index URL taken from the entries in the `config` file. Note that there is no date or time present in the file—the credentials are cached forever until we tell Docker to remove them, using the logout command.

 Credentials stored in the local file are not encrypted—it's just a `username:password` string encoded using Base64 encoding. Do not share this file with anyone.

If you no longer want to cache your credentials in the local storage, issue the logout command:

```
docker logout
```

Docker will reply, saying that the entry from the `config.json` file has been removed and thus you have been logged out from the registry:

Remove login credentials for https://index.docker.io/v1/

The local credentials file can be useful if you are experimenting with the Docker Hub and security is not the thing you especially care for. In other cases, like working with private registries or doing some serious work, storing the credentials in some other storage can be a more appropriate and secure solution. Using an external store is more secure than storing credentials in the Docker configuration file. Luckily, the Docker Engine can make use of an external credentials store, such as the native keychain of the operating system. This will be, for example, Apple OS X keychain or Microsoft Windows Credential Manager.

 Using external storages will require additional helpers available on a system `$PATH`. The helper program interacts with a specific keychain or external store. You can download helpers from GitHub `https://github.com/docker/docker-credential-helpers/releases`. The list of currently available credential helpers include: D-Bus Secret Service, Apple OS X keychain, and Microsoft Windows Credential Manager.

If you want to use external storage for your credentials, you need to make helpers available on a system `$PATH` and instruct Docker, that it needs to use this external storage by modifying `.docker/config.json`:

```
{
   "credsStore": "osxkeychain"
}
```

If you will ever need to store the credentials in a storage that is not officially supported by Docker, there are some third-party storage helpers available on the Internet. For example, there is Amazon ECR Credentials helper available on GitHub (`https://github.com/awslabs/amazon-ecr-credential-helper`). It makes use of the same credentials as the AWS command-line tools and the AWS SDKs. In case you don't find a credentials helper you need, Docker allows using your own developed credential helpers. Basically, a helper can be any program that can read values from the standard input. It exposes just three operations: `store` (to save credentials, where the input is JSON containing the server URL, name, and password), `get`, and `erase` to get and remove credentials from the storage, respectively. `Get` and `erase` takes only server URL as an input parameter.

The simplest way to implement your own credentials store will be to browse the source code for the existing helpers at GitHub `https://github.com/docker/docker-credential-helpers`.

Now that we understand what happens when you log into the registry, it's time to make use of it and search for an image.

Searching for images

To effectively search for a specific image, first we need to understand the Docker image naming schema and tags concept. We have already mentioned it before; let's look at it now in detail.

Image naming and tags

The full image name has the following syntax:

```
{registry_host}/(_|/{user_or_org_namespace})/{repository}:{tag}
```

Let's explore it in detail, image names start with a namespace and a slash. For example, the image named `hello-world` created and uploaded by user `tutum` (which is an Apache image responding with `hello-world` message on port `80`, by the way) will begin with this part: `tutum/hello-world`.

There can also be images with no namespace prefix-these will be images from the so-called **official repositories**. The official repositories are certified repositories from vendors and contributors to Docker such as Red Hat, Oracle, and Canonical. And of course, you can use them to build your own applications and services. An example of the official images can be the most-starred `ubuntu`, `nginx`, or the official version of `hello-world`-images that we have been using in the previous chapters. Official images are usually supported by the people who have created the application that is containerized in Docker, for example, `nginx` image from the official repository is supported by the Nginx team.

 If you decide to use an image from the official repository as the base for your own work, you can be pretty sure you're using a maintained, optimized, and up-to-date image.

Each repository can contain multiple images. For example, the `nginx` repository will contain different versions of the web server image, such as `1.10.1-alpine`, `stable`, `latest`, and so on. Each of these images is identified by tags. As we have mentioned before, tags usually represent different versions of the same application or service and are used to distinguish images from each other. A tag is simply an alphanumeric identifier attached to the image, which could be, for example, `1.0` or `latest`, but it's considered good practice to provide a build hash to clearly and unambiguously identify the image. A tag name may not start with a period or a dash and may contain a maximum of 128 characters. Docker's automated builds, which we are going to cover later, let you link image tags either to a branch or a tag in your git history.

The `latest` tag is kind of a special one. Also, it may not work as you may expect. Well, to cut the long story short, it doesn't mean anything special unless the image creator (`ubuntu` or `nginx`, for example) has a specific `build`, `tag`, and `push` pattern. The `latest` tag assigned to an image simply means that it's the image that was last built and executed without a specific tag provided. It's easy to understand that it may be confusing-pulling the image tagged `latest` will not fetch the latest version of the software.

> Docker will not take care of checking if you are getting the newest version of the software when pulling the image tagged `latest`.

If you pull the image without specifying a tag, Docker will download the image tagged `latest`. But this will not be necessary with the latest and greatest version of the software you wanted to run. Instead, you should always consult the other tags present in the repository to pick the version of software you need.

Also, the same `latest` tag behavior will apply if we build our own images later in this book. If you do not specify a tag after the repository name, it will be automatically assigned the `latest` tag in the repository.

Last but not least, the image name can be prefixed with a hostname or IP of the Docker registry. For example, the image name `localhost:5000/hello-world` will reference a `hello-world` repository in your local registry. But what if you need to pull the official image from the registry other than Docker Hub? Following the image name schema, just use the single underscore character instead of user or organization name. For example, consider the following command:

```
docker pull somerRegistry.com/_/someOfficialImage:1.0
```

This will pull the image tagged `1.0` from the `someOfficialImage` official repository located on `somerRegistry.com`. You can also shorten the command by omitting the user or organization name completely. Our command will then look just like this:

```
docker pull somerRegistry.com/someOfficialImage:1.0
```

As you remember, if you do not provide a registry hostname, Docker will default to its own official registry, the Docker Hub.

Now we should have a full understanding of what the image name consists of. It should be easier to precisely locate an image to pull. You can find public repositories and images from Docker Hub in two ways. You use the Docker Hub website or you can use the Docker command-line tool to run the `docker search` command. Let's search for an image now.

Searching through the web interface

Looking for an image using the web interface of Docker Hub is as simple as using the `Search` field in the right upper corner:

In response, Docker Hub will list images with names or authors matching your search term. Note that only public repositories will be presented on the result list.

 Private repositories will not appear in the repository search results.

In the search results, you can notice the stars and the download count. This can give you an idea about how popular the repository is. Also, you can see if the repository is official or public and if it is built using the automated build:

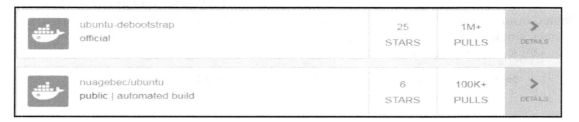

Searching using the web interface can be useful if you would like to get some more detailed information about the repository. If you click on the `repository` name, you will be presented with the repository details page, often containing a lot of useful information. The second tab on the details page contains a list of tags, so you can quickly look around and pick the version you need. This view also shows you the size of the associated image. Image sizes are the cumulative space taken up by the image and all its parent images—this is also the disk space used by the contents of the tar file formed when you execute the `docker save` command to export an image. If the image listed on the search results page is being built automatically, Docker Hub will present two additional tabs: The **Dockerfile** and **Build Details**. The **Dockerfile** tab will contain the Dockerfile being used during the build (it can be very useful when learning how to create your own Dockerfiles) and a linked source repository (as you remember, this may be GitHub or BitBucket):

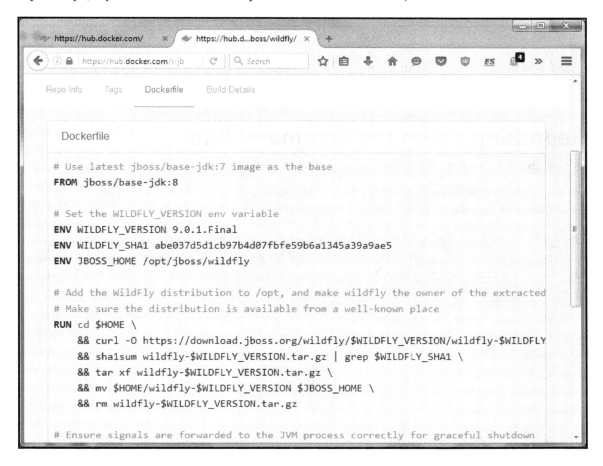

The **Build Details** list the automated build job status (such as success or failure) and information like the date of the build:

Status	Tag	Created	Last Updated
Repo Info Tags Dockerfile **Build Details**			
✓ Success	xenial	12 hours ago	12 hours ago
✓ Success	14.04	12 hours ago	12 hours ago

As you can see, the web interface of Docker Hub can give you a lot of details about the image you are looking for, but it's not very convenient. A faster solution is to search for an image using the command line.

Searching using the command line

Docker gives you a command for searching for an image: `docker search`.

For example, if you were looking for an `ubuntu` image, you might run the following command line search: `docker search Ubuntu`.

The syntax of the `search` command is rather straightforward, you can see it by issuing the `docker help search` command. By default, it takes only one argument—what to look for. Searching can find images by image name, username, or description. This will show you a list of the currently available repositories on the Docker Hub, which match the provided keyword. This is an example output of searching for the Ubuntu image:

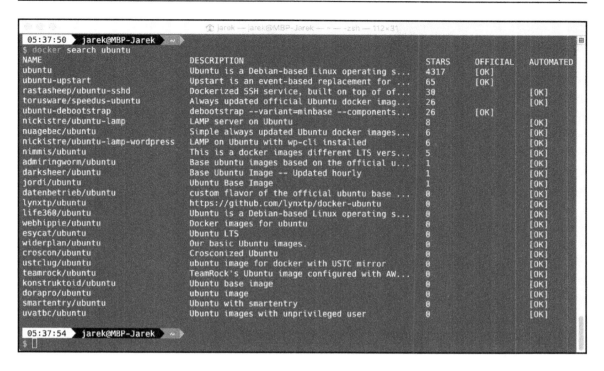

```
05:37:50  jarek@MBP-Jarek  ~
$ docker search ubuntu
NAME                           DESCRIPTION                                  STARS  OFFICIAL  AUTOMATED
ubuntu                         Ubuntu is a Debian-based Linux operating s... 4317  [OK]
ubuntu-upstart                 Upstart is an event-based replacement for ... 65    [OK]
rastasheep/ubuntu-sshd         Dockerized SSH service, built on top of of... 30              [OK]
torusware/speedus-ubuntu       Always updated official Ubuntu docker imag... 26              [OK]
ubuntu-debootstrap             debootstrap --variant=minbase --components... 26    [OK]
nickistre/ubuntu-lamp          LAMP server on Ubuntu                         8               [OK]
nuagebec/ubuntu                Simple always updated Ubuntu docker images... 6               [OK]
nickistre/ubuntu-lamp-wordpress LAMP on Ubuntu with wp-cli installed         6               [OK]
nimmis/ubuntu                  This is a docker images different LTS vers... 5               [OK]
admiringworm/ubuntu            Base ubuntu images based on the official u... 1               [OK]
darksheer/ubuntu               Base Ubuntu Image -- Updated hourly          1               [OK]
jordi/ubuntu                   Ubuntu Base Image                            1               [OK]
datenbetrieb/ubuntu            custom flavor of the official ubuntu base ... 0               [OK]
lynxtp/ubuntu                  https://github.com/lynxtp/docker-ubuntu      0               [OK]
life360/ubuntu                 Ubuntu is a Debian-based Linux operating s... 0               [OK]
webhippie/ubuntu               Docker images for ubuntu                     0               [OK]
esycat/ubuntu                  Ubuntu LTS                                   0               [OK]
widerplan/ubuntu               Our basic Ubuntu images.                     0               [OK]
croscon/ubuntu                 Crosconized Ubuntu                           0               [OK]
ustclug/ubuntu                 ubuntu image for docker with USTC mirror     0               [OK]
teamrock/ubuntu                TeamRock's Ubuntu image configured with AW... 0               [OK]
konstruktoid/ubuntu            Ubuntu base image                            0               [OK]
dorapro/ubuntu                 ubuntu image                                 0               [OK]
smartentry/ubuntu              Ubuntu with smartentry                       0               [OK]
uvatbc/ubuntu                  Ubuntu images with unprivileged user         0               [OK]
05:37:54  jarek@MBP-Jarek  ~
$
```

There is a lot of information at a glance. Notice that the command output lists the image names, a short description, also the number of stars, a marker saying if it's the official repository and a status of the last automated build.

If a repository is private, it won't be listed on the repository search results, unless you are the image creator, member of an organization, or a collaborator.

> Private repositories will not appear in the repository search results. To see all the repositories you can access and their status, view the Dashboard on Docker Hub.

The reason for this is that Docker first asks the index if you have enough permissions to list and pull the image (if you are the creator, member of the organization, or a collaborator). Actually, a lot of actions are being taken in the background:

- You execute the request to the index to list or download the image.
- In response, the index returns an information:
  - The registry in which the image is located
  - Checksums for the image, including all its layers
  - A token for authorization purposes (*not mandatory for public repositories*):
    - You contact the registry with the token that was returned in the index's response.
    - In return, the registry asks the index if the token is authorized and valid.
    - Lastly, the index now sends a `true/false` message back to the registry, allowing or forbidding you to list or pull the needed image.

Using the shell (or command line) commands to find an image is the fastest way of finding the image. Once you have found the image you want—now comes the part you already know—just download the image with the `docker pull` command. But you are not limited only to docker `search/pull` commands and the Docker Hub web interface to deal with the images. Docker provides a comprehensive set of remote APIs and one of them is the Docker Hub and Docker registry REST API.

Docker Hub and docker registry REST API

Let's discuss Docker Registry API and Docker Hub API and list the API endpoints related to searching and downloading the images. We will be using the command-line tool `curl`, but you can use any REST client of your choice, even your web browser.

First, let's check the status of the remote registry, by issuing a call to `/_ping` endpoint, by executing an HTTP GET:

```
curl -k https://registry.hub.docker.com/v1/_ping
```

The registry will reply with a simple `true` value, that it's up and running.

First, we need to login or verify if we are logged in. Authorization is done with Basic Auth over SSL. To deal with user accounts, the API exposes the `/users` endpoint. Now, issue a `GET` on the following URL:

```
https://registry.hub.docker.com/v1/users
```

This will reply with an **OK** response if you are logged in or return the `HTTP 401 Unauthorized` status if you are not:

The Docker Hub API is not read-only, it also accepts `POST` requests. For example, you can register your new account issuing a `POST` to the `/users` endpoint. The `POST` request payload needs to contain the registration data, such as e-mail, username, and a password, for example:

```
{
    "email": "someUser@someHost.com",
    "username": "myNewAccount",
    "password": "mySecret"
}
```

To execute such an API call, you can use the `curl` command or any other tool or command for performing HTTP requests. An example `curl` command would look like this:

```
$ curl -H "Content-Type: application/json" -X POST -d '{" email ":"
someUser@someHost.com"," username":" myNewAccount", "password":"
mySecret"}' https://registry.hub.docker.com/v1/users
```

The response to this call will be just a string `User Created`, coming with the `HTTP 201 User Created` return code. In case of any errors, the response will have `HTTP 400 Error` code.

To update the user account, for example, to change a password or e-mail address for a given user, you will need to send similar JSON payload to the same `/users` endpoint, but with the PUT request. If you pass in an e-mail, it will add it to your account, it will not remove the old one. Passwords will be updated.

To look up images in the specific repository, we will use the `/images` endpoint. The URL for listing images is:

```
/v1/repositories/(namespace)/(repo_name)/images
```

So, to list the images in the official `ubuntu` repository, for example, we need to perform an HTTP `GET` operation on the following:

```
https://registry.hub.docker.com/v1/repositories/ubuntu/images
```

Let's execute the call (in a web browser this time—there will be a lot of output). Simply enter the URL in your web browser and execute the `GET` request. In return, the Hub will reply with a JSON containing the image IDs:

Not very readable, but there's another endpoint for listing tags, which the repository has. To obtain all tags or a specific tag of a repository, execute `GET` on the /tags endpoint. This has a similar URL:

```
/v1/repositories/(namespace)/(repository)/tags
```

Let's try it to lookup tags in the ubuntu repository, by executing the GET request on https ://registry.hub.docker.com/v1/repositories/ubuntu/tags:

https://registry.hub.docker.com/v1/repositories/ubuntu/tags

https://registry.hub.docker.com/v1/repositories/ubuntu/tags

[{"layer": "3db9c44f", "name": "10.04"}, {"layer": "c5881f11", "name": "12.10"}, {"layer": "463ff6be", "name": "13.04"}, {"layer": "195eb90b", "name": "13.10"}, {"layer": "5ba9dab4", "name": "14.04.1"}, {"layer": "63e3c102", "name": "14.04.2"}, {"layer": "8693db7e", "name": "14.04.3"}, {"layer": "dce38fb5", "name": "14.10"}, {"layer": "314a1f07", "name": "15.04"}, {"layer": "3db9c44f", "name": "lucid"}, {"layer": "1f80e9ca", "name": "precise-20150212"}, {"layer": "5898adab", "name": "precise-20150228.11"}, {"layer": "9610cfc6", "name": "precise-20150320"}, {"layer": "ac6b0eaa", "name": "precise-20150427"}, {"layer": "5c97af89", "name": "precise-20150528"}, {"layer": "78cef618", "name": "precise-20150612"}, {"layer": "6d021018", "name": "precise-20150626"}, {"layer": "d0e008c6", "name": "precise-20150729"}, {"layer": "57bca513", "name": "precise-20150813"}, {"layer": "61994089", "name": "precise-20150924"}, {"layer": "0ac5b09d", "name": "precise-20151020"}, {"layer": "04c3793b", "name": "precise-20151028"}, {"layer": "bad926a6", "name": "precise-20151208"}, {"layer": "32190de3", "name": "precise-20160108"}, {"layer": "aaf78e4d", "name": "precise-20160217"}, {"layer": "fe2d3b64", "name": "precise-20160225"}, {"layer": "f8440fa5", "name": "precise-20160303"}, {"layer": "af263f35", "name": "precise-20160311"}, {"layer": "33eb06bb", "name": "precise-20160318"}, {"layer": "25b0d242", "name": "precise-20160330"}, {"layer": "a77ec755", "name": "precise-20160425"}, {"layer": "550ac17d", "name": "precise-20160503"}, {"layer": "9227b87c", "name": "precise-20160526"}, {"layer": "c5881f11", "name": "quantal"}, {"layer": "463ff6be", "name": "raring"}, {"layer": "195eb90b", "name": "saucy"}, {"layer": "2d24f826", "name": "trusty-20150218.1"}, {"layer": "2103b00b", "name": "trusty-20150228.11"}, {"layer": "b7cf8f0d", "name": "trusty-20150320"}, {"layer": "07f8e8c5", "name": "trusty-20150427"}, {"layer": "fa81ed08", "name": "trusty-20150528"}, {"layer": "6d494699", "name": "trusty-20150612"}, {"layer": "d2a0ecff", "name": "trusty-20150630"}, {"layer": "63e3c102", "name": "trusty-20150730"}, {"layer": "8251da35", "name": "trusty-20150806"}, {"layer": "91e54dfb", "name": "trusty-20150814"}, {"layer": "cdd47452", "name": "trusty-20151001"}, {"layer": "a005e6b7", "name": "trusty-20151009"}, {"layer": "a5a467fd", "name": "trusty-20151021"}, {"layer": "ca4d7b1b", "name": "trusty-20151028"}, {"layer": "d55e68e6", "name": "trusty-20151208"}, {"layer": "af88597e", "name": "trusty-20151218"}, {"layer": "8693db7e", "name": "trusty-20160119"}, {"layer": "c29e52d4", "name": "trusty-20160217"}, {"layer": "1997914a", "name": "trusty-20160226"}, {"layer": "56063ad5", "name": "trusty-20160302"}, {"layer": "c917d649", "name": "trusty-20160315"}, {"layer": "ab035c88", "name": "trusty-20160317"}, {"layer": "901e234d", "name": "trusty-20160323"}, {"layer": "41cc538f", "name": "trusty-20160405"}, {"layer": "a572fb20", "name": "trusty-20160412"}, {"layer": "66e0fb0f", "name": "trusty-20160424"}, {"layer": "d4751aa1", "name": "trusty-20160503.1"}, {"layer": "9bc95376", "name": "trusty-20160526"}, {"layer": "dce38fb5", "name": "utopic"}, {"layer": "78949b1e", "name": "utopic-20150211"}, {"layer": "525b6e4a", "name": "utopic-20150228.11"}, {"layer": "59a878f2", "name": "utopic-20150319"}, {"layer": "0b79d1c2", "name":

Now, in the response we have some more information like the layer ID and a name of the tag, often including the latest tag.

Apart from the endpoints for listing user login and validation, listing images and tags, the Registry Hub API contains some more. Let's summarize them in the following table:

Purpose	Request type and endpoint
Status check of registry	GET /v1/_ping
Create a new user account	POST /v1/users
Update user details	PUT /v1/users/(username)/
Authorize a token for a library	PUT /v1/repositories/(repo_name)/auth

Authorize a token for user's repository	`PUT /v1/repositories/(namespace)/(repo_name)/auth`
Verify a user login	`GET /v1/users`
Create a new library repository	`PUT /v1/repositories/(repo_name)/`
Create a new user repository	`PUT /v1/repositories/(namespace)/(repo_name)/`
Update user repository images	`PUT /v1/repositories/(namespace)/(repo_name)/images`
Update library repository images	`PUT /v1/repositories/(repo_name)/images`
Delete the existing library repository	`DELETE /v1/repositories/(repo_name)/`
Delete the user repository	`DELETE /v1/repositories/(namespace)/(repo_name)/`
List images in the library repository	`GET /v1/repositories/(repo_name)/images`
List images in user's repository	`GET /v1/repositories/(namespace)/(repo_name)/images`
Retrieve an image	`GET /v1/images/(image_id)/json`

Obtain all tags or a specific tag of a repository	`GET /v1/repositories/(namespace)/(repository)/tags`
Delete a tag	`DELETE /v1/repositories/(namespace)/(repository)/tags/(tag*)`
Extract image layer	`GET /v1/images/(image_id)/layer`
Insert image layer	`PUT /v1/images/(image_id)/layer`
Retrieve roots of an image	`GET /v1/images/(image_id)/ancestry`

All of the API commands are pretty well documented on the Docker documentation website, available at `https://docs.docker.com`. There you can find example JSON payloads you need to provide for your API calls, altogether with example responses and HTTP return status codes. The exposed REST API is a great way if you want to develop your own applications or automation scripts dealing with the Registry. This is another proof of extensibility and flexibility Docker provides for administrators or developers.

After reading this chapter, you should now be familiar with the ways you can look for images, be it using the web interface, command-line tool, or remote API. You should be able to easily find an image that will become a base for your own images, which we are going to create in the next chapter, actually.

Summary

After reading this chapter, you should have the understanding about the concept of Docker's remote storages-Docker Registries. We also know how to create and manage user's account on the most popular Docker registry, the Docker Hub. We are able to find an image that can be useful and appropriate as a base for our own image. In fact, in `Chapter 6`, *Creating Images*, we will use all of it in practice—we will create an image based on the image found in the Docker Hub.

6
Creating Images

After reading the previous chapters, you should be familiar on how to find images suitable as a base for your own software. You can pull them from the remote repository, run and make changes to them during runtime and then export as new images. We saw building our own image earlier via running a container, installing our software in it, and doing a commit to create the image in Chapter 3, *Understanding Images and Containers*. This is not very practical and sometimes very cumbersome. Luckily, there's a solution for that. Docker has a scripting engine that we can use to create a new image with a predefined list of instructions and properties. We call these scripts Dockerfiles. This time, we are going to create an image based on a Dockerfile. This chapter will cover the following topics:

- Introduction to Dockerfiles
- Creating and editing Dockerfiles
- Dockerfile instructions
- Building images

Let's understand what a Dockerfile is first. It's nothing more than a plain text file containing instructions on how to build an image. Docker will process this file and build images step-by-step (or rather, layer-by-layer), automatically, taking a source (base) image as a foundation. We can, for example, use the base Ubuntu image, install the application server such as Wildfly, configure your own application or service, and publish the resulting image as a whole–a complete application that others can use. Using Dockerfile has a lot of benefits–you edit and work on a text file, rather than making all the changes directly and saving the image back to disk. You treat the Dockerfile as a part of the source code of your application–you should put it into the version control system like GIT to be able to track changes and share it with members of your team. In fact, writing a Dockerfile is a more consistent and repeatable way to build your own images. Also, using Dockerfile is the recommended way of building images on the fly, for example, in the continuous deployment setup.

This chapter will cover the following topics:

- Creating and editing Dockerfiles
- Dockerfile instructions
- Building images

Let's begin by creating a Dockerfile. We are going to create images in a more programmatical way using the Dockerfile. To edit Dockerfile, you can use any text editor of your choice, but it would be a lot more convenient to use an IDE with syntax highlighting support for Dockerfiles. For example, IntelliJ IDEA has a Docker integration plugin I can highly recommend. By the way, we will be using this plugin a lot in the next chapter–there is a new IDEA `Run/Debug Configuration` for Docker deployments, which will allow you to specify the cloud deployment target, an appropriate Dockerfile, and give your container a name. This plug-in lets you download and build images, create and start containers, and carry out other Docker-related tasks. Apart from that, you will get editor completion and syntax highlighting when editing Dockerfiles, as you can see in the following screenshot:

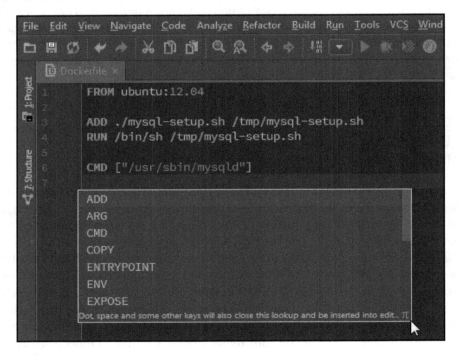

The image creation flow in Docker is pretty straightforward and consists basically of two steps:

- First, you prepare Dockerfile, which is just a text file that has a series of instructions on how to build the image. It supports a not very large set of commands that you can use in your Dockerfile, to instruct Docker how to create an image.
- Next, you will use the docker build command to create a Docker image based on the Dockerfile that you have just created.

The standard name for a Dockerfile is just Dockerfile and it's just a plain text file. Dockerfiles use simple, clean, and clear syntax, which makes them strikingly easy to create and use. They are designed to be self-explanatory, especially because they allow commenting just like a good and properly written application source code.

The instructions in this file are not case-sensitive, however, the good idea is to stick to a convention and write them in uppercase–this will make a Dockerfile more readable. You can write comments in the Dockerfile using the hash symbol #. Docker will skip commented lines unless it contains a parser directive, which we are going to cover in a while. While some commands, such as MAINTAINER, can be placed anywhere in a Dockerfile, most of them such as ADD must be placed in the order you would like them to be executed when building an image. CMD and ENTRYPOINT are exceptions–only the last CMD or ENTRYPOINT instruction in a Dockerfile will have an effect.

> The order of instructions in a Dockerfile is important–they will be executed in the same order as in the Dockerfile.

Let's start with the description of possible Dockerfile instructions, one by one.

Dockerfile instructions

In this section, we are going to cover Dockerfile instructions one by one. Let's begin with the instruction that should be the first one in the Dockerfile we are going to create, the FROM instruction.

FROM

The syntax for the FROM instruction is very simple. It can have three forms. It can be as simple as that:

```
FROM <image>
```

By default, Docker will use the image tagged latest. If you need to build upon different tags, you will need to add the tag name after the name of the image. The FROM instruction will take this form then:

```
FROM <image>:<tag>
```

Last but not least, you can even more precisely pick the image using its digest. As you remember from the previous chapters, images with the same tag can change in time, if their author decides so. If you like to lock your base image to the fixed version, you can specify its digest as the image name. This way your own image will be always built using the specific version of the base image, regardless of tags. To specify base image using digest, use the following syntax of the FROM instruction:

```
FROM <image>@<digest>
```

The FROM instruction tells Docker what will be the base for the image being created. Here you can use your skills of finding images on the Docker Hub, learned in Chapter 5, *Finding Images*. Now this is important–as it will be starting point–choose wisely. Of course you can pick whatever you want to be base for your own image, it's up to you–but my recommendation would be to always prefer the official repositories. By choosing the official image, you can be pretty sure it will be of high quality, tested, supported, and maintained.

 You can use your own images in the FROM instruction.

If a FROM image is not found on your Docker host (on your local machine, for example), Docker will try to find and download it from the Docker image index. Again, the Docker Hub will be picked by default.

All subsequent instructions in the Dockerfile will use the image specified in FROM as a base starting point. That's why it's mandatory–a valid Dockerfile must have it at the top. Although you can have multiple FROM instructions in your image, it's probably not a good and recommended practice–while interesting, isn't fully supported. In particular, the nonfinal images that are produced by using multiple FROM are not easily found without some parsing of the build output. Actually, there is an ongoing discussion on Docker's GitHub about removing the support for multiple FROM instructions from a Dockerfile specification.

The FROM instruction takes a tag or digest as a parameter. If you decide to skip them, Docker will assume you want to build your image from the latest tag. As you remember from Chapter 5, *Finding Images*, it will not always be the latest version of the image you want to build upon. Docker will throw an error during the build if it cannot find a tag or digest you provide.

MAINTAINER

By using the MAINTAINER instruction, you set the Author field of the generated image. This can be your name, username, or whatever you would like it to be referenced with, as an author of the image that will be created using this Dockerfile. This command can be placed anywhere in a Dockerfile, but the good practice is to place it on top of the file, just after the FROM instruction. This is the so-called **non-executing** command, which means that it will not make any changes to the generated image. The syntax, again, is very simple:

```
MAINTAINER authors_name
```

ADD

The ADD basically copies the files from the source on the host into the Docker image's own filesystem at the desired destination. It takes two arguments; the source (<source path or URL>) and a destination (<destination path>):

```
ADD <source path or URL> <destination path >
```

The source path can be a file or a directory relative to the directory in which the build process is going to be started (the build context). This means you cannot have, for example, `../../config.json` placed as a source path parameter of the ADD instruction. The build context can be changed using the PATH option in the `docker build` command and the source path is relative to the build context.

The source can contain wildcards. These are the same as in conventional filesystem: * for any text string, or ? for any single character.

Consider the following examples:

- ADD myFiles* /myDirectory/: This will add all the files starting with myFiles
- ADD file?.txt /myDirectory/: This will replace with any single character so that it will match file1.txt, fileB.txt, and so on.

 The destination path, on the other hand, cannot contain wildcards.

You can specify multiple source paths, separated with a comma. All of them must be relative to the building context, the same as if you have just a single source path. If your source or destination paths contain spaces, you will need to use a special syntax, adding the square brackets around:

```
ADD ["<source path or URL>" "<destination path>"]
```

A trailing slash / is quite important when adding files or directories to an image. If the source path doesn't end with a trailing slash, it will be considered as a single file and just copied into the destination. If the source path ends with a trailing slash, it will be considered as a directory; all of its contents will then be copied into the destination path, but the directory itself will not be created at the destination path.

If the source path points to the compressed archive in one of the common formats such as zip, tar, and so on, it will be decompressed into the destination path. Docker doesn't recognize an archive by the filename, it checks the contents of the file.

If the archive is damaged or unreadable by Docker in another way, it will not be extracted and you will not be given an error message–the file will be just copied into the destination path.

The same trailing slash rules apply to the destination path: if it ends with a trailing slash, it means that it's a directory. Otherwise, it will be considered as a single file. This gives you great flexibility when constructing filesystem contents of your image–you can add files into directories or just add whole directories.

Note that when using `ADD` with more than one source file, the destination must be a directory and end with a slash `/`.

The `ADD` command is not only about copying files from the local filesystem–you can use it to get the file from the network. If the source is a URL, then the contents of the URL will be automatically downloaded and placed at the destination. Note that file archives that were downloaded from the network will not be decompressed. Again, the trailing slash is important when downloading files–if the destination path ends with a slash, the file will be downloaded into the directory. Otherwise, the downloaded file will be just saved under the name you provided as the destination path.

The `<destination directory>` is either an absolute path or a path that is relative to the directory specific by the `WORKDIR` instruction (we will cover it in a while). The source (or multiple sources) will be just copied into the destination specified. Consider the following example:

- `ADD config.json projectRoot/` will add the `config.json` file to `<WORKDIR>/projectRoot/`
- `ADD config.json /absoluteDirectory/` will add the `config.json` file to the `/absoluteDirectory/`

When it comes to the ownership of the files created in the image, they will always be created with the user ID (`UID`) 0 and group ID (`GID`) 0. Permissions will be the same as in the source file, unless it's a file downloaded from the remote URL. In this case, it will get permissions value `600` (only the owner can read and write the file). If you need to change these values (ownership or permissions), you will need to provide more instructions in your Dockerfile, after the `ADD` instruction.

If the files that you need to add to the image are placed on the URL that needs authentication, the ADD instruction will not work–you will need to use the shell command to download the file, such as wget or curl.

COPY

The COPY instruction will copy new files or directories from `<source path>` and adds them to the filesystem of the container at the path `<destination path>`.

It's very similar to ADD instructions, even the syntax is identical:

```
COPY <source path or URL> <destination path >
```

The same rules from ADD apply to COPY–all source paths must be relative to the context of the build. Again, the presence of the trailing slash at the end of source and destination path is important. If it's present, the path will be considered as a file, otherwise it will be treated as a directory.

Of course, as in ADD, you can have multiple source paths. If source or destination paths contain spaces, you will need to wrap them in to square brackets:

```
COPY ["<source path or URL>" "<destination path>"]
```

The `<destination path>` is an absolute path (it begins with a slash), or a path relative to the path specified by the WORKDIR instruction.

As you can see, the functionality of COPY is almost the same as that of the ADD instruction with one difference. COPY supports only the basic copying of local files into the container. On the other hand, ADD features some more, such as archive extraction, downloading files through URL, and so on. Docker's best practices say, that you should prefer COPY if you do not need those additional features of ADD. The Dockerfile will be cleaner and easier to understand thanks to the transparency of the COPY command.

There is one common, important aspect for both ADD and COPY instructions, a cache. Basically, Docker caches the files that go into the image during the build. The contents of the file or files in the image is examined and a checksum is calculated for each file. During the cache lookup, the checksum is compared against the checksum in the existing images. If anything has changed in the file(s), such as the contents and metadata, then the cache is being invalidated. Otherwise, if the source file has not changed, then an existing image layer is being reused.

If you have multiple Dockerfile steps that use different files from your context, copy them individually, rather than all at once. This will ensure that each step's build cache is only invalidated (forcing the step to be re-run) if the files that are specifically required change.

As you can see, the COPY instruction has almost identical syntax and behavior as the ADD instruction, but their feature set is somehow different. For files and directories that do not require the ADD feature of archive unpacking or fetching from the URL, you should always use COPY.

CMD

The purpose of a CMD instruction is to provide defaults for an executing container. You can think about the CMD instruction as the *starting point* of your image, when the container is being run later on. This can be an executable, or if you specify the ENTRYPOINT instruction (we are going to explain it in a while later in this chapter) you can omit the executable and provide the default parameters only.

The CMD instruction syntax be as follows:

- CMD ["executable","parameter1","parameter2"]: This is the so-called exec form. It's also the preferred and recommended form. The parameters are enclosed in square brackets–it's a JSON array. It also means that you must use double quotes (") around words, not single quotes ('). The important note is that the exec form does not invoke a command shell when the container is run. It just runs the executable provided as the first parameter. It means also that normal shell processing will not happen, for example, the following environment variables substitution will not work:

  CMD ["parameter1","parameter2"]

  This form of CMD instruction just provides a default set of parameters for the ENTRYPOINT instruction.

- CMD command parameter1 parameter2: This a shell form of the instruction. This time, the shell (if present in the image) will be processing the command. The specified binary will be executed with an invocation of the shell using /bin/sh -c. It means that if you display the container's hostname, for example, using CMD echo $HOSTNAME you should use the shell form of the instruction.

We have said before that the recommended form of CMD instruction is the exec" form. Here's why everything started through the shell will be started as a subcommand of /bin/sh -c, which does not pass signals. This means that the executable will not be the container's PID 1–and will not receive Unix signals–so your executable will not receive a SIGTERM from docker stop <container>. There is another drawback–you will need a shell in your container. If you're building a minimal image, it doesn't need to contain a shell binary. The CMD instruction using the shell form will simply fail.

> When Docker is executing the command, it doesn't check if the shell is available inside the container; if there is no /bin/sh in the image, the container will fail to start.

The difference between exec and shell forms of the instruction can be easily shown in the running example. Consider the following Dockerfile, using the shell form:

```
FROM ubuntu
CMD echo $HOSTNAME
```

The output will be just the unique hostname generated by Docker when the container is run:

```
MINGW64:/c/Users/jarek/dockerfiles                                    —    □    ×

jarek@DESKTOP-1G11EK0 MINGW64 ~/dockerfiles
$ docker run 5c9f6d57b18e
31847a5aad30

jarek@DESKTOP-1G11EK0 MINGW64 ~/dockerfiles
$
```

On the other hand, if we will change the CMD to the exec form, Docker will be looking for an executable named echo, which, of course, will fail, because echo is a shell command.

Because CMD is like a starting point for the Docker Engine when running a container, there can only be one single CMD instruction in a Dockerfile.

> If there are more than one CMD instructions in a Dockerfile, only the last one will take effect.

The parameters for the CMD command can be overridden when starting the image–if you specify arguments to docker run. While launching the container, you can override the default CMD parameters by providing them at the command line, as shown in the following screenshot. In this example, we are asking you to launch the /bin/sh -c shell again, because we are using the shell form of the CMD, this time overriding the default CMD instruction from the Dockerfile:

```
docker run 00bd948ecdff "echo" "Hello world!"
```

Notice that this time it will not print out the hostname, but Hello world instead, taken from our overridden CMD parameters:

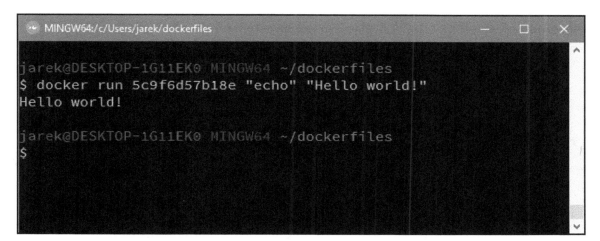

We are going to cover this in detail in Chapter 7, *Running Containers*.

ENTRYPOINT

The official Docker documentation says that the ENTRYPOINT instruction allows you to configure a container that will run as an executable. It's not very clear, at least for the first time. The ENTRYPOINT instruction is related to the CMD instruction. In fact, it can be confusing at the beginning. The reason for that is simple; CMD was developed first, then ENTRYPOINT was developed for more customization, and some functionality overlaps between those two instructions. Let's explain it a bit. The ENTRYPOINT instruction specifies a command that will always be executed when the container starts. The CMD instruction, on the other handspecifies the arguments that will be fed to the ENTRYPOINT instruction. Consider this example. Let's say that the image we want to run (ubuntu) has an ENTRYPOINT which is /bin/sh -c but does not have a default CMD and we execute the following command:

```
docker run ubuntu "echo" "hello world"
```

In this case, the image will be the latest ubuntu, the ENTRYPOINT instruction will be the /bin/sh -c, and the command passed to the ENTRYPOINT instruction will be echo "hello world".

The syntax for the ENTRYPOINT instruction can have two forms, similar to CMD:

- ENTRYPOINT ["executable", "parameter1", "parameter2"]: This is the exec form, preferred, and recommended. Exactly the same as in the exec form of CMD instruction, this will not invoke a command shell. This means that normal shell processing will not happen. For example, ENTRYPOINT ["echo", "$HOSTNAME"] will not do variable substitution on the $HOSTNAME variable. If you want shell processing, then you need to either use the shell form or execute a shell directly, for example:

  ```
  ENTRYPOINT [ "sh", "-c", "echo $HOSTNAME" ]
  ```

  Variables that are defined in the Dockerfile using ENV (we are going to cover this in a while), will be substituted by the Dockerfile parser.

- ENTRYPOINT command parameter1 parameter2: It's a shell form. Normal shell processing will occur. This form will also ignore any CMD or docker run command-line arguments. Also, your command will not be PID 1, because it will be executed by shell. As a result, if you then run docker stop <container>, the container will not exit cleanly–the stop command will be forced to send an SIGKILL command after the timeout.

You need to know that, exactly the same as with CMD instruction, only the last ENTRYPOINT instruction in the Dockerfile will have an effect. Overriding the ENTRYPOINT in the Dockerfile allows you to have a different command processing your arguments when the container is run. If you need to change the default shell in your image, you can do this by changing an ENTRYPOINT:

```
FROM ubuntu
ENTRYPOINT ["/bin/bash"]
```

From now on, all parameters from CMD or provided when starting the container using docker run, will be processed by Bash shell instead of default /bin/sh -c.

Consider another example Dockerfile:

```
FROM busybox
ENTRYPOINT ["/bin/ping"]
CMD ["localhost"]
```

If you now run the container built from this Dockerfile, the ping command, as an image ENTRYPOINT will be processing arguments from the supplied CMD argument: localhost, in our case. As a result, you will have a /bin/ping localhost command-line response:

```
MINGW64:/c/Users/jarek/dockerfiles                                    —    □    ×

jarek@DESKTOP-1G11EK0 MINGW64 ~/dockerfiles
$ docker build .

jarek@DESKTOP-1G11EK0 MINGW64 ~/dockerfiles
$ docker run 6ef1568d3d05
PING localhost (127.0.0.1): 56 data bytes
64 bytes from 127.0.0.1: seq=0 ttl=64 time=0.032 ms
64 bytes from 127.0.0.1: seq=1 ttl=64 time=0.092 ms
64 bytes from 127.0.0.1: seq=2 ttl=64 time=0.092 ms
64 bytes from 127.0.0.1: seq=3 ttl=64 time=0.089 ms
64 bytes from 127.0.0.1: seq=4 ttl=64 time=0.091 ms
64 bytes from 127.0.0.1: seq=5 ttl=64 time=0.092 ms

jarek@DESKTOP-1G11EK0 MINGW64 ~/dockerfiles
$
```

As you remember from the CMD instruction description, it sets the default command and/or parameters, which can be overwritten from the command line when Docker container runs. The ENTRYPOINT command and parameters will not be overwritten from the command line. Instead, all the command-line arguments will be added after ENTRYPOINT parameters.

> Unlike the CMD parameters, the ENTRYPOINT command and parameters are not ignored when Docker container runs with the command-line parameters.

That's why we can run our ping image with different parameters passed to the ENTRYPOINT instruction:

```
MINGW64:/c/Users/jarek/dockerfiles                                    —    □    ×

$ docker run 6ef1568d3d05 yahoo.com
PING yahoo.com (206.190.36.45): 56 data bytes
64 bytes from 206.190.36.45: seq=0 ttl=47 time=218.232 ms
64 bytes from 206.190.36.45: seq=1 ttl=47 time=231.793 ms
64 bytes from 206.190.36.45: seq=2 ttl=47 time=195.860 ms
64 bytes from 206.190.36.45: seq=3 ttl=47 time=199.852 ms
64 bytes from 206.190.36.45: seq=4 ttl=47 time=208.578 ms
64 bytes from 206.190.36.45: seq=5 ttl=47 time=204.701 ms
64 bytes from 206.190.36.45: seq=6 ttl=47 time=217.937 ms
64 bytes from 206.190.36.45: seq=7 ttl=47 time=223.408 ms
64 bytes from 206.190.36.45: seq=8 ttl=47 time=197.937 ms
64 bytes from 206.190.36.45: seq=9 ttl=47 time=204.191 ms

jarek@DESKTOP-1G11EK0 MINGW64 ~/dockerfiles
$
```

> You can use the exec form of ENTRYPOINT to set fairly stable default commands and arguments and then use either form of CMD to set additional defaults that are more likely to be changed.

Having the ENTRYPOINT instruction gives us a lot of flexibility. And, last but not least, an ENTRYPOINT can be also overridden when starting the container using the --entrypoint parameter for the docker run command. Note that you can override the ENTRYPOINT setting using –entrypoint, but this can only set the binary to execute (no sh -c will be used). We will cover this in detail in Chapter 7, *Running Containers*.

As you can see, both CMD and ENTRYPOINT instructions define what command gets executed when running a container. Let's summarize what we have learnt about the differences and their co-operation:

- Dockerfile should specify at least one of the CMD or ENTRYPOINT instructions
- Only the last CMD and ENTRYPOINT in a Dockerfile will be used
- ENTRYPOINT should be defined when using the container as an executable
- You should use the CMD instruction as a way of defining default arguments for the command defined as ENTRYPOINT or for executing an ad-hoc command in a container
- CMD will be overridden when running the container with alternative arguments
- The ENTRYPOINT argument sets the concrete default application that is used every time a container is created using the image
- If you couple ENTRYPOINT with CMD, you can remove an executable from CMD and just leave its arguments, which will be passed to the ENTRYPOINT instruction
- The best use for the ENTRYPOINT instruction is to set the image's main command, allowing that image to be run as though it was that command (and then use CMD as the default flags).

LABEL

To add the metadata to our image, we use the LABEL instruction. A single label is a key-value pair. If you need to have spaces in the label value, you will need to wrap it into the pair of quotes. Labels are additive. They include all labels taken from the image that is the base of your own image (the one from the FROM instruction). If Docker encounters a label that already exists, it will override the label having the same key with the new value.

There are some rules that you must stick to when defining labels: keys can only consist of lowercase alphanumeric characters, dots, and dashes and must begin and end with an alphanumeric character.

To prevent naming conflicts, Docker recommends using namespaces to label keys using reverse domain notation. On the other hand, keys without namespaces (dots) are reserved for command line use.

The syntax of the `LABEL` instruction is straightforward:

```
LABEL "key"="value"
```

To have a multiline value, separate the lines with backslashes, for example:

```
LABEL description="This is my \ multiline description of the software."
```

You can have multiple labels in a single image. Provide them separated with a space or a backslash, for example:

```
LABEL key1="value1" key2="value2" key3="value3"
LABEL key1="value1" \
key2="value2" \
key3="value3"
```

Actually, if you need to have multiple labels in your image, it's recommended to use the multilabel form of the `LABEL` instruction, because it will result in just one additional layer in the image.

> Each `LABEL` instruction creates a new layer. If your image has many labels, use the multiple form of the single `LABEL` instruction.

If you want to inspect what labels an image has, use the `docker inspect` command you already know from the previous chapters:

```
MINGW64:/c/Users/jarek/dockerfiles                                    —    □    ×

jarek@DESKTOP-1G11EK0 MINGW64 ~/dockerfiles
$ docker inspect a5e28372fe98 | grep Labels -A1
            "Labels": {
                "version": "0.0.1"
--

            "Labels": {
                "version": "0.0.1"

jarek@DESKTOP-1G11EK0 MINGW64 ~/dockerfiles
$
```

The ENV Dockerfile instruction sets the environment variable `<key>` to the value `<value>`. It has two forms:

- The first form, ENV `<key>` `<value>` will set a single variable to a value. The entire string after the first space will be treated as the `<value>`. This will include any character, also spaces and quotes. Consider the following example: ENV JAVA_HOME /var/lib/java8
- The second form is ENV `<key>=<value>` ..., and allows setting multiple environment variables at once. The difference is the equal to sign. If you need to provide spaces in the values, you will need to use quotes. If you need quotes in the values, use backslashes: ENV CONFIG_TYPE=file CONFIG_LOCATION="home/Jarek/my \ app/config"

Note that you can use ENV to update the PATH environment variable, and then CMD parameters will be aware of that setting. This will result in a cleaner form of CMD parameters in the Dockerfile. Consider the following example:

```
ENV PATH /var/lib/tomcat8/bin:$PATH
```

Setting this will ensure that CMD `["startup.sh"]` works, because it will find the `startup.sh` file in the system PATH. You can also use ENV to set the often modified version numbers so that upgrades are easier to handle, as shown in the following example:

```
ENV TOMCAT_VERSION_MAJOR 8
ENV TOMCAT_VERSION 8.5.4
RUN curl -SL
http://apache.uib.no/tomcat/tomcat-$TOMCAT_VERSION_MAJOR/v$TOMCAT_VERSION/b
in/apache-tomcat-$TOMCAT_VERSION.tar.gz | tar zxvf apache-tomcat-
$TOMCAT_VERSION.tar.gz  -c /usr/Jarek/apache-tomcat-$TOMCAT_VERSION
    ENV PATH /usr/Jarek/apache-tomcat-$TOMCAT_VERSION/bin:$PATH
```

In the preceding example, Docker will download the version of Tomcat specified in the ENV variable, extract it to the new directory with that version in its name and also set up the system PATH to make it available for running.

The environment variables set using ENV will persist when a container is run from the resulting image. The same as with labels created with LABEL, you can view the ENV values using the `docker inspect` command. The ENV values can be also overridden just before the start of the container, using docker run `--env <key>=<value>`.

EXPOSE

The EXPOSE instruction informs Docker that the container listens on the specified network ports at runtime. We already have mentioned the EXPOSE instruction in Chapter 4, *Networking and Persistent Storage*. As you remember, the EXPOSE in a Dockerfile is the equivalent for the --expose command line option. Docker uses the EXPOSE command followed by a port number to allow incoming traffic to the container. We already know that EXPOSE does not make the ports of the container automatically accessible to the host. To do that, you must use either the -p flag to publish a range of ports or the -P flag to publish all of the exposed ports at once.

Let's look at the Nginx web server Dockerfile, as an example. As always, looking at an existing source is the best of way to create your own. It's no different, when it comes to Dockerfiles. The Nginx Dockerfile is quite nice and small, it's available on GitHub (https://github.com/dockerfile/nginx/blob/master/Dockerfile):

```
# Pull base image.
FROM ubuntu:14.04
# Install Nginx.
RUN \
  add-apt-repository -y ppa:nginx/stable && \
  apt-get update && apt-get install -y nginx && \
  rm -rf /var/lib/apt/lists/* && \
  echo "\ndaemon off;" >> /etc/nginx/nginx.conf && \
  chown -R www-data:www-data /var/lib/nginx

# Define mountable directories.
VOLUME ["/etc/nginx/sites-enabled", "/etc/nginx/certs",
"/etc/nginx/conf.d", "/var/log/nginx", "/var/www/html"]

# Define working directory.
WORKDIR /etc/nginx

# Define default command.
CMD ["nginx"]

# Expose ports.
EXPOSE 80
EXPOSE 443
```

As you can see in the preceding Dockerfile, it uses EXPOSE to expose two ports: standard HTTP (80) and SSL (443). These ports will be available for the other containers on this host, and–if you expose them during runtime–also for the external world. You can either run the image using a specified port explicitly:

```
docker run nginx -p 80
```

Alternatively, you can tell Docker that we want all of the exposed ports published at once:

```
docker run nginx -P
```

The good practice is to use common, known port numbers for your application. For example, if your application runs on nginx web server, you should do the EXPOSE with port number 80, so that the users of your application will not be surprised with some exotic port numbers. Of course, if there's a specific need for exposing nonstandard port numbers, you are free to go, it's just a good practice.

RUN

The RUN instruction is the central executing instruction for Dockerfiles. In essence, the RUN instruction will execute any commands in a new layer on top of the current image and then commit the results. The resulting committed image will be used as a base for the next instruction in the Dockerfile. As you remember from Chapter 3, *Understanding Images and Containers*, layering is the core concept in Docker. RUN takes a command as its argument and runs it to form the image. The RUN instruction can run any command (or application), which is similar to the CMD instruction we got to know earlier. There is a key important difference–the time of execution. The command supplied through the RUN instruction is executed during the build time, whereas the command specified through the CMD instruction is executed when the container is launched by executing docker run on the newly created image. Unlike CMD, the RUN instruction is actually used to build the image, by creating a new layer on top of the previous one which is committed.

 CMD is runtime instruction, where RUN is the build-time instruction.

This also means that CMD and ENTRYPOINT set parameters that can be overridden at runtime, so if you don't change anything, after starting your container, the result will always be the same. RUN, however, will be executed at build time and no matter what you do at runtime, its effects will be seen here.

RUN, similarly to CMD and ENDPOINT, can take two forms:

- RUN <command>: This is a *shell* form. The supplied command and its arguments will be executed in a shell, which is /bin/sh -c on Linux or cmd /S /C on Windows. The default shell for the RUN instruction can be changed using the SHELL command.

- RUN ["executable", "parameter1", "parameter2"]: This an *exec* form. The same rules apply as in CMD. Using this form, you can execute commands using a base image that does not contain the specified shell executable. RUN in this form will not invoke a command shell. And again, the same as with CMD or ENTRYPOINT, normal shell processing such as variable substitution, for example, will not happen.

 To make your Dockerfile more readable and easier to maintain, you can split long or complex RUN statements on multiple lines separated with backslashes.

The RUN commands from the Dockerfile will be executed in the order they appear in it. Each RUN instruction will create a new layer in the image. Layers, as you already know from Chapter 3, *Understanding Images and Containers*, are being cached and reused by Docker. The cache for RUN instructions isn't invalidated automatically during the next build. For example, the cache for an instruction such as RUN apt-get upgrade -y will be reused during the next build. What makes the cache important? For the most part, the cache is exceptionally helpful and can save you tremendous amount of time while building your images. If the objects on the filesystem that Docker is about to produce are unaffected between builds, reusing a cache of a previous build on the host is a great time-saver. It makes building a new container really, really fast. None of those file structures have to be created and written to disk this time–the reference to them is sufficient to locate and reuse the previously built structures. However, there are times when the caching can be dangerous and provide unexpected results. Cache is used pretty heavily during the build process and this may cause issues when you want the updated output of a RUN command to make it into the new container.

If the `RUN` command doesn't change between two builds, Docker's cache will not get invalidated. In effect, Docker will reuse the previous results from cache. This is clearly harmful, when, for example, the `RUN` command is a source code checkout, for example, a Git clone as the first step of a project's build.

 Beware that cache needs to be invalidated sometimes, otherwise you will get unexpected results with your image builds.

That's why it's good to know how to selectively invalidate the cache. In the Docker world, this is called cache busting.

Consider the following example. Probably the most common use-case for RUN is an application of `apt-get`, which is a package manager command for downloading packages on Ubuntu. Let's say we have the following Dockerfile, installing a MongoDB in image:

```
FROM ubuntu
RUN apt-get update
RUN apt-get install -y mongodb-server
```

If we build an image from this Dockerfile, all layers from two RUN instructions will be put into the layers cache. But, after a while you decide you want the `node.js` package in your image, so now the Dockerfile looks like this:

```
FROM ubuntu
RUN apt-get update
RUN apt-get install -y mongodb-server
RUN apt-get install -y nodejs
```

On the second build, Docker will reuse the layers by taking them from the layer's cache. As a result the `apt-get` update will not be executed, because the cached version will be used. In effect, your newly created image will potentially have an outdated version of the MongoDb and node-js packages. You should always have the cache concept in mind when creating RUN instructions. In our example, we should always combine RUN `apt-get` `update` with `apt-get install` in the same RUN statement, which will create just a single layer. Consider the following example:

```
RUN apt-get update \
&& apt-get install -y mongodb-server \
&& apt-get install -y nodejs
```

Yet better than this, you can also use a technique called **version pinning** to avoid cache problems. It's nothing else than just providing a specific, concrete version for the package you want to install:

```
RUN apt-get update \
&& apt-get install -y mongodb-server \
&& APT-GET INSTALL -Y NODEJS= 0.6.12~DFSG1-1UBUNTU1
```

Using `apt-get update` alone in a `RUN` statement is not recommended because of the caching issues.

The cache for `RUN` instructions can be invalidated by `ADD` instructions or using the `--no-cache` flag, for example:

```
docker build --no-cache
```

USER

The `USER` instruction is very simple. It sets the user name or UID to use when running the image. It also affects the user for any `RUN`, `CMD`, and `ENTRYPOINT` instructions that follow it in the Dockerfile.

The syntax of the instruction is just USER `<user name or UID>`, for example:

```
USER tomcat
```

You can use the `USER` command if an executable can be run without privileges. The Dockerfile can contain the user and group creation instruction like this one:

```
RUN groupadd -r tomcat && useradd -r -g tomcat tomcat
```

Switching USER back and forth frequently will increase the number of layers in the resulting image and will also make a Dockerfile more complex.

VOLUME

As you remember from `Chapter 3`, *Understanding Images and Containers*, Docker filesystems are kind of temporary by default. If you start up a Docker image (that is, run the container) you'll end up with a read-write layer on top of the layers stack. You can create, modify, and delete files as you wish, then commit the layer to persist the changes. Also, using Dockerfile will create a read-only image. In `Chapter 4`, *Networking and Persistent Storage* we have learned how to create volumes–a great way of storing and retrieving data from the Docker container. We can do the same in the Dockerfile, using the `VOLUME` instruction.

The syntax couldn't be simpler, it's just `VOLUME ["/volumeName"]`.

The parameter for `VOLUME` can be a JSON array, a plain string with one or more arguments, for example:

```
VOLUME ["/var/lib/tomcat8/webapps/"]
VOLUME /var/log/mongodb /var/log/tomcat
```

The `VOLUME` instruction creates a mount point with the specified name and marks it as holding externally mounted volumes from native host or other containers.

The `VOLUME`command will mount a directory inside your container and store any files created or edited inside that directory on your host's disk out side the container file structure. Using `VOLUME` in the Dockerfile lets Docker know that a certain directory contains permanent data. Docker will create a volume for that data and never delete it, even if you remove all the containers that use it. It also bypasses the union filesystem so that the volume is in fact an actual directory that gets mounted, either read/write or read-only, in the right place in all the containers that share it (if they are started with `--volumes-from` option, for example). To understand `VOLUME`, let's look at the simple Dockerfile:

```
FROM ubuntu
VOLUME /var/myVolume
```

If you now run your container and save some files in `/var/myVolume`, they will be available to other containers for sharing.

Basically, the `VOLUME` and `-v` options are almost equal. A difference between the `VOLUME` and `-v` options is that you can use the `-v` option dynamically and mount your host directory on your container when starting it by executing `docker run`. The reason for this is that Dockerfiles are meant to be portable and shared. The host directory volume is something that is 100% host dependent and will break on any other machine, which is a little bit off the Docker idea. Because of this, it is only possible to use portable instructions within a Dockerfile.

The fundamental difference between VOLUME and -v is this: -v will mount the existing files from your operating system inside your Docker container and VOLUME will create a new, empty volume on your host and mount it inside your container.

WORKDIR

The WORKDIR instruction adds a working directory for any CMD, RUN, ENTRYPOINT, COPY, or ADD instruction that follow in the Dockerfile. The syntax for the instruction is WORKDIR /PATH. You can have multiple WORKDIR instructions in one Dockerfile, if the relative path is provided, it will be relative to the path of the previous WORKDIR instruction.

ARG

If you need to pass an argument at build time to the Docker during the docker build command, you can use the ARG instruction in the Dockerfile. An ARG variable definition comes into effect from the line on which it is defined in the Dockerfile. Later on, during the build, any value can be passed to the docker build command using the --build-arg switch:

```
--build-arg <variable name>=<value>
```

The value from the --build-arg switch will be passed to the daemon building the image. If you specify the build time argument that is not defined using the ARG instruction, the build will fail with an error. You can specify multiple arguments using multiple ARG instructions, for example:

```
FROM ubuntu
ARG user
ARG version
```

Also, the default value can be specified for an argument in a Dockerfile–if none will be specified during the build time, the default value will be used:

```
FROM ubuntu
ARG user=jarek
```

Parameters can be passed to the builder by calling:

```
docker build --build-arg user=somebodyElse .
```

 It is not recommended to use ARG for passing secrets such as GitHub keys, user credentials, passwords, and so on, because it will be visible to any user of the image by using the docker history command.

ONBUILD

The ONBUILD instruction specifies additional instructions, which will be triggered when some other image is built by using this image as its base image. In other words, the ONBUILDinstruction is an instruction the parent Dockerfilegives to the childDockerfile (downstream build). Any build instruction can be registered as a trigger and those instructions will be triggered immediately after the FROM instruction in the Dockerfile.

The syntax of the ONBUILD instruction is as follows:

```
ONBUILD <INSTRUCTION>
```

Within this, <INSTRUCTION> is another Dockerfile build instruction, which will be triggered later when the *child* image is going to be built. There are some limitations: the ONBUILD instruction does not allow the chaining of another ONBUILD instruction and it does not allow the FROM and MAINTAINER instructions as ONBUILD triggers.

This is useful if you are building an image that will be used as a base to build other images, for example, an application build environment or a daemon, which may be customized with user-specific configuration. The ONBUILD instruction is very useful for automating the build of your chosen software stack. Consider the following example with Maven and building Java applications. (yes, Maven is also available as a Docker container). Basically, all your project's Dockerfile needs to do is reference the base container containing the ONBUILD instructions:

```
FROM maven:3.3-jdk-8-onbuild
CMD ["java","-jar","/usr/src/app/target/app-1.0-SNAPSHOT-jar-with-
    dependencies.jar"]
```

There's no magic, and everything becomes clear if you look into the parent's Dockerfile; in our case, it will be the `docker-maven` Dockerfile available on GitHub:

```
FROM maven:3-jdk-8 RUN mkdir -p /usr/src/app WORKDIR /usr/src/app
ONBUILD ADD . /usr/src/app ONBUILD RUN mvn install
```

There's a base image that has both Java and Maven installed and a series of instructions to copy files and run Maven.

The `ONBUILD` instruction adds to the image a trigger instruction to be executed at a later time–when the image is used as the base for another build. The trigger will be executed in the context of the *child* build, as if it had been inserted immediately after the `FROM` instruction in the *child* Dockerfile.

When Docker encounters an `ONBUILD` instruction during the build process, the builder adds kind of a trigger to the metadata of the image being built. But this is the only way this image is being affected. At the end of the build, a list of all triggers is stored in the image manifest, under the key `OnBuild`. You can see them using the `docker inspect command`, which we already know.

Later, the image may be used as a base for a new build, using the `FROM` instruction. As part of processing the `FROM` instruction, the Docker builder looks for `ONBUILD` triggers, and executes them in the same order they were registered. If any of the triggers fail, the `FROM` instruction is aborted which will make the build fail. If all triggers succeed, the `FROM` instruction completes and the build resumes.

 The `ONBUILD` triggers are removed from the final image after being executed. They will be inherited any further.

STOPSIGNAL

To specify what system call signal should be sent to the container to exit, use the `STOPSIGNAL` instruction. This signal can be a valid unsigned number that matches a position in the kernel's `syscall` table, for instance, 9, or a signal name in the format `SIGNAME`, for instance, `SIGKILL`.

HEALTHCHECK

This is a rather new feature, introduced in Docker 1.12. You can use the HEALTHCHECK instruction to tell Docker, how to test a container to check that it is still working. This can be checking if the database responds to remote calls or if a web application still listens on a specified port.

If you specify the HEALTHCHECK instruction, the running container will heave additional status in addition to its normal status. We have been talking about container statuses in Chapter 3, *Understanding Containers and Images*. As you remember, a container can have several statuses that can be listed using the docker ps command. These can be created, restarting, removing, running, paused, or exited. But sometimes this is not enough–the container may be still "alive" from the Docker point of view, but the application can hang or fail in some other way–an additional checking for the application status can be useful and the HEALTCHECK instruction comes in handy.

The HEALTHCHECK status is initially starting. Whenever a health check passes, it becomes healthy (whatever state it was previously in). After a certain number of consecutive failures, it becomes unhealthy.

The syntax for a HEALTHCHECK instruction is as follows:

```
HEALTHCHECK --interval=<interval> --timeout=<timeout>  CMD
<command>
```

The <interval> (the default value is 30 seconds) and <timeout> (again, the default is 30 seconds) are time values, specifically checking interval and timeout accordingly. The <command> is the command actually being used to check if the application is still running. The exit code of the <command> is being used by Docker to determine if a health check failed or succeeded. The values can be 0, which means that the container is healthy and ready for use and 1, which means that something is wrong and the container is not working correctly.

Consider the following example:

```
HEALTHCHECK --interval=5m --timeout=2s --retries=3  CMD curl -f
http://localhost/ || exit 1
```

In the preceding example, the `curl -f http://localhost` command will be executed every five minutes, for the maximum timeout of 2 seconds. If a single run of the check takes longer than 2 seconds, then the check is considered to have failed. If three consecutive retries fail, the container will get the `unhealthy` status.

 There can only be one `HEALTHCHECK` instruction in a Dockerfile. If you list more than one, then only the last `HEALTHCHECK` will take effect.

The `HEALTCHECK` instruction gives you the possibility to fine tune container monitoring and thus be sure that your container is working fine. It's better than just `runningexited` or `dead` standard Docker status.

SHELL

As we have seen before, some instructions such as RUN and CMD can use the shell form of execution. The default shell on Linux is `["/bin/sh", "-c"]`, and on Windows is `["cmd", "/S", "/C"]`. If you need to, you can use the SHELL instruction to override the default shell used for the shell form of commands. It can be `zsh`, `csh`, or `tcsh` for Linux or PowerShell for Windows, for example. The syntax for the instruction is:

```
SHELL ["executable", "parameters"]
```

Note that `SHELL` can take only the JSON array as a parameter. The `SHELL` instruction could also be used to modify the way in which a shell works. For example, using `SHELL cmd /S /C /V:ON` on Windows, the behavior of the default cmd shell (it will be delayed environment variable expansion in this case) can be modified.

The `SHELL` instruction can appear multiple times. Each `SHELL` instruction overrides all the previous declarations, but be aware that every `SHELL` line in your Dockerfile will result in a new layer in the resulting image.

Now we have addressed all of the Dockerfile instructions and roles in creating the image. Let's focus on the process of building an image now.

Using Dockerfiles

Now that we understand what every other Dockerfile instruction does, we can prepare our first Dockerfile. As mentioned earlier, it's just a plain text file. Once you've created a Dockerfile and added all your instructions, you can use it to build an image using the `docker build` command. The format for this command is:

```
docker build [OPTIONS] <PATH or URL> | -
```

The docker build command takes some arguments and options, you can display them with a short description using the `-help` switch, as with any other Docker command:

```
docker build -help
```

There are options to tweak the build process by specifying the CPU and memory setup or turning off the cache, for example. You can also tag the new repository after the build, using the `-t` option, for example:

```
docker build -t jarek/myapp .
```

To tag the image into multiple repositories at once, you can also add multiple `-t` parameters:

```
docker build -t jarek/myapp:1.0.0 -t jarek/myapp:latest .
```

The default set of parameters related to CPU and memory tweaking should be a good enough starting point, so you can omit them at the beginning.

The `docker build` command builds an image from a Dockerfile and a context. The build's context is the files at a specified location under the `PATH` or `URL`. The `PATH` is a directory on your local filesystem, while the `URL` is a the location of a Git repository. It works recursively, so a `PATH` includes any subdirectories and the URL includes the repository and its submodules. If you run the build command from the directory where your actual Dockerfile is, use just a dot as the `PATH` parameter. The simplest form of docker build, with the current directory as a build context will then be:

```
docker build
```

The build is being run by the Docker daemon. The first that will happen is that the entire context will be sent as a single bundle to the daemon. That's why you should be careful when specifying the build context. You can observe the size of the context being pushed to the daemon just after you have started the build:

```
MINGW64:/c/Users/jarek/dockerfiles                                    —  □  X

jarek@DESKTOP-1G11EK0 MINGW64 ~/dockerfiles
$ docker build .
Sending build context to Docker daemon 6.144 kB
Step 1 : FROM ubuntu
 ---> 42118e3df429
Step 2 : CMD "echo Hello World!"
 ---> Using cache
 ---> 89a2b43fca54
Successfully built 89a2b43fca54
SECURITY WARNING: You are building a Docker image from Windows against a non-Windows Docker ho
st. All files and directories added to build context will have '-rwxr-xr-x' permissions. It is
 recommended to double check and reset permissions for sensitive files and directories.

jarek@DESKTOP-1G11EK0 MINGW64 ~/dockerfiles
$
```

It's good practice to start with a directory containing only your Dockerfile as context and add only the files that are needed for building the Dockerfile.

Anyway, you can have your Dockerfile anywhere in the system. To build an image using the file outside of the current directory, you can use the -f switch for the docker build command, for example:

docker build -f /usr/Jarek/myDockerfiles/Dockerfile .

In the preceding example, Docker will use a Dockerfile from the specified path, but the build context will be the current directory, as specified by a dot.

As we have mentioned earlier in this chapter, instructions from Dockerfile, such as COPY, for example, will look for the file in the context of the build if the source path is specified without a trailing space. In real life, the docker build context will contain many other working files and directories, which should never be included in the image, like temporary files, logs, and so on. Nevertheless, the Docker build system would still send those files to the daemon.

To increase the build's performance and make the image as clean as possible, you can exclude files and directories by adding a .dockerignore file to the context directory. It's similar to the .gitignore file–all paths contained in the .dockerignore file will be simply ignored. You can use standard wildcards when specifying paths to ignore. Consider the following example of the .dockerignore file:

```
*/tmp*
*/*/tmp*
**/*.log
tmp?
```

In the preceding example, file and directory names start with tmp in any immediate subdirectory of the root. Also files and directories starting with tmpf from any subdirectory that is two levels below the root and files and directories in the root directory whose names are a one-character extension of tmp, such as tmp1 or tmp2 will also be ignored. The special mapping in the form of **/* can also be used–it matches any number of directories (including zero). For example, **/*.log will exclude all the log files found in all the directories. You can exclude some files from being matched to ignored. Consider the following example:

```
*.log
!important.log
```

The preceding example will match all log files, except the important.log file. When doing exclusions, be advised that the order of lines in the .dockerignore file is important. If you exclude a file and then declare similar matching below that exclusion, it will not be excluded.

Using .dockerignore can result in a much more cleaner image. There's another way of customizing the build process. As we have mentioned before, environment variables that are declared with the ENV instruction can be used in Dockerfile instructions, such as ADD, COPY, ENV, EXPOSE, LABEL, USER, WORKDIR, VOLUME, STOPSIGNAL, or ONBUILD.

The build command, if parsed and processed successfully, results in a new image that you can start using `docker run`, just like any other image, taken, for example, from Docker Hub. The output after executing the `docker build` command will be the ID of the new Docker image. It will also be present if you list your images using the command you already know: `docker images`, as shown in the following screenshot:

Summary

Docker provides a small but very flexible set of instructions for creating images using Dockerfiles. We have illustrated all the commands, their syntax, and their usage techniques in order to effectively create Docker images. Instructions have a rather simple syntax and are very well documented in the official Docker documentation. Creating your own images will not be very tricky. However, you will need to stick some best practices and guidelines, recommended by Docker. First of all, you should keep in mind that the containers created by your images should be ephemeral, that is, they should be able to be stopped, destroyed, and recreated with absolute minimum configuration. The images should be clean as far as possible, so starting from an empty build context, adding only what is necessary and using a .dockerignore is a way to go. Also, the YAGNI (You ain't gonna need it) principle, known from clean-code development practices has a very important meaning when it comes to creating Dockerfiles.

Keep it at absolute minimum, don't install something because it's nice to have it in a container. Always keep in mind the cache mechanism Docker uses and try to minimize the number of layers, by combining similar command into one instruction. Bare minimum, working as fast as it can and weighting as less as possible should be the goal. Also, if it's possible, consider running only one process per container–it will scale easier and allow for container reuse. If one service depends on another service, they should run in different, but linked containers.

Working with Dockerfile needs some practice and experimenting, but will pay later–when you will be able to create and adjust your images quickly. In the next chapter, we will focus more on running the images.

7
Running Containers

In previous chapters, we have learned about the Docker architecture, networking, persistent storage, and the structure of Dockerfile. At this point, you should be able to create your own Docker image and start using it. Actually, we did run the containers several times, but without going into details; we are going to do that in this chapter. In this chapter, we are going to focus more on running the containerized software. This will include the following concepts:

- Container running modes
- Overriding the CMD and ENTRYPOINT
- Monitoring containers
- Exit codes and restart policies
- Runtime constraints on resources
- Docker Swarm mode

You will learn how to set up your containers to behave well when running by specifying the restart policy and runtime constraints. In Chapter 6, *Creating Images*, we already discussed the CMD and ENTRYPOINT commands of Dockerfile. In this chapter, we will focus on how to override them during the container startup, this time in detail. We will learn how to read containers logs and output them not only to the text file, but to some specialized log tools, such as Splunk or Fluentd, for further analysis or processing. At the end of the chapter, we will learn about the new Docker feature – the Swarm mode, which allows you to manage the cluster of your Docker containers.

Let's recall what we have learned so far about Docker. Docker runs processes in isolated containers. A container is a process that runs on a host; however, the host might be local or remote. When you execute the docker run command, the container process that runs is isolated and has its very own filesystem, networking stack, and isolated process tree separate from the host. You run the image using the docker run command. Keep in mind that every docker run creates a new container with the specified image and starts a command inside it (CMD or ENTRYPOINT specified in the Dockerfile). By default, the file system of a container is persistent, even after the container shut down. These file systems can grow in size very quickly if you run short-term foreground processes again and again. The solution is that instead of cleaning it manually by hand, tell Docker to automatically clean up the container and remove the file system when the container exits. You can do this by adding the -rm flag, so that the container data is removed automatically after the process is finished.

 The --rm flag will make Docker remove the container after it has been shut down.

For example, use the run command, as shown in the following example:

```
docker run --rm -it Ubuntu /bin/bash
```

The preceding command tells Docker to remove the container if it's shut down.

Docker is very flexible, so it's no wonder that there are a lot of parameters for the docker run command. They are important and we will cover them in detail in the upcoming sections.

Let's recall the basic docker run syntax:

```
docker run [OPTIONS] IMAGE[:TAG|@DIGEST] [COMMAND] [ARG...]
```

The docker run command takes an image you would like to run; with it comes a lot of possible options that you might find useful, such as the runtime mode, either detached or foreground, and network settings or runtime restrictions on processor and memory. Of course, you can execute the run command without almost any arguments but the image name. It will run and take the default options coming from an image. Docker gives you the possibility to *override* the options specified by the author of the image.

When starting a Docker container, you can decide whether you want to run the container in the default mode, in the foreground, or in the background in the so-called **detached** mode. Let's explain what the difference is.

Runtime modes – detached and foreground

When running a container, you have a choice to run it in the foreground or detached mode. Let's start with the detached mode.

Detached

You can start a Docker container in a detached mode with adoption. The container starts up and runs in the background. After the container startup, you can use the console for executing other commands. Dockerfile can launch only one process at a time. Take note of the fact that the containers started in detached mode exit when the root process used to run the container exits. Understanding this is important even if you have some process running in the background (started from the instruction in the Dockerfile). Docker will stop the container if the command that started the container finishes. In other words, Docker requires your command to keep running in the foreground; otherwise, it thinks that your application stops and shuts down the container. For example, if the default command in your container is bash, when you run the image in background using the -d command line option, the shell will exit immediately and Docker will stop the container.

> Your container immediately stops, unless the commands are not running in the foreground.

But there is a solution for this. You can cheat Docker by executing a foreground command forever. The trick to make your container run continuously is to keep your main process running. Consider the following example:

```
docker run -d myImage tail -f /dev/null
```

Executing the tail command on /dev/null will keep the main bash shell busy and will not allow Docker to shut the container down.

In detached mode, you can display the standard output of your Docker container using the `docker logs` command. You can access the log files because everything that is written to `stdout` for the process that is `pid 1` inside the container will get captured in a special history file on the Docker host. To view the log entries, execute the following command:

```
docker logs -f <container name>
```

We are going to cover Docker logging in a short while. To retain control over a detached container, use the `dockerattach` command. The syntax for `docker attach` is:

```
docker attach [OPTIONS] <container ID or name>
```

The `docker attach` command can come in handy if you want to see what is written to the `stdout` stream in real time. It will basically reattach your console to the process running in the container. In other words, it will stream the `stdout` into your screen and map the `stdin` to your keyboard, thus allowing you to enter the commands and see their output. To detach from the process, use the default *Ctrl* + P, *Ctrl* + Q keyboard sequence.

Foreground

The foreground mode is the default one. It's the opposite of the detached mode and it's used when you simply do not specify the `-d` option. In the foreground mode, the console you are using to execute `docker run` will be attached to the standard input, output, and error streams. Actually, by default, Docker will attach all the standard streams to your console; these will be STDIN, STDOUT, and STDERR. You can change this default behavior and use the `-a` switch for the `docker run` command. As a parameter for the `-a` switch, you use the name of the stream you want to attach to the console. For example:

```
docker run -a stdin -a stdout -i -t centos /bin/bash
```

The preceding command will attach both `stdin` and `stdout` streams to your console.

There are `-i` or `--interactive` (for keeping the STDIN stream open even if not attached) and `-t` or `--tty` (for attaching a `pseudo-tty`) switches, commonly used together as `-it`, which you will need to allocate a `pseudo-tty` console for the process running in the container. It is used to attach the command line to the container after it has started. As you may remember from the previous chapters, we already did this, when we were running the interactive Ubuntu bash shell:

```
docker run -it ubuntu
```

When you run your container and want to interact with it later, updating the restrictions for example, you must tell Docker the image that you want to execute the command for. Images can be identified in the Docker world in a couple of ways. Until now, we have been executing images using long or short UUID identifiers. Let's see some options here.

Identifying images and containers

As you remember from the previous chapters, images that you want to run can be identified simply by there name, such as Ubuntu. In this case, Docker will pick the image tagged by *latest* by default. You can also use the tag syntax or the digest syntax:

```
Image[:tag]
Image[@digest]
```

For example, if you want to run Ubuntu tagged as version *14.04*, you simply execute the command:

```
docker run ubuntu:14.04
```

The image can contain an identifier called a **digest**. The digest is calculated as the sha256 checksum of the image manifest, excluding the signature portion. The manifest comprises of the image's name, its tag (latest), architecture, fsLayers (a list of the image's layers, referenced by their digests), history, schema version, and signatures. You can list the digest by specifying the –digests option to the `docker images` command. A digest can be used with the `docker create`, `docker pull`, and `dockerrmi` commands and with the `FROM` instruction in a Dockerfile. Also, it can be used in the `docker run` command, to precisely run the specified image. The digest value is predictable and referenceable and allows of picking the image very precisely.

The following example will run the Ubuntu image that was selected using a digest:

```
docker -it run
ubuntu@sha256:1ffcb21397aa4012a9d88cff8582224ff06aa13ba2de2e9f96c9814bfda95
e0 /bin/bash
```

The containers can be identified in three ways using there name or short or UUID identifier. The identifiers are generated by the Docker daemon. Probably, the most convenient option is to identify a container by its name. It's always easier to remember a friendly name than a long alphanumeric identifier. Defining a name will add meaning to a container, so you will know at the first glance what the container is responsible for. Let's say the name will be `myWildfly` – you will know that the container is your application server. Having `abbb3434aa43` as a container identifier doesn't make things clear. To provide a name for the `docker run` command, use the `--name` switch. If you don't provide a name for a container with the `--name` option, then Docker will create a name for you. I recommend that you always create meaningful names for your containers, since it will be a lot easier to remember them. If you specify a name, you can use it when referencing the container within a Docker network. This works for both the background and foreground Docker containers.

When containers run on default bridge network, they must be linked to communicate by name.

Docker makes use of the PID namespace, thus giving you options to monitor the processes being run within the containers and also limit their number.

PID settings

To set the PID namespace mode, you have three options for setting the PID namespace mode for the container:

- `--pid=""`: This will set the PID (Process) namespace mode for the container
- `--pid=container`: This `<name|id>` joins another container's PID namespace
- `--pid=host`: This will use the host's PID namespace inside the container

The PID namespace is enabled for all containers by default. The PID namespace is useful for the separation of processes. By default, the container PIDs are isolated from the host but you can change this behavior by running your container with the `--pid host` option, the container PID will be visible from the host. Also, your container will share the host's process namespace. This means that the processes within the container will see all of the processes on the host. You can join the container you are starting with another container's PID namespace using `--pid=container:id`. This may be useful for debugging that container from another; for example, you can also easily limit the number of active processes running inside a container to prevent fork bombs.

A fork bomb (also known as rabbit virus or wabbit) is a denial-of-service attack, wherein a process continually replicates itself to deplete the available system resources, slowing down or crashing the system due to resource usage. To limit the number of active processes within the container, execute the `docker run` command with `--pids-limit` value set:

```
docker run --pids-limit=64
```

Getting the current PID of the container is easy using the `docker inspect` command:

```
docker inspect --format '{{.State.Pid}}'<containerID or name>
```

On the other hand, getting the container name by PID is more tricky, but doable. To do this, you will need to use some grepping, as shown in the following example:

```
dockerps -q | xargsdocker inspect --format '{{.State.Pid}}, {{.ID}}' |
grep "^${PID},"
```

Similar to how some programs write their process ID to a file (you've seen them as PID files), Docker can write the container ID to a file you choose. To write the process ID to a file, use the `--cidfile` switch:

```
--cidfile=""
```

Apart from the PID namespace, you can also set the UTS namespace for your containers.

UTS settings

As you remember Docker tries to isolate the container from the host system. The UTS namespace is for setting the hostname and the domain, which is visible, to run processes in that namespace. UTS is the abbreviation for UNIX Timesharing System. By default, all containers have the UTS namespace enabled. It means the process has a separate copy of the hostname and the (now mostly unused) NIS domain name, so it can set it to something else without affecting the rest of the system.

The hostname is set via `sethostname` and is the `nodename` member of the `struct` returned by `uname`. The NIS domain name is set by `setdomainname` and is the `domainname` member of the `struct` returned by `uname`.

The syntax of setting the UTS namespace in Docker is very similar to the `--pid` syntax, you will just use `--uts` instead of `--pid`. To set the UTS namespace for the container, use the `--uts="value"` switch. You can also use the `--uts=host` to bind the host's UTS namespace within your container.

Now we know how to identify containers, we want to run and set up their namespaces. Let's learn how to override the default commands provided in the Dockerfile of the image. We have been doing this in previous chapters, but without going much into details. Let's do it again now.

Overriding default commands from Dockerfile

As you can recall from Chapter 6, *Creating Images*, when we create a Docker image, we provide the default command or options either using the CMD instruction or default command to execute at runtime using the ENTRYPOINT instruction. But without the possibility to influence the container startup process by providing different commands or parameters, other than the image author provided, it wouldn't be possible to use Docker in many cases. Images would be rather static and sometimes just useless. Luckily, Docker supports overriding those defaults and this feature makes it very flexible tool. As you remember from the previous chapter, there's an important difference between ENTRYPOINT and CMD instructions: the ENTRYPOINT defines the process that runs as PID 1 in the container and the CMD provides options for it. If the ENTRYPOINT has not been specified in the Dockerfile, but CMD was, then the shell /bin/sh -c will be the image's entry point. The CMD instruction, the same as ENTRYPOINT, can be specified on the command line when the docker run command is executed, which makes it powerful tool for modifying container's behavior. So, in this section we are interested in overriding the startup commands and their parameters; let's begin with the CMD.

Overriding the CMD

As you remember from the beginning of the current chapter, the syntax for the docker run command includes the COMMAND parameter:

```
docker run [OPTIONS] IMAGE[:TAG|@DIGEST] [COMMAND] [ARG...]
```

The COMMAND parameter is not required because the author of the image may have already provided a default COMMAND using the CMD instruction in the image's Dockerfile. This is usually very often the case.

The CMD instruction should be used in a Dockerfile only once to run the software contained in the image. It's usually the last command in a Dockerfile, but when starting the container from such an image, we can override the CMD instruction simply by providing our own command or parameters as the COMMAND parameter for the docker run. Anything that appears after the image name in the docker run command is passed to the container and treated as CMD arguments. As a result, if the image also specifies an ENTRYPOINT then the CMD or COMMAND gets appended as arguments to the ENTRYPOINT. But guess what, we can override the ENTRYPOINT as well.

Overriding the ENTRYPOINT

Every Docker image has an entry point. It can be the default one or the one specified by the ENTRYPOINT instruction, it's a default command to be executed at runtime; it specifies what executable to run when the container starts, but it is more difficult to override. The ENTRYPOINT makes a running container more like a complete *command* to execute, which takes parameters from the COMMAND value. But sometimes when running the container, you will want to run something else, so you can override the default ENTRYPOINT at runtime using a string to specify the new ENTRYPOINT. The syntax for overriding an entry point is as follows:

```
docker run -it --entrypoint /bin/bash Ubuntu
```

Let's take at look of the MongoDB Dockerfile, which has the ENTRYPOINT defined:

```
FROM dockerfile/ubuntu
RUN mkdir -p /data/db /data/configdb \
&&chown -R mongodb:mongodb /data/db /data/configdb
VOLUME /data/db /data/configdb
COPY docker-entrypoint.sh /entrypoint.sh
ENTRYPOINT ["/entrypoint.sh"]
EXPOSE 27017
CMD ["mongod"]
```

As you can see, there is a custom entry point defined; it will be an entrypoint.sh shell script. If you run this container now, the main process of the container will come from this script. We can override this entry point using the command:

```
docker run -it --entrypoint /bin/bash mongo
```

After executing the previous command, the ENTRYPOINT from the Dockerfile will be overridden by the one you have provided during the docker run command. Of course, MongoDB will not start the property in this case (you will see the bash prompt instead), but this can give you an idea of how you can influence the default container behavior, sometimes executing something completely different from what the image author intended.

Apart from overriding the CMD or ENTRYPOINT from the Dockerfile during the startup of the container, there's another way of executing a command worth mentioning. It will be the dockerexec command.

Executing arbitrary commands with exec

It's maybe the most powerful all–around tool when working with Docker images. The exec command allows you to run arbitrary commands inside a running container.

In opposite of the overriding the CMD or ENTRYPOINT, the command started using docker exec will only run while the container's primary process (PID 1) is running.

 If the container is paused, then the docker exec command will fail with an error.

Also, the syntax of the exec command is different. It's not a part of the Docker run command, it's rather a new separate command, executed after you run your container with the docker run. Consider the following example and run the following in one shell terminal:

```
docker run -it ubuntu bash --name myUbuntuBash
```

Then run the next command in the second shell terminal window:

```
dockerexec -d myUbuntuBash touch /tmp/myFile
```

In the preceding example, the first command fill starts the interactive bash shell from the Ubuntu container, ok that is nothing new; however, the second command, docker exec will actually execute a touch shell command within the running container.

The `docker exec` can be a little confusing with the `docker attach` command we have already mentioned when learning about the detached containers. It's worth noting, that the `docker attach` isn't for running an extra thing in a container, it's useful for attaching to the running process. Also, if the main process is a shell, then we can run a new process using attach. The `docker exec`, on the other hand, is specifically designed for running new things in a container that is already started. Of course, it can also be a shell or some other process, as can be seen in the following screenshot:

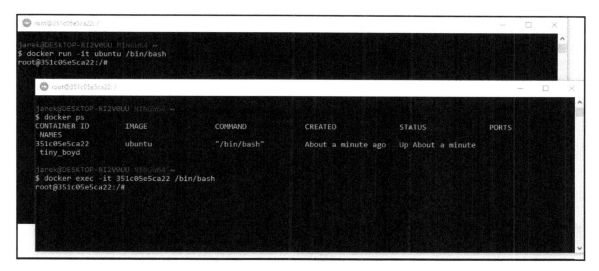

We now know how to run containers, either in foreground or in background; we know how to override default startup process or how to execute our custom commands in the running containers. It's now time to take a look at the running containers and monitor how well they behave; or how bad, for that matter.

Monitoring containers

There are a few ways of monitoring the running Docker containers. They includes viewing the log files, looking at the container events and statistics, and also inspecting container properties. Let's begin with the logging. Docker has powerful logging features. An access to the log entries is crucial, especially if you have your container running in the detached runtime mode. Let's see what Docker can offer when it comes to a logging mechanism.

Viewing logs

Most applications output their log entries to the standard stdout stream (normally you just see in in the console when you run the application). However, when running from Docker in detached mode, we see nothing on the console because the container runs in the background. To view the log entries from the container, execute the following command:

```
docker logs -f <container name>
```

The -f flag acts as the same flag in Linux tail command; it will continuously display new log entries on the console. When you are done, hit ctrl-c to stop displaying log files on the console.

The log file is available even after the container stops, as long as its file system is still present on disk (until of course it is removed with the dockerrm command). The data is stored in a JSON file located in the /var/lib/docker directory. You can see the complete path of the log file using the docker inspect command and using a template to extract the LogPath (we will cover inspect and templates in a while):

```
docker inspect -f {{.LogPath}} 351c05e5ca22
```

```
MINGW64:/c/Users/jarek                                                    —    □    ×

jarek@DESKTOP-RI2V0UU                 ~
$ docker inspect -f {{.LogPath}} 351c05e5ca22
/mnt/sda1/var/lib/docker/containers/351c05e5ca222d2505e4a643152cbb1843d09480cad0e2422272f720f714ec5d/351c05e5ca222d250
5e4a643152cbb1843d09480cad0e2422272f720f714ec5d-json.log

jarek@DESKTOP-RI2V0UU                 ~
$
```

Docker utilizes the concept of logging drivers, to store containers log entries. The default driver is the json-file driver, which just writes out the JSON entries into the file. It can take some tweaking parameters, for example:

```
--log-opt max-size=[0-9+][k|m|g]
--log-opt max-file=[0-9+]
```

The `max-size` specifies the maximum file size that can be created. Docker will create a new file if it reaches the specified size. You can use the size suffixes k, m, or g, where k will be for kilobytes, m for megabytes and g for gigabytes. If you do not provide the `max-size`, Docker will write all the log output into a single file, which is not very handy, if you need to download, upload, or search through the log file for example. The `max-file` option specifies the maximum number of files that a log is rolled over before being discarded. Note that if `max-size` is not set, the `max-file` option will be ignored.

> The `docker log` command only displays log entries from the newest log file.

However, the `json-file` driver is not the only log driver implementation available. Actually, there are a couple of implementations to choose from:

- `none`: It will switch off logging completely
- `syslog`: It's a `syslog` logging driver for Docker and writes log messages to the system `syslog`.
- `journald`: It will log messages to `journald`. `systemd-journald` is a daemon responsible for event logging with append-only binary files serving as its log files.

Apart from the preceding, there are a couple of more specialized drivers you can choose from:

- `splunk`: This provides writing log messages to Splunk using **Event Http Collector**. Splunk can be used as an `enterprise-grade` log analyzer. You can read more about it at https://www.splunk.com.
- `gelf`: This will write log entries into a GELF endpoint similar to Graylog or Logstash. Graylog, available at https://www.graylog.org, is an open source log management, supporting search, analysis, and alerting across all of your log files. Logstash, which you can find at `https://www.elastic.co/products/logstash`, is a pipeline for processing any day source.
- `fluentd`: This writes log messages to fluentd. Fluentd is an open source data collector for unified logging layer. The main feature of Fluentd is that it separates data sources from backend systems by providing a unified logging layer in between. It's small, fast, and has hundreds of plugins that make a very flexible solution out of it. You can read more about fluentd on its website https://www.fluentd.org.

- `gcplogs`ta (including log data) from any source. fluentd: This writes log messages to fluentd. Fluentd is an open source data collector for unified logging layer. The main feature of Fluentd is that it separates data sources from backend systems by providing a unified logging layer in between. It's small, fast, and has hundreds of plugins that make a very flexible solution out of it. You can read more about fluentd on its website https://www.fluentd.org. gcplogs: This will send the log entries to Google Cloud Logging
- `awslogs`: This driver will write log messages to the Amazon CloudWatch Logs.

As you can see, again the Docker's pluggable architecture gives you almost infinite flexibility when running the container. To switch to the other log driver, use the `--log-driver` switch for the `docker run` command, for example:

```
docker run --log-driver=syslog ubuntu
```

The `docker logs` command is available only for the `json-file` and `journal` logging drivers. To access logs written to other log engines, you will need to use the tools provided by the vendor of the log solution, such as Splunk.

Apart from using the `docker log` command, another way of seeing the console output is using the attach command that we learned about earlier in this chapter; attach it to the running container, to see its console output.

Container events

To get the real-time events from the server, we use the `docker events` command. When something has changed during the container runtime, such as `stop`, `pause` or `kill`, container will store and publish an event for that case. This can be very useful if you would like to know what has happened during the container runtime; it's a powerful monitoring feature. Docker containers report a huge list of events, which you can list with the `docker events` command:

```
    attach, commit, copy, create, destroy, detach, die, exec_create,
 exec_detach, exec_start, export, health_status, kill, oom, pause, rename,
    resize, restart, start, stop, top, unpause, update
```

The `docker events` command can take the `-f` switch, which will filter the output if you are looking for something specific (the filter is empty by default, so it will return all the events). Currently, the list of possible filters includes:

- `container` (container=<name or id>)

- event (event=<event action>)
- image (image=<tag or id>)
- plugin (experimental) (plugin=<name or id>)
- label (label=<key>orlabel=<key>=<value>)
- type (type=<container or image or volume or network or daemon>)
- volume (volume=<name or id>)
- network (network=<name or id>)
- daemon (daemon=<name or id>)

The `docker events` command can take `--since` and `-until` switches, which can be used to specify a timeframe you want to get the events from. Docker supports common RFC3339 formats for date and time, for example `2016-09-10T05:10:00`, `2016-09-10T05:05:00.999999999`, `2016-09-10Z07:00`, and `2016-09-10`.

By default, the `docker events` will stream the events to the console, similar to the tail -f command. As you can see in the following screenshot, t he sample output will contain timestamp of the event, container ID, and, of course, the occurred event itself:

```
jarek@DESKTOP-RI2V0UU                    ~
$ docker events -f container=351c05e5ca22
2016-09-10T05:08:12.655249466+02:00 container start 351c05e5ca222d2505e4a643152cbb1843d09480cad0e2422272f720f714ec5d (
image=ubuntu, name=tiny_boyd)
2016-09-10T05:08:19.500733774+02:00 container kill 351c05e5ca222d2505e4a643152cbb1843d09480cad0e2422272f720f714ec5d (i
mage=ubuntu, name=tiny_boyd, signal=15)
2016-09-10T05:08:19.500945713+02:00 container die 351c05e5ca222d2505e4a643152cbb1843d09480cad0e2422272f720f714ec5d (ex
itCode=0, image=ubuntu, name=tiny_boyd)
2016-09-10T05:08:19.544860602+02:00 container stop 351c05e5ca222d2505e4a643152cbb1843d09480cad0e2422272f720f714ec5d (i
mage=ubuntu, name=tiny_boyd)
```

Inspecting a container

We have been using the `dockerps` command heavily since now. It can give you a lot of useful information about your running containers, such as their ID, status, command executed, exposed ports, and so on. There's another command, `docker inspect` that can also give you some useful information about your containers. The syntax for the `docker inspect` command is as follows:

```
docker inspect [OPTIONS] CONTAINER|IMAGE|TASK [CONTAINER|IMAGE|TASK...]
```

By default, the inspect command will output the information about the container or image in a JSON array format. You can provide a template for processing the output, using the `--format` or `-f` for short as a switch for the command. The `docker inspect` command accepts templates in Go. The simplest use case for the `inspect` command is just to provide short template to extract the information you need, for example:

```
docker inspect -f '{{.State.ExitCode}}'jboss/wildfly
```

As the `inspect` command accepts the provided Go template to form the output of the container or image metadata, this feature gives you almost infinite possibilities of processing and transforming the results. The Go templating engine is powerful, so instead of piping the output through grep, which is quick but messy, you can use the template engine to further process the result.

The argument to `--format` is a just a template that we want to apply to the metadata of container. In this template, we can use conditional statements, loops, and other Go language features. For example, to find the names of all containers with a non-zero exit code:

```
docker inspect -f '{{if ne 0.0 .State.ExitCode }}{{.Name}}
{{.State.ExitCode}}{{ end }}' $(dockerps -aq)
```

Note that we provide `$(dockerps -aq)` instead of container ID or name. As a result, all of the running containers IDs will be piped to the `docker inspect` command, which can be a very handy shortcut. The curly brackets `{{}}` means that the Go template directives anything outside of them will be printed out literally. The dot (`.`) in Go templates means context. Most of the time, the current context will be the complete data structure for the metadata, but it can be rebound when needed, including using the with action. For example, the following two inspect commands will print out exactly the same result:

```
docker inspect -f '{{.State.ExitCode}}'wildfly
docker inspect -f '{{with .State}} {{.ExitCode}} {{end}}'wildfly
```

If you are inside the bound context, the dollar sign (`$`) will always get you the root context. Execute the following command:

```
docker inspect -f '{{with .State}} {{$.Name}} exited with {{.ExitCode}}
exit code \ {{end}}'wildfly
```

This will output:

```
/wildfly exited with 0 exit code.
```

The template engine supports logical functions, such as and, or, and not – they will return a Boolean result. Also the comparison functions are supported, such as eq (equals), ne (not equals), lt (less than), le (less than or equal to), gt (greater than), ge (greater than or equal to). Comparison functions can compare strings, floats, or integers. All of these can be very useful together with the conditional functions, such as if, when creating some more sophisticated output from the inspect command:

```
docker inspect -f '{{if eq .State.ExitCode 0.0}} \
Normal Exit \
{{else if eq .State.ExitCode 1.0}} \
Not a Normal Exit \
{{else}} \
Still Not a Normal Exit \
{{end}}'wildfly
```

Sometimes the huge output of the docker inspect command can be confusing. Since the output comes in JSON format, the jq-tool can be used to get an overview of the output and pick interesting parts.

The jq-tools is available for free at https://stedolan.github.io/jq/. It's a lightweight and flexible command-line JSON processor, similar to the sed command for the JSON data. For example, let's extract the container IP address from the metadata:

```
docker inspect <containerID> | jq -r '.
[0].NetworkSettings.IPAddress'
```

As you can see, the docker inspect command provides useful information about Docker containers. Combined with the Go template features, and optionally with the jq tool, it gives you the powerful tool to get the information about your containers and can be used further in scripting. But there's another source of valuable information apart from the metadata. It's runtime statistics, which we are going to focus on now.

Statistics

To see the runtime statistics for running containers, use the docker stats command. The measured statistics include CPU, memory, and network I/O usage.

The syntax for the docker stats command is as follows:

```
docker stats [OPTIONS] [CONTAINER...]
```

The options can include `--no-stream` that will disable the streaming stats and only pull the first result and `--all` (or `-a` for short), which will show all containers, by default the command shows statistics just for running containers.

The simplest form of the command will be just `docker stats`. It will list all statistics for all running containers. You can limit the returned data to one or more specific containers, by specifying a list of container IDs or names, separated with a space:

`docker stats b4fd15acfcb1 d15acb4ffcbb`

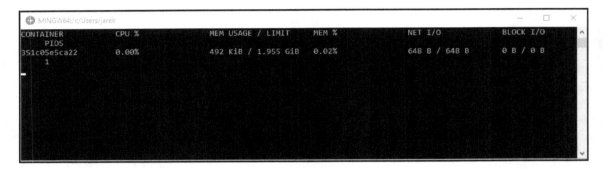

Viewing logs, container events, and runtime statistics gives you almost infinite possibilities when monitoring your running containers. But how can we assure that the container will run continuously, let's say on a production server? The Docker contains the exit codes and the restart policies come to the rescue.

Container exit codes and restart policies

You can specify the so called **restart policy** using the `--restart` switch with the `docker run` command. Restart policy tells Docker how to behave on container shutdown. It can be restarted to minimize downtime, for example if running on production server. However, before we explain the Docker restart policy, let's focus on the exit codes. The exit code is crucial information, it tells why the container failed to run or why it exited. Sometimes it's related to the contained command you will give to `docker run` as a parameter.

When the `dockerrun` command ends with a non-zero code, the exit codes follow the `chroot` standard, as you can see in the following example:

- exit code `125`:The `docker run` command fails by itself
- exit code`126`: The supplied command cannot be invoked
- exit code `127`: The supplied command cannot be found
- Other, non-zero, application dependent exit code.

As you can recall, in the previous chapters we have been using the `dockerps` command to list the running containers. To list the non-running containers as well, we can add the `-a` switch for the `dockerps` command. The exit code can be found in the output of the `dockerps-a` command in a status column when a container completes, as you can see in this screenshot:

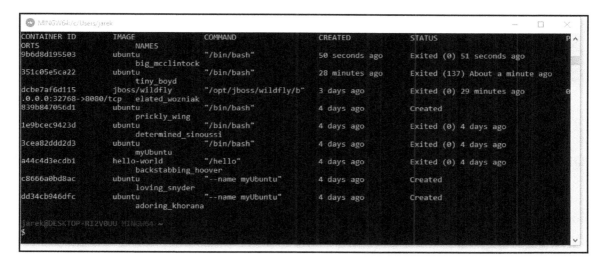

It's possible to automatically restart crashed containers by specifying a restart policy when starting the container. Specifying the desired restart policy is done by the restart switch for the `docker run` command, as in the example:

```
dockerrun --restart=always mongo
```

Currently Docker has four restart policies. Let's get to know them now one by one, starting with the simplest: *no*.

no

The **no** policy is the default restart policy and simply will not restart a container under any case. Actually you do not have to specify this policy, because this is the default behavior. Unless you have some configurable setup to run Docker containers, then the *no* policy can be used as an *off* switch.

always

If we want the container to be restarted no matter what exit code the command would have, we can use the always restart policy. Basically, it does what it says-Docker will restart the container in every case. The restart policy will always restart the container. This is true even if the container has been stopped before the reboot. Whenever the Docker service is restarted, containers using the always policy will also be restarted, it doesn't matter whether they were executing or not.

> With the restart policy, the Docker daemon will always try to restart the container indefinitely.

on-failure

This is a special restart policy and probably the most often used one. Using the `on-failure` restart policy, you can instruct Docker to restart your container whenever it exits with a non-zero exit status and not restart otherwise. That's why we have begun explaining restart policies with the exit codes. You can optionally provide a number of times for Docker to attempt to restart the container. The syntax of this restart policy is also a little bit different, because using this policy, you can also specify a maximum number of tries that Docker will make to automatically restart the container.

Consider the following example:

```
dockerrun --restart=on-failure:5 mongo
```

The preceding command will run MongoDBimage and will try to restart it five times in case of failure before giving up. The main benefit of a `on-failures` restart policy is that when an application exits with a successful exit code (that means there were no error in the application, it just finished executing) the container will not be restarted. The number of restart tries for a container can be obtained via the `docker inspect` command. For example, to get the number of restarts for container with specific ID or name:

```
docker inspect -f "{{ .RestartCount }}"<ContainerID>
```

You can also get the last time the container was started again:

```
docker inspect -f "{{ .State.StartedAt }}"<ContainerID>
```

You should know that Docker uses a delay between restarting the container, to prevent flood-like protection. This is an increasing delay, it starts with the value of 100 milliseconds, and then Docker will double the previous delay. In effect, the daemon will wait for 100 ms, then 200 ms, 400ms, 800ms, and so on, until either the `on-failure` limit is reached or when you stop the container using `docker stop` or execute the force removal by executing the `dockerrm -f` command.

> If a container is successfully restarted the delay is reset to the default value of 100 milliseconds.

unless-stopped

Again, similar to `always` if we want the container to be restarted regardless of the exit code, we can use `unless-stopped`. The `unless-stopped` restart policy acts the same as `always` with one exception, it will restart the container regardless of the exit status, but do not start it on daemon startup if the container has been put to a stopped state before. This means that with `unless-stopped` restart policy is that if the container was running before the reboot, the container would be restarted once the system restarts. Wher. an application within a Docker container exits, that container is halted. If an application that is running within a container crashes, the container stops and that container will remain stopped until someone or something restarts it.

Before you apply the restart policy to your container, it's good to think what kind of work the container will be used to do. That also depends on the kind of software that will be running on the container. A database for example, should have probably `always` or `unless-stopped` policy applied. If your container has some restart policy applied, it will be shown as `Restarting` or `Up` status when you list your container using the `dockerps` command.

Updating a restart policy on a running container

Sometimes there's a need to update the Docker runtime parameters after the container has already started, such as *on-the-fly*. The sample case can be if you want to prevent containers from consuming too many resources on the Docker host. To set the policy during the runtime, we can use the `docker update` command. Apart from other runtime parameters (such as memory or CPU constraints for example, about which we are going to tell in a while later in this chapter), the `docker update` command gives you the possibility to update the restart policy on a running container. The syntax is straightforward, you will just need to provide the new restart policy that you would like the container to have and the containers ID or name:

```
docker update --restart=always <CONTAINER_ID or NAME>
```

A new restart policy will take effect immediately after you run the `docker update` command on a container. On the other hand, if you execute the `update` command on the container that is stopped, the policy will be used when you start the container later on. The possible options are exactly the same as those you can specify when starting the container:

- `no` (which is default)
- `always`
- `on-failure`
- `unless-stopped`

If you have more than one container running on the Docker host, and want to specify new restart policy on all of them at once, just provide all of their IDs or names separated with space.

You can also see what restart policy was applied using the `docker events` command you already know from the previous section. The `docker events` that can be used to observe the history of runtime events that the container has reported, will also report the `docker update` event, providing you the details what has changed.

If the container has been applied the restart policy, the event will be present in the history, as you can see in the following screenshot:

If you want to check the restart policy of a running container use `docker inspect` with the container ID or name with the `--format` argument set for the path of the value:

```
docker inspect --format '{{ .HostConfig.RestartPolicy.Name }}'<ContainerID>
```

The preceding command will simply display the currently applied restart policy, as seen on the screenshot:

The ability to set a restart policy on a container by container basis is great for those cases where your images are self-contained and you don't need to do more complex orchestration tasks. The restart policy is not the only parameter you can change on the running containers. To be sure that your containers behave well when running on the Docker host, you can put constraints on them. We are going to cover them now.

Runtime constraints on resources

It may be useful to restrict the Docker container usage on resources when running. Docker gives you a lot of possibilities to set constraints on the memory, CPU usage or disk access usage. Let's begin with setting the memory constraints.

Memory

It's worth knowing, that by default, that is if you use the default settings without any constraints, the running container can use all of the host memory. To change this behavior we can use the `--memory` (or `-m` for short) switch for the `docker run` command. It takes a usual suffixes k,m, or g for kilobytes, megabytes and gigabytes respectively.

The syntax of the `docker run` command with memory constraints set will be as follows:

```
docker run -it -m 512m ubuntu
```

The preceding command will execute the Ubuntu image with the maximum memory that can be used by container of half of gigabyte.

> If you do not set a limit on the memory container can allocate can lead to random issues where a single container can easily make the whole host system unstable and/or unusable. So it's a wise decision to always use the memory constraints on the container.

Apart from user memory limit, there are also memory reservation and kernel memory constraint. Let's explain what memory reservation limit is. Under normal working conditions, a running container can, and probably will use as much of the memory as needed up to the limit you have set using the `--memory` (-m) switch for the `docker run` command. When memory reservation is applied, Docker will detect low memory situation and will try to force container to restrict it's consumption up to a reservation limit. If you do not set the memory reservation limit, it will be the same as the hard memory limit set with the -m switch.

Memory reservation is not a hard limit feature. There's no guarantee the limit won't be exceeded. The memory reservation feature will attempt to ensure that memory will be allocated based on the reservation setting.

Consider the following example:

```
docker run -it -m 1G --memory-reservation 500M ubuntu /bin/bash
```

The preceding command sets the hard memory limit to one gig, and then sets the memory reservation to half a gig. With those constraints set, when the container consumes memory more than 500M and less than 1G, Docker will attempt to shrink container memory below 500M.

In the next example, we are going to set the memory reservation without setting the hard memory limit:

```
docker run -it --memory-reservation 1G ubuntu /bin/bash
```

In the previous example, when the container starts, it can use as much memory as it's processes need. The `--memory-reservation` switch setting will prevent the container from consuming too much memory for long time, because every memory reclaim will shrinks the container's memory usage to the size specified in the reservation.

The kernel memory is something entirely different from the user memory–the main difference is that kernel memory can't be swapped out to disk. It includes stack pages, slab pages, sockets memory pressure, and TCP memory pressure. You use the `--kernel-memory` switch setup kernel memory limit to constrain these kinds of memory. The same as in setting the user memory limit, just provide a number with a suffix like k, b, g for kilobyte, megabyte or gigabyte respectively-although setting it in kilobytes may be a really rare case.

For example, every process eats some stack pages. By restricting kernel memory, you can prevent new processes from being started when the kernel memory usage is too high and because the host cannot swap the kernel memory to disk, the container can block the whole host services by consuming too much kernel memory.

Setting the kernel memory limit is straightforward. We can set the `--kernel-memory` alone, without limiting the total memory with −m, as seen in the following example:

```
docker run -it --kernel-memory 100M ubuntu  /bin/bash
```

In the previous example, the process in the container can take memory as it needs, but it can only consume 100M kernel memory. We can also set up the hard memory limit, as in the following command:

```
docker run -it -m 1G --kernel-memory 100M ubuntu /bin/bash
```

In the previous, we set memory and kernel memory altogether, so the processes in the container can use 1G memory in total, and this 1G will include 100M of the kernel memory.

One more constraint related to the memory which can be useful when running containers, is the `swappines` constraint. We apply the constraint by using the `--memory-swappiness` switch to the `docker run` command. It can be helpful when you want to avoid performance drops related to memory swapping. The parameter for the `--memory-swappiness` switch is the percentage of anonymous memory pages that can be swapped out, so it takes values from 0 to 100. A value of 0 turns off anonymous page swapping completely. On the contrary, a value of 100 sets all anonymous pages as candidates for swapping out. For example:

```
docker run -it --memory-swappiness=0 ubuntu/bin/bash
```

In the previous command we turn the swapping completely for our `ubuntu` container.

Apart from setting the memory usage constraint, you can also instruct Docker how the processor power should be assigned to containers it's going to run.

Processors

Using the `-c` (or `--cpu-shares` as an equivalent) for the `docker run` command switch it's possible to specify a value of shares of the CPU that container can allocate. By default, every new container has 1024 shares of CPU and all containers get the same part of CPU cycles. This percentage can be altered by shifting the container's CPU share weighting relative to the weighting of all other running containers. But take note, that you cannot set the precise processor speed that container can use. This is a relative weight and has nothing to do with the real processor speed. In fact, there is no way to say precisely that a container should have right to use only to 2GHz of host's processor.

 CPU share is just a number – it's not related at all to the CPU speed.

If we start two containers and both will use 100% CPU, the processor time will be divided equally between the two containers. The reason for that is two containers will have the same number of processor shares. But if you constraint one container's processor shares to512it will receive just a half of the CPU time. This does not mean that it can use only half of the CPU – the proportion will only apply when CPU-intensive processes are running. If the other container (with 1024 shares) is idle – our container will be allowed to use 100% of the processor time. The real amount of CPU time will differ depending on the number of containers running on the system. It's easier to understand on a tangible example.

Consider three containers, one (let's call it `Container1`) has `--cpu-shares` set for `1024` and two others (`Container2` and `Container3`) have a `--cpu-shares` setting of `512`. When processes in all three containers attempt to use all of the CPU power, the `Container1` would receive 50% of the total CPU time, because it has half of the CPU usage allowed in comparison to the sum of other running containers (`Container2` and `Container3`). If we add a fourth container (`Container4`) with a `--cpu-share` of `1024`, our first `Container1` will only get 33% of the CPU, because it now has one third of the total CPU power assigned, relatively. `Container2` will receive 16.5%, `Container3` also 16.5% and the last one, `Container4`, again, will be allowed to use 33% of the CPU.

While the `-c` or `--cpu_shares` flag for the `dockerrun` command modifies the container's CPU share weighting relative to the weighting of all other running containers, it does not restrict the container's use of CPU from the host machine. But there's another flag to limit the CPU usage for the container: `--cpu-quota`. Its default value is `100000` which means allowance for 100% of the CPU usage. We can use the `--cpu-quota` to limit CPU usage, for example:

```
docker run -it  --cpu-quota=50000 ubuntu/bin/bash
```

In the preceding command, the limit for the container will be 50% of a CPU resource. The `--cpu-quota` is usually used in conjunction with `--cpu-period` flag for the `docker run`. This is the setting for CPU **CFS** (**Completely Fair Scheduler**) period. The default period value is `100000` which is 100 milliseconds. Take a look at the example:

```
docker run -it --cpu-quota=25000 --cpu-period=50000  ubuntu /bin/bash
```

It means that the container can get 50% of the CPU usage every 50ms.

Limiting CPU shares and usage is not the only processor-related constraint we can set on the container. We can also assign the container's processes to a particular processor or processor core. The `--cpuset` switch of the `docker run` command comes in handy when we want to do this. Consider the following example:

```
docker run -it --cpuset 4 ubuntu
```

The preceding command will run the `ubuntu` image and allow container use all of four processor cores. To start the container and only allow usage on one processor core, you can change the `--cpuset` value to 1:

```
docker run -it --cpuset 1 ubuntu
```

You can of course mix the option `-cpuset` with `--cpu_shares` to tweak your container's CPU constraints.

Updating constraints on a running container

As with the restart policies, the constraints can be updated also when the container is already running. This may be helpful, if you observe your containers eating too much of the Docker host system resources and would like to limit this usage. Again, we use the `docker update` command to do this.

The same as with restart policies, the syntax for the `docker update` command will be the same as when starting the container – you specify the desired constraints as an argument for the `docker update` command and then give the container ID (taken from the `dockerps` command output for example) or its name. Again, if you would like to change the constraints on more than one container at once, just provide their IDs or names separated with a space. Let's look at some examples how to update constraints at the runtime:

```
docker update --cpu-shares 512 abbdef1231677
```

The previous command will limit the CPU shares to the value of `512`. Of course, you can apply CPU and memory constraints at the same time, to more than one container:

```
docker update --cpu-shares 512 -m 500M abbdef1231677 dabdff1231678
```

The previous will update CPU shares and memory limit to two containers, identified by `abbdef1231677` and `dabdff1231678`.

Of course, when updating the runtime constraints, you can also apply the desired restart policy in one single command, as in the following example:

```
docker update --restart=always -m 300M aabef1234716
```

As you can see, the ability to set constraints gives you a lot of flexibility when running Docker containers. But it's worth noting, that applying constraints is not always possible. The reason for that is the constraint setting features depend heavily of the internals of the Docker host, especially it's kernel. For example, it's not always possible to setup kernel memory limit or memory swappinnes, for example – sometimes all you will get is **Your kernel does not support kernel memory limit or kernel does not support memory swappiness capabilities** messages. Sometimes those limitations can be configurable, sometimes not. For example if you get **WARNING: Your kernel does not support cgroup swap limit** on Ubuntu, you can tweak your `Grub` bootloader with the `cgroup_enable=memory swapaccount=1` setting. It's important to read logs printed out by Docker, to make sure your constraints are in place.

> Always take note on the warnings Docker outputs during the container startup or after updating your constraints on the fly – it may happen that your constraints will not take action!

At this time, we know about the container runtime modes (foreground and detached). We are able to monitor running containers and update their restart policies and runtime constraints. But there's some more when it comes to running containers and scaling your applications – the Docker Swarm mode. It couldn't be missed in a chapter about running containers, so let's cover it now.

Docker Swarm mode

We have mentioned the Swarm mode briefly in the `Chapter 4`, *Networking and Persistent Storage*, when we were learning about multi-host networks. This time, we will look closer to the container clustering features of Docker. The Swarm mode is quite new feature in Docker – it's available in Docker version 1.12 and up. It means, that you can only use this in Linux, which is obvious, but if you run Docker in Windows or Mac, you can use the native Docker for Windows or Docker for Mac application. However, what Swarm is? Let's explain what was the purpose behind including the Swarm in latest Docker versions.

The purpose

Running a single application in a Docker container is easy. We already did it a number of times. But what about scaling and fail-over? Imagine that you have an application or service that will need to respond swiftly even under heavy load. If a single container cannot handle the load, then you will probably want to run multiple containers. Using Docker Swarm, you can establish and manage a cluster of Docker hosts as a single virtual system. By enabling the cluster, you basically create a cooperative group of Docker hosts If one them fails and is down, other can still serve an application to the user. Having Docker Swarm cluster running, you also have the ability to add or subtract container instances whenever the load changes. And here comes the best part: we don't have to make the decision on which host to start every container on. It will be made automatically by Swarm – in the background, Docker running in swarm mode decides which nodes to start them on. It may seem complex, but in real life running Docker Swarm is as easy as running single Docker containers. If you will get familiar with Docker commands, you will be familiar with Docker Swarm commands as well. Let's get started with explaining some Swarm mode terminology.

Terminology

There are some key names in Docker Swarm. We need to understand their meaning to easily understand the rest of the chapter and also external resources. Let's list them one by one:

- **Swarm**: This is simply a cluster of running Docker containers. It's a pool of Docker hosts that acts a bit like a single large Docker host.
- **The Swarm manager**: This is a Docker host on which you have initialized the Swarm. The manager node serves the special purpose: it maintains the cluster state, schedules services and serves swarm mode HTTP API endpoints.

- **Node**: All containers running in a swarm are called `nodes` – they run in a so-called **swarm mode**. To make a container run in this mode, you will need to initialize the swarm (this will create a new swarm) or join the container to the existing Swarm. In Docker's swarm mode, you can deploy manager and worker nodes at runtime. A node can be also promoted to be Manager by using the `docker node promote` command.

- **Scheduling**: It's just a name for launching containers in a Swarm cluster. Currently, there are three algorithms implemented in Docker Swarm to help it decide on which nodes in the cluster the container should be run: spread, BinPack and random. The spread setting is the default one-Docker will balance the containers based on the CPU and RAM resources available on each node. BinPack scheduler is quite the opposite -it will utilise the given node first to its max capacity, the will run containers on the next node. Random, as its name says, is just a random scheduling.

- **Service**: It's a container that is going to be run on the cluster together with the command that will be executed on the container.

Docker Engine provides some commands for dealing with the swarm. Most of them are very similar to the commands we already know – those for working with the containers. Let's list them altogether with their description.

Swarm mode commands

- `swarminit`: To initialize the Swarm and also make to current Docker host the Swarm manager.
- `swarm join`: To join a node to the Swarm.
- `service create`: To schedule a service (container) to the Swarm.
- `service inspect`: To display details about container running as a Swarm service.
- `service ls`: To list running services. The command output will also contain the number of nodes that this specific service is being run on.
- `servicerm`: To remove a service.
- `service scale`: To add a replicas of the given service. You can also scale multiple services at once.

- `serviceps`: Will list the tasks of the service (which is the command that was run with the container).
- `service update`: Allows you to update the service's – you can set service command line arguments, runtime constraints, like CPU or memory, add or modify environment variables and so on.

To initialize the Swarm (which also make the host you are currently on a Swarm manager), you'll need to execute the `swarm init` command:

```
docker swarm init --advertise-addr<IP>
```

As an output, Docker will give you the token that you will need to user if you would like to connect another Docker host to you Swarm. You can see it on the following screenshot:

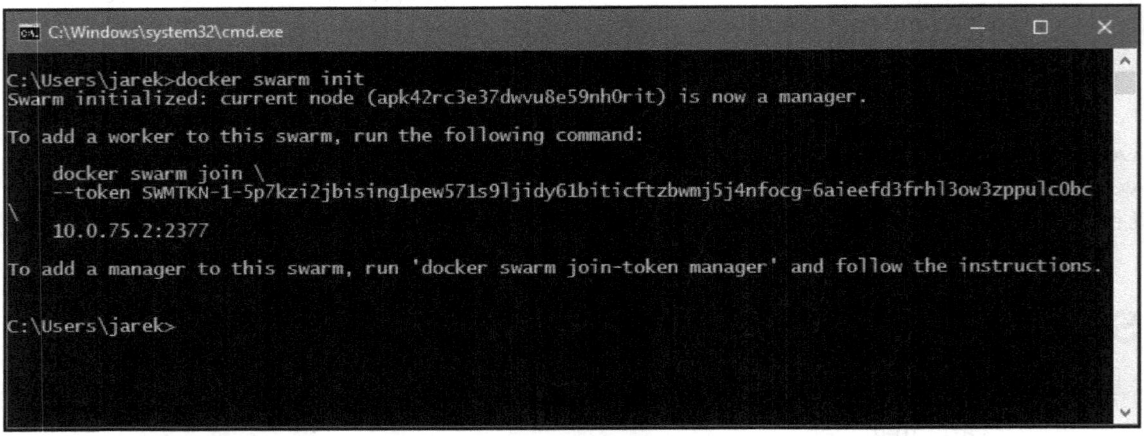

To connect a node to the Swarm, execute the docker `swarm join` command, including the token you were given from the `docker swarm init` command, for example:

```
docker swarm join \
    --token
SWMTKN-1-5p7kzi2jbising1pew571s9ljidy61biticftzbwmj5j4nfocg-6aieefd3frhl3ow
3zppulc0bc
```

Now we have simple (two nodes) Docker Swarm. It's time to install (schedule) a service. Scheduling a service to be run on Docker Swarm is very similar to running the standalone container. You can schedule the service using the `docker service create` command:

```
docker service create --replicas 1 -p80:80 --name nginx nginx
```

In the previous case we run nginx web server as a Docker Swarm service. Most of the commands that we have been using to deal with containers, such as `ps`, and `ls`, `inspect` – they will also work with the `docker service` command, as you can see on the following screenshot:

```
C:\Windows\system32\cmd.exe                                            —   □   ×
C:\Users\jarek>docker service ls
ID              NAME    REPLICAS  IMAGE   COMMAND
ad5b71qaac5w    nginx   1/1       nginx

C:\Users\jarek>docker service inspect nginx
[
    {
        "ID": "ad5b71qaac5wwijgfa394fg1g",
        "Version": {
            "Index": 12
        },
        "CreatedAt": "2016-11-06T12:28:45.2801102Z",
        "UpdatedAt": "2016-11-06T12:28:45.2801102Z",
        "Spec": {
            "Name": "nginx",
            "TaskTemplate": {
                "ContainerSpec": {
                    "Image": "nginx"
                },
                "Resources": {
                    "Limits": {},
                    "Reservations": {}
                },
                "RestartPolicy": {
                    "Condition": "any",
                    "MaxAttempts": 0
                },
                "Placement": {}
            },
            "Mode": {
                "Replicated": {
                    "Replicas": 1
                }
            },
            "UpdateConfig": {
                "Parallelism": 1,
                "FailureAction": "pause"
            },
            "EndpointSpec": {
                "Mode": "vip"
            }
        },
        "Endpoint": {
            "Spec": {}
        },
        "UpdateStatus": {
            "StartedAt": "0001-01-01T00:00:00Z",
            "CompletedAt": "0001-01-01T00:00:00Z"
        }
    }
]
C:\Users\jarek>
```

The way service related commands mimic those container related commands makes the service related command easier to remember. To scale the service, which will be increasing the number of service instances, execute the `docker scale` command, for example:

```
docker service scale nginx=3
```

As you can see, having the Docker Swarm is not that tricky as it may seem. The beauty of the Docker cluster implementations is its simplicity. With the swarm mode you create a swarm with the `init` command, and add workers to the cluster with the `join` command. That's it. The commands to create and join a swarm literally take a second or two to complete.

Summary

You may have an impression, that there is a huge flexibility when it comes to running Docker containers. And you are right, definitely there is much we can do. We can override the images RUN, CMD, ENTRYPOINT instructions to change the container run behavior, sometimes even totally change the container's purpose if needed. Docker provides a lot of powerful commands to inspect the container runtime state, viewing logs, events and statistics. They surely make devop's daily job a lot easier. Also, setting the container restart policies and runtime constraints on CPU or memory can result of run-and-forget way of working with Docker containers. If you need your applications to scale easily, there is nothing simpler than bringing a Docker Swarm to life. Setting up Docker Swarm is easy, straightforward and flexible. Of course, detailed setup of a cluster may take some time, but running a basic cluster of Docker containers in seconds is possible.

Now that we know how to create images, how to run and test them during runtime – it's time for another step – to show world out work. In the next Chapter 8, *Publishing Images*, we are going to publish our images to the Docker Hub and do some more interesting tricks, like creating the automated builds for our images.

8
Publishing Images

So far you have learned how to use the command line to run Docker on your local machine, how to pull down images to build containers from existing images, and how to create your own images. In this chapter, we are going to learn how to publish our images in the Docker Hub registry. We will also cover the process of doing an automatic build of the image using the Webhooks. We have already discussed the process of pulling an image from the registry in `Chapter 5`, *Finding Images*. Now, however, instead of pulling images, we are going to publish our work. As you might remember, to do this, you will need to have a Docker Hub account. You can refer to `Chapter 5`, *Finding Images*, for the instructions on how to create an account, if you haven't done so already. The Docker Hub service is free for public Docker images. Once you have created your account, you can push the image that you created previously, to make it available for others to use. In this chapter, we are going to cover the following topics:

- Managing image tags and pushing to the remote registry
- Integrating GitHub and Bitbucket
- Webhooks and automated builds

Let's begin with publishing our images to the repository.

Publishing images

When dealing with images on the remote registry, the concept of tag is very important. We were going to find the images and identify those using tags. This is also crucial if you are going to publish your own image; you will need to tag it first. Let's do that now.

Tagging

We use the `docker tag` command to tag an image. You can identify an image you want to tag by either using its ID or its name. Also, you can pick the image to tag using other tags. The syntax of the `docker tag` command is as follows:

```
docker tag IMAGE[:TAG] IMAGE[:TAG]
```

For example, you will need to execute the following command to tag a local image with name `myHelloWorld` and tag `test` into the `myRepo` repository with `version1.0.test`:

```
docker tag myHelloWorld:test myRepo/myHelloWorld:version1.0.test
```

If you run the `docker images` command now, you will see your newly tagged image.

Your newly tagged image is now ready to be pushed to the remote registry. The concept of tags is used heavily by the Docker Hub's automated builds. A tag lets you link a `version` tag to either a branch or a tag in the `git` history. A branch in this case will refer either to a different Git branch or a different sub-directory. We will get back to it in a while when we discuss the automated build feature.

Untagging the image

Sometimes it may be useful to remove a tag from the image. There is no docker `untag` command, but if you are careful, you can use the `docker rmi` command to untag the image. Normally, we use the `docker rmi` command to remove the image; however, if your image is tagged with more than one tag, then the `docker rmi` command will remove the tag but not the image.

 Be cautious, because if the image has no more tags, the `docker rmi` command will remove the image.

For example, execute the following command if you need to remove the `version1.0.test` tag from your image:

```
docker rmi <image ID or name>:version1.0.test
```

Pushing the image

Once your image is properly tagged, you can log in to the Docker Hub using the `docker login` command, the same way that we did in `Chapter 5`, *Finding Images*. To log in into the remote registry, execute the `docker login` command:

```
docker login --username=yourUsername --email=yourEmail@address.com
```

After successful authentication, you just simply push the image using the `docker push` command:

```
docker push yourUsername/myRepo
```

Of course, pushing the image can take some time, depending on the image size and the speed of your internet connection. When finished, the image is available for pulling. If you need to check if the image is available and ready on the remote registry, you can just pull it.

 If you want to pull your own image from the Docker Hub, first delete the original image from your local machine. Docker will compare the one you have locally and the one you have on the remote registry and will not pull as the local and the remote images are identical.

If publishing to a public repository in the Docker hub, logging in and executing the `docker push` command will make the new image available to the world. However, you are, of course, not limited to the public registry, you can also push the image to your own private registry. In case you want to use a private registry, you need to set the URL to your private registry as the username. First, you will need to tag it properly and then push it. If your registry is listing on `localhost port 5000`, you can execute the following commands:

```
docker tag yourUser/myRegistry localhost:5000/myRegistry
docker push localhost:5000/myRegistry
```

You can create your own private registry by making use of the Docker Distribution toolset, available freely on GitHub: `https://github.com/docker/distribution`. The main utility you can find in this GitHub repository is the Docker registry 2.0 implementation for storing and distributing Docker images. It replaces the old docker-registry project with a new API design, focused on security and performance. This new registry implementation provides the following benefits over the old one: faster push and pull, simplified deployment, pluggable storage backend, and webhooks notifications. It supports multiple storage backends, you can choose, for example, the local file system or a cloud similar to the Amazon S3.

Tagging and pushing images to the remote registry, either public or private, is rather straightforward and not a complicated process. But there's more in what Docker Hub offers and automated builds. Let's explain them in the succeeding sections.

Webhooks and automated builds

As you may recall from Chapter 5, *Finding Images*, one of the coolest Docker Hub features are the automated builds. An automated build is triggered by webhooks when changes are made to a source code of the image (that is, to Dockerfile). Webhooks let you execute different actions after pushing an image to a repository. Automated Builds repository automate the building and updating of images from the most popular git repositories, namely GitHuborBitbucket, directly on Docker Hub. Automated builds repository can be created either for private or public repositories. It works by adding a commit hook to your selected GitHub or Bitbucket repository; thus, triggering a build and update when you push a commit. Automated Builds repository have several advantages, images built this way are built exactly as specified, the Dockerfile is available to anyone with access to your Docker Hub repository, and your Docker repository is automatically always up-to-date with source code changes.

Setting up the automated build

In Chapter 6, *Creating Images*, we discussed that Docker builds images using the so called **build context**. The build context is a Dockerfile and any files in a specific location that are referenced by the Dockerfile. For an Automated Build, the build context will be a source code repository containing a Dockerfile. This means that the source code repository must contain all the files that you would usually need to build the image locally, with mandatory Dockerfile in the first place.

 For automated builds, the source code repository is the build context.

To set up the Automated Build you will need to login into Docker Hub first. After that, open the create dropdown and choose **Create Automated Build**, as you can see in the following screenshot:

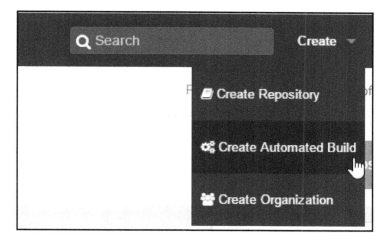

Docker Hub uses the GitHub or Bitbucket as a source code repository, so you will need to link your GitHub or Bitbucket account to your Docker Hub account, if you haven't done this earlier. The steps will include authenticating with GitHub or Bitbucket and granting Docker Hub limited or full access to your repository account. That access is required for the Docker Hub to find your repositories and register appropriate webhooks for you. To do this, click on the **Link Account** button and choose either GitHub or Bitbucket, as shown:

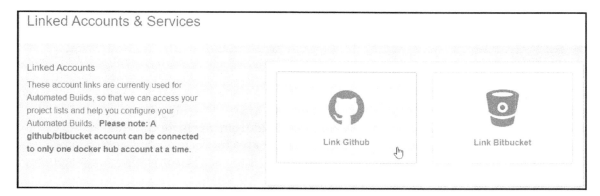

If you select **Link GitHub,** you will need to do one more choice. You can give Docker Hub public and private access or a limited, read-only, public access to your repositories, as you can see on the following screenshot:

Public and Private (Recommended)

- Read and Write access to public and private repositories. (We only use write access to add service hooks and add deploy keys)
- Required if you want to setup an Automated Build from a private GitHub repository.
- Required if you want to use a private GitHub organization.
- We will automatically configure the service hooks and deploy keys for you.

Select

Limited Access

- Public read only access.
- Only works with public repositories and organizations.
- You will need to manually make changes to your repositories in order to use Automated Build.

Select

There's a big difference between the two. The first option gives read and write access to public and private repositories, it means that Docker Hub will be able to add service hooks and deploy keys to your repositories automatically. Also, this read-write access is mandatory, if you want to set up an Automated Build from a private GitHub repository. The limited, read-only access means that you will be able to create an Automated Build repository only with public repositories. Also, in order to use the automated build feature, you will need to make changes to the repository on your own.

Giving Docker Hub access to your private repository is a lot more convenient and recommended, but consider using only the limited access if you have security concerns.

Once you give access to your repository, you will be taken to the OAuth summary screen, where GitHub will ask for your confirmation before giving access to your account:

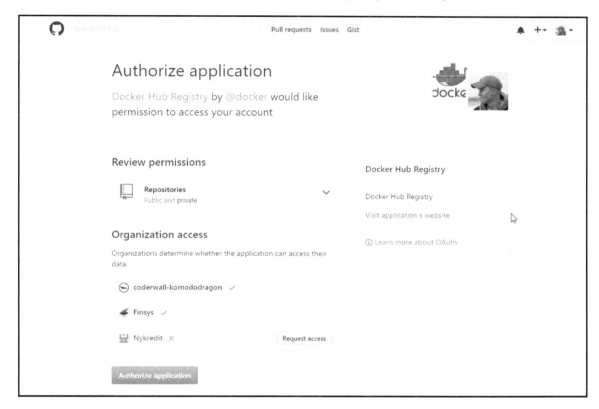

After authorizing the access to your GitHub account, the list of your repositories on GitHub will be shown if you pick the **Create Automated Build** option from the **Create** dropdown.

> The repository you want to have automatic build created from needs to have a Dockerfile in that you want to build.

For the purpose of this example, I've forked the `hello-world` Docker image repository available on GitHub at `https://github.com/docker-library/hello-world`.

All you need to do now is pick up the repository from the list. You will be presented with the `Automated Build` configuration screen. Here, you can set the visibility of the resulting image (public or private). By default, Docker Hub will tag the resulting images with the names of the branches in your Git repository. The Git `push` command to the `master` branch will trigger a build and tag the image with the `latest` tag. A git `push` to a branch other than `master` will trigger the build of an image from that Git branch. The result will then be tagged with this branch name.

 You can create multiple Automated Builds per repository and configure them to point to specific Dockerfile's or Git branches.

This is usually sufficient and it's a very effective setup, but you can customize the behavior if you need to. Just click on the **Click here to customize** link to open a rule editor:

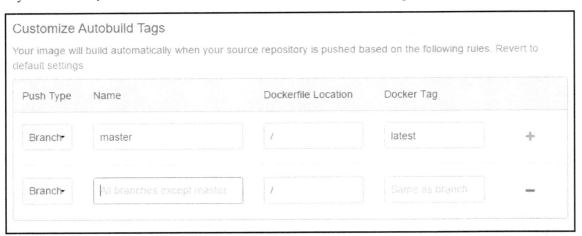

In the **Autobuild Tags** editor, you can specify the tags that specific kind of git push (branch or tag) will have. As you can see, the result of the `master` git branch build will be tagged `latest` by default. There is a lot of flexibility here, you can add or remove rules as you like. For example, a build result of push to the specific branch will be always tagged differently from the other branches.

 You can always change the tagging configuration later, after creating an `Automated Build` in the `Build Settings` page.

After clicking on the **Create** button, your automated build will be created. Docker Hub will list it along with your other repositories; note that the repository you have just created is a result of the automated build:

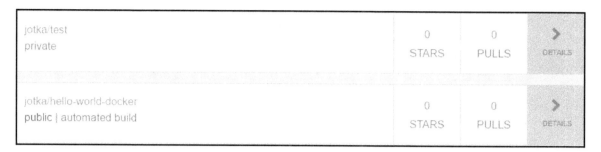

Once you've created an `Automated Build` repository, you can deactivate or delete it later. Docker will list your automated build as a normal repository, however with two differences. The first one difference is that you cannot push an image to `Automated Build` repository.

> You cannot push to an Automated Build with the `docker push` command. You can only manage it by committing and pushing your source code to GitHub or Bitbucket repository.

The second difference is that if you go to the repository details, two additional tabs will be present: **Build Details** and **Build Settings**. The `Build Details` screen, as shown in the following example, will present the history of the latest builds and their statuses, such as `Queued`, `Success`, or `Failure`.

The statuses you can see include:

- `Queued`: Your image waits in the queue to be built. Just wait for a while and it will be ready.
- `Building`: The image is being currently built.
- `Success`: There were no issues during the building process and the image is now available for pulling.
- `Error`: There were some issues during the build (like an error in the Dockerfile or a missing file in the context). If you click on the status row, you will be taken to the Builds Details screen, where you can view the build logs to quickly find a reason for the build failure.

The **Build Settings** page contains the detailed list of settings you can change for that specific automated build. You will find it here on the **Autobuild Tags** editor, the one you saw when creating the Automated Build repository at the beginning. You can always tweak your tagging scheme here.

Although the main trigger for the start of the image build is the git push command, you can also trigger a build issuing the `HTTP POST` command to the specific endpoint. This feature is called a Build Trigger.

Build Triggers

The build trigger is simply an HTTP endpoint, which—if called using an HTTP post command will trigger a build of the image of your choice. You can set up the trigger URL using the **Build Triggers** part of the setup.

It's available when you scroll down the page until you see the *Build triggers* section, as you can see in the following screenshot:

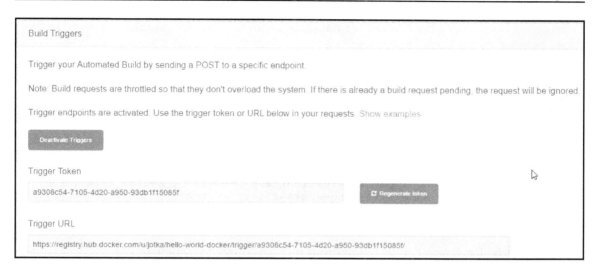

Docker will generate a special unique trigger initially, you can regenerate it if you wish. The token is being used as a part of the trigger URL. Having this set up, you can now trigger a build from your own processes, for example, your continuous integration or delivery flow. The example use case can be if your image uses some external dependencies. You can rebuild the image on demand, not only while pushing the new code to the source code repository.

To test the build trigger, you can execute the POST using the HTTP client of your choice, such as postman for Chrome or PAW for Mac. The simplest and fastest tool is the curl command probably. It's a command line HTTP client, available, by default, in Linux, but you can download it for almost all possible platforms from its homepage: https://curl.haxx.se/download.html. The POST call to the build trigger takes JSON payload with instruction do Docker Hub what to do and how to do it. Consider the following examples of triggering a build. If you want to trigger all tags/branches, execute:

```
    curl -H "Content-Type: application/json" --data '{"build": true}' -X
POST
https://registry.hub.docker.com/u/jotka/hello-world-docker/trigger/a9308c54
-7105-4d20-a950-93db1f15085f/
```

To trigger a build using the Docker tag name, you will need to provide the tag name in the JSON payload of the POST command:

```
curl -H "Content-Type: application/json" --data '{"docker_tag":
"master"}' -X POST
https://registry.hub.docker.com/u/jotka/hello-world-docker/trigger/a9308c54
-7105-4d20-a950-93db1f15085f/
```

To trigger a build by a source branch, such as feature/NIS-234 the JSON payload needs to carry the branch name, as shown:

```
curl -H "Content-Type: application/json" --data '{"source_type":
"Branch", "source_name": " feature/NIS-234"}' -X POST
https://registry.hub.docker.com/u/jotka/hello-world-docker/trigger/a9308c54
-7105-4d20-a950-93db1f15085f/
```

Last but not the least, you can trigger a build using a source tag, such as 1.1:

```
curl -H "Content-Type: application/json" --data '{"source_type": "Tag",
"source_name": "v1.1"}' -X POST
https://registry.hub.docker.com/u/jotka/hello-world-docker/trigger/a9308c54
-7105-4d20-a950-93db1f15085f/
```

Docker Hub and its Automated Build feature is a great tool to keep your source code and published images in sync. But there's also another great feature that allows executing an action in another application in response to an event in the repository—these are Webhooks. Let's take a look at them now.

Webhooks and continuous deployments

Docker Hub fires Webhooks when an image is built or a new tag is added to your Automated Build repository.

When defining the Webhook, you specify its name and target URL to call when build finishes or a new tag comes. This can be done on the `Webhooks` tab in the `Automated Build` repository details, as you can see in the following screenshot:

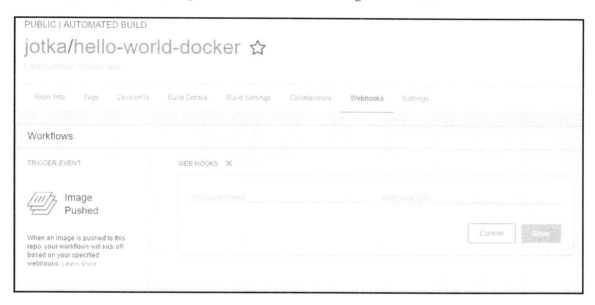

The Webhook call will be an HTTP `POST` request. The JSON payload of this request will contain all the details of the event that just happened. The easiest way to see what that payload is and also test your Webhook is to register a temporary REST endpoint at `http ://requestb.in`and enter use it as a Webhook URL.

The requestb.in is a web application, available free of charge, which allows you to create a URL (the endpoint) that will listen for requests made to it and let you inspect them in a readable form. Just click on the Create Request Bin button, to create your own URL, as you can see in the following screenshot:

The resulting page will present the URL value and also some examples on how you can call the newly created URL. Those examples are not interesting for us at the moment; it's the Docker Hub that is going to call the URL. The **Bin URL** is the URL you will want to enter in the setup of the Webhook in the Docker Hub, as you can see on the following screenshot:

The URL created in the `http://request.in`will listen for incoming connections and present the incoming `POST` data after the webhook has been called. If you trigger a build on the Docker Hub, either by pushing a commit to the `GIT` repository, using a build trigger or executing a build manually from the Docker Hub web interface. Docker Hub will use the defined Webhook to call the listening endpoint, where you will actually see the incoming data. You can see the result in the following screenshot:

As you can see in the `RAW BODY` section, Docker Hub posts a JSON payload with all the details of the event:

```
{
    "push_data":{
        "pushed_at":1475303709,
        "images":[
        ],
        "tag":"latest",
        "pusher":"jotka"
    },
    "callback_url":"https://registry.hub.docker.com/u/jotka/hello-world-docker2
/hook/2ec10hea0aade410aeih2c1gjdi2b3e50/",
```

```
"repository":{
    "status":"Active",
    "description":"desc",
    "is_trusted":true,
    "full_description":null,
    "repo_url":"https://hub.docker.com/r/jotka/hello-world-docker2",
    "owner":"jotka",
    "is_official":false,
    "is_private":false,
    "name":"hello-world-docker2",
    "namespace":"jotka",
    "star_count":0,
    "comment_count":0,
    "date_created":1475303673,
    "repo_name":"jotka/hello-world-docker2"
    }
}
```

In the payload, we have all the details related to the event that made Webhook to be called `repo_name`, `date_created`, `tag`, and so on. These can be of course used in the Webhook implementation, to, for example, pull the resulted image and deploy it somewhere.

Webhooks can be used to further automate some things and create continuous deployment setup. All you need to is define the POST endpoint and have some application (a web server, actually) that listen for requests at the specified endpoint, Docker will do the POST with all the details. Probably the best use for Webhooks is a continuous deployment setup. There's a Docker management tool, for example, called Shipyard, available at `https://shipyard-project.com`. If Docker Hub builds a new Docker image (either triggered by a push to the source code repository or using the `Build Trigger`), it will send a Webhook notification to Shipyard using the HTTP `POST` request. Shipyard will check the Webhook key for authorization, and then pull latest image from the Docker Hub. As a result, Shipyard will stop and remove your current containers and will deploy a new one. Another useful application which allows you to set up a continuous deployment pipeline is the Swarm Inception. It's a simple application available at GitHub `https://github.com/giant swarm/swarm-inception`. This is actually a small server, which listens for POST requests. Using `Swarm Inception` you can do continuous container delivery using Docker Hub's image builder and `Giant Swarm`. Again, when the build completes, Docker Hub will call this service's Webhook handler, which in turn triggers a deployment or update of the image built by Docker Hub onto Giant Swarm's public cloud. Giant Swarm is a cloud application, where you can simply deploy your Docker Containers on your fully-managed Kubernetes Cluster in seconds.

While the Swarm Inception can be used out-of-the-box to implement continuous deployment, it's also a very good reference document for implementing your own Webhook handlers and doing continuous deployments with Docker Hub's builder service. While Giant Inception uses Giant Swarm's APIs to deal with the containers, you can easily fork or copy the repository and implement your own continuous delivery with other services.

There are some other great starting points to implement your own Webhook listening servers. The first one is the project called dockerhook-webhook-listener, available on GitHub https://github.com/cpuguy83/dockerhub-webhook-listener. It's just a plain and simple web server written in Go (the same language in which Docker itself is developed, by the way). Another great one is the Captain Hook, again available on GitHub: https://github.com/bketelsen/captainhook. It's a generic Webhook endpoint that runs scripts based on the URL called. Each script you create in the configdir of the Captain Hook will be executed when the corresponding endpoint is called.

Captain Hook itself is available as a Docker image, so you can pull and use it in no time.

You can pull Captain Hook from the Docker Hub by executing well-known docker pull command:

```
docker pull ablas/docker-captainhook
```

Next, you run Captain Hook using the docker run command, exposing the 8080 port and providing the scripts path for your Webhooks handlers as a HOOKS_PATH environment variable:

```
docker run -d -p 8080:8080 -v `${HOOKS_PATH}`:/webhooks ablas/docker-captainhook
```

You can put your Webhook handlers in any folder, just note that you'll need to map it to the /webhooks directory. Each one script will correspond to one listening endpoint. For example, if you put a script called deployMyContainer.json, it will be executed if Docker Hub create a POST request to the following URL:

```
http://your.captainhook.url/deployMyContainer
```

The handler script can contain a reference to the shell script. After the specific POST endpoint has been hit, the shell script will take over and,for example, deploy a fresh image. Take a look at this Captain Hook script:

```
{
    "scripts": [
        {
            "command": "/usr/jarek/webhook.sh",
            "args": [
                "3"
            ]
        }
    ]
}
```

In the referenced shell script, we need to do something useful, actually. All we have to do is to parse the incoming JSON payload. We can do it using the JSON parsing jq tool, about which we know from the previous Chapter 7, *Running Containers*.
It's available at https://stedolan.github.io/jq/. We have been using jq to parse the docker inspect command output. At this time we can use the jq tool to parse the incoming data and to pull the image from the Docker Hub and run it.

After reading this chapter, you should be aware that Webhooks are powerful feature. The listening endpoint can be written in any language of your choice, let it be Java, Scala, or C#. There is a lot of ready-to-use API for dealing with Docker containers available for free. You can, of course, use them in your Webhook handler implementation to pull and deploy images. We are going to cover some of them in the next chapter. To give you some inspirations, here are some you can pick from:

- **Java Docker API client**: Available on GitHub https://github.com/docker-java/docker-java. It's based on Jersey REST library.
- **Docker.DotNet**: |It's a C# client available on GitHub https://github.com/ahmetalpbalkan/Docker.DotNet.
- **docker-client**: It's for Groovy https://github.com/gesellix/docker-client
- **tugboat:** It's available at https://github.com/softprops/tugboat, is a Scala library for dealing with the Docker containers.

 An always up-to-date API list is available at Docker website at the https://docs.docker.com/engine/reference/api/remote_api_client_libraries/address.

There's so many of them that there's a huge chance you will find something for the programming language of your choice. Knowing the incoming payload structure and having a Docker API library it's easy to implement your own listening Webhook handlers. If you have Webhooks defined in your automated builds, Webhook handlers running and listening for calls, your deployments can be launched seamlessly from GIT `push` command. It will work smoothly without needing any manual intervention from anyone. It's true continuous deployment. Docker can be useful also in your existing development or continuous delivery flow, using Jenkins, or Maven for example. This is what we are going to cover in the next chapter.

Summary

In this chapter, we have learned how to tag and push our images to the remote registry making it available for others to use. We also know how to setup the automated build feature using the integrated GitHub or BitBucket account. Automatic Build repository is a great feature; it allows you to keep the source of your images (including of course, Dockerfiles) and the images on the DockerHub in sync. We also know how to use Webhooks feature to do some more automation, for example continuous deployment. In the next chapter, we will go a little bit more into using Docker, we will be utilizing Docker to package our Java and JavaScript application into the container.

9
Using Docker in Development

After reading the past chapters, you should be able to pull a image and use it as the base for your own image. We already know how to create an image, attach volumes, expose ports, and run it in a container. We can also publish it into the Docker Hub for others to use. This is the last chapter in which we are going to cover some practical examples of how you can put Docker to use in your daily life as a developer. First of all, you will learn how to make Docker work with the most popular Java build system: Maven. Then we can put our applications into containers in practice; we will run Spring Boot Java application from inside a Docker container. Next, we will pack the Angular.js frontend application, which runs on Node.js in a Docker container. These examples should give you an idea and some inspiration on how you can create Docker containers with your own applications. In particular, we are going to cover the following topics in this chapter:

- Using Docker with Maven
- Packaging Java Spring Boot application into the container
- Packaging node.js Angular application into the container

Let's begin with explaining how to incorporate Docker in our Java Maven build.

Using Docker with Maven

If you develop in Java, you probably know Maven. It's used widely to build Java applications or libraries. The Maven's build process uses the concept of an artifact. An artifact is a file, usually a JAR (containing Java libraries or application) or WAR/EAR, which is a Java web application. The artifacts are deployed to a Maven repository. A Maven build produces one or more artifacts and each artifact has a group ID (usually a reversed domain name, such as `com.example.foo`), an artifact ID (just a name), and a version string. The three together uniquely identify the artifact. Your application dependencies are also specified as artifacts.You already know Docker pretty well, so you could probably imagine what a useful Maven plug in for Docker should do. It should allow to:

- Pull images from the registry
- Build container images
- Start containers
- Optionally link containers
- Expose the needed ports (useful for integration tests)
- Push images to the registry

Including Docker in your Maven build setup can be especially useful in your development flow. Imagine that after Maven build, the resulting image containing your application could be automatically pushed to the registry, thus making it ready for your colleagues, testers, or clients. Your high-level build process could include the following steps:

1. Build from sources
2. Execute unit tests
3. Create Docker image (the `dockerbuild` command needs to be executed here)
4. Run integration tests on the container (Docker commands, such as `run`, `start`, `expose`, `link`, and `stop` will be probably executed here)
5. Publish the image (the last step is usually the `docker publish` command)

There are a lot of Docker plugins for Maven; we will focus on probably the two most interesting ones. The first one is Spotify's Maven Docker Plugin.

Spotify's Maven Docker plugin

It's available as open source and you can get the sources and documentation from GitHub: h
ttps://github.com/spotify/docker-maven-plugin. You can use this plugin to create a
Docker image with artifacts built from your Maven project. For example, the build process
for a Java service can output a Docker image that runs the service.

The usage of the Spotify's docker-maven-plugin is pretty straightforward. You will just
have to include it as a plugin in your build and provide a dockerDirectory value in the
configuration. The plugin will expect the Dockerfile in this directory, so if you specify that
directory, it must contain valid Dockerfile. You can also build the image without Dockerfile.
In this case, you will need to provide additional plugin configuration, such as baseImage
(it will be used in the FROM instruction-the starting point in every Dockerfile, as you
remember from Chapter 6, *Creating Images*), maintainer, cmd and entrypoint.

The contents of the directory specified as the dockerDirectory value will be copied into
${project.build.directory}/docker. This will be the build context when the docker
build command starts. Using the resource element, you can include additional artifacts
to the Docker's build context. Take a look at the following example fragment of the
pom.xml build file:

```xml
<build>
  <plugins>
    <plugin>
      <groupId>com.spotify</groupId>
      <artifactId>docker-maven-plugin</artifactId>
      <version>0.4.13</version>
      <configuration>
        <imageName>myImage</imageName>
        <dockerDirectory>docker</dockerDirectory>
        <resources>
          <resource>
            <targetPath>/</targetPath>
            <directory>${project.build.directory}</directory>
            <include>${project.build.finalName}.jar</include>
          </resource>
        </resources>
      </configuration>
    </plugin>
  </plugins>
</build>
```

In the preceding example we have included the plugin in the plugins section of the
`pom.xml` file. One `jar` file from the `${project.build.directory}`, which will be the
`/target` directory by default will be included in the build context. This time it will be a `jar`
file named as your application name, containing your built application.

Having this setup, altogether with a proper Dockerfile referencing the application `jar` from
the `/target` directory is enough to create a Docker image from the Maven's `pom.xml`. You
have to simply execute the following Maven target:

```
mvn clean package docker:build
```

If you decide to push the resulting image into the registry, the additional `-DpushImage`
parameter is needed:

```
mvn clean package docker:build -DpushImage
```

If you need the image to be built, tagged, and pushed when you run just `mvn deploy`, you
will need to bind Docker commands to Maven phases, similar to how you normally do with
every other build plugin. Spotify's plugin is nice, quick, and simple. If you just need to
build images, it can be a starting point. But it has one limitation: it doesn't allow running
containers. Since this plugin can be only used to build an image, it's quite limited. Let's look
at another one: fabric8io Docker plugin.

fabric8io Maven Docker plugin

Its configuration is different. The fabric8 plugin uses a configuration section for all images
to maintain. It has configuration item for each section, which are divided into build and run
parts for building instructions and runtime configurations. Some of the features include a
progress bar when pulling images, dynamic and flexible port mapping and assignment to
variables, and building images via plugin configuration or Dockerfile (the same as Spotify's
plugin). It also logs output of the containers' standard out during integration test and has
full support for waiting on time, specific URL or log output after container startup.

Fabrio8.io Docker Maven plugin is very powerful and flexible when it comes to the
configuration. To setup the image configuration, you will need to create `<image>` element
in the `<configuration><images>` element, as shown on the following example:

```
<configuration>
  <images>
    <image>
      <alias>myApplication</alias>
      <name>me/my-application:${project.version}</name>
      <build>
```

```
      <from>java:8</from>
      <assembly>
        <descriptor>artifact</descriptor>
      </assembly>
      <cmd>
        <shell>java -jar maven/myApplication.jar</shell>
      </cmd>
    </build>
    <run>
      <ports>
        <port>8080:8080</port>
      </ports>
    </run>
  </image>
 </images>
</configuration>
```

You can have multiple `<image>` elements, for each image you are going to create or use.

The image build process is configured within the `<build>` element. Fabric8.io plugin takes two approaches for the build configuration; you can either use the existing Dockerfile or use the inline configuration (as seen in the previous example). If you want to use the existing Dockerfile, you need to provide additional `dockerFileDir` and `dockerFile` elements. The first one will specify a directory containing a Dockerfile, the second one will point to the specific Dockerfile in that directory. All files in the directory that are specified as the `dockerFileDir` element will also be included in the image build context.

The inline configuration, on the other hand, will describe the image building process in the `pom.xml` itself. You will need to provide elements, such as `<from>`, which will contain the base image (as FROM instruction in the Dockerfile). The assembly descriptor contains all the files that will go into the image and `<cmd>` contains the command to run when a container is created. As we discussed in Chapter 6, *Creating Images*, this setup resembles a standard Dockerfile and of course you have the full support for all Dockerfile standard features. You can expose ports (the same way as we did in Chapter 6, *Creating Images*, with the EXPOSE Dockerfile instruction).

To expose ports, you will need to define `<port>` sub-elements in the `<ports>` element. In the following example, we are exposing port number `8080` that we can map to the host's port later when running the container:

```
<ports>
  <port>8080</port>
</ports>
```

To define volumes, similar construction is needed and each `<volume>` element that is contained inside the `<volumes>` element will represent the volume. Exactly the same as the VOLUME instruction, it creates a mount point with the specified name and marks it as holding externally mounted volumes from native host or other containers.

```
<volumes>
  <volume>/path/to/volume</volume>
</volumes>
```

To define the entry point of the image, you will need, as you may have guessed already, an `<entrypoint>` element, as shown in the following example:

```
<entryPoint>
  <exec>
    <arg>java</arg>
    <arg>-jar</arg>
    <arg>/maven/myApplication.jar</arg>
  </exec>
</entryPoint>
```

The `<entrypoint>` specifies a command that will always be executed when the container starts, the same way the ENTRYPOINT instruction in the normal and traditional Dockerfile.

The `<assembly>` element in the build configuration specifies how build artifacts and other files your application may need will be put in the resulting Docker image. There are a couple of predefined assembly descriptors, such as `artifact-with-dependencies` (which will attach the project's artifact and all its dependencies into the image), `artifact` (where only the project's artifact will be put into the image, `project` (attaches the whole Maven project into the image), and `rootWar` (which will copy the artifact as `ROOT.war` into the exposed directory).

All files coming from assembly descriptor will go to the image automatically. You can see what was included in the image by looking into the contents of the `target/docker/yourProject/build/maven` directory.

As you can see, the configuration from the `<build>` element matches the structure and contents of Dockerfile almost exactly. It will be taken into account when you execute the `docker:build` command using Maven:

```
mvn -PmyProfile docker:build
```

The `<run>` element of the `<image>` contains the runtime setup; this is going to be used when you create and run the Docker container using Maven using the following command:

```
mvn -PmyProfile docker:build docker:start
```

In the runtime configuration, you can define port mappings as shown in the following example:

```
<ports>
  <port>8080</port>
</ports>
```

In the preceding case, the container port `8080` will be mapped to the Docker host port `8080`. This will be the same as what we did in the Chapter 4, *Networking and Persistent Storage*, we have mapped the exposed ports using the `-p` or `-P` option for the `docker run` command:

```
docker run --name nginx -d -P nginx
```

Apart from mapping ports, you can also map volumes. This will again resemble the mapping which we did previously using the `-v` option for the `docker run` command:

```
docker run -it -v data:/data ubuntu
```

As we had seen in Chapter 4, *Networking and Persistent Storage*, a container can mount volumes from various sources when starting up. It can be a directory of the host system or from another container which exports one or more directories. The mount configuration is specified within a `<volumes>`section of the `<run>` configuration.

```
<volumes>
  <bind>
    <volume>/logs</volume>
    <volume>/opt/hostDirectory:/opt/containerDirectory</volume>
  </bind>
</volumes>
```

To import volumes from another image (as we did with `--volumes-from` earlier), you can use the `<from>` and `<image>` elements in your volumes configuration. To provide an image name or alias, specify the volumes you would like to use in the `<image>` element, as shown in the following example:

```
<volumes>
  <from>
    <image>test/myApplication2</image>
  </from>
</volumes>
```

The fabric8.io Maven plugin is a complete solution and contains all Docker-related build and runtime configurations. You can link images, provide runtime network settings, and define runtime restart policy (we have been talking about restart policies in detail in the Chapter 7, *Running Containers*). It also has a full set of Maven related goals, such as `docker:build` for building images, `docker:start` or `docker:run` and `docker:stop` for managing the container's lifecycle, `docker:push` for uploading containers to the registry, and `docker:logs` to output the container log. You can even include the resulting Docker image into Maven artifacts for further processing using maven:source goal.

To execute the whole chain of actions, that is, create image, start the container, execute unit test, stop the container, and do the cleanup, execute the `install` command:

```
mvn -PmyProfile install
```

The fabric8.io plugin has a lot to offer when working with Maven and Docker. You can always refer to the newest documentation present on the plugin's website at `https://dmp.fabric8.io/`. It's the first class choice if you need to build or run Docker containers from your Maven build.

Now we know how to create and run Docker containers from our own build process. Let's focus now on packaging actual applications into containers. We are going to cover example setups, such as Java application and Angular.js frontend application. Let's begin with Java; we are going to *containerize* the Spring Boot application. We will use the fabric8 Docker Maven plugin that we already know about.

Spring Boot application in Docker container

For the purpose of our example, we will start with a simple hello-world type Spring Boot application. We are going to run in on top of official Java image: openjdk. If you prefer to run it on the Oracle Java image, you can search for it in the DockerHub registry. There are a lot of images that are ready to use, some of them are based on the official images, such as Ubuntu for example. As we saw in Chapter 6, *Creating Images*, it's always good to pick an official image as the base image. Official images are tested, supported, and usually of very high quality. The basic steps for creating Java application in the container are:

- Using a base image pulled out from the Docker Hub
- Installing the application itself, it will be an executable jar file in our case
- Exposing ports, if your application needs to communicate with the outside world using a network
- Running the container

Of course, if you would like to put another kind of application in the container, the preceding steps would not be enough; you would want to install a web server on top of your base image, such as Tomcat or Wildfly. Also, the application itself would probably be packaged in a WAR or EAR file.

The application that we are going to put in the container will be just a very simple Spring Boot helloâ⊚⊚world sample application. We are not going to cover Spring Boot in detail, we just need to have something to package and run from the Docker container.

Let's begin with creating our Maven pom.xml build file, as shown in the following example:

```xml
<?xml version="1.0" encoding="UTF-8"?>
<project>
  <modelVersion>4.0.0</modelVersion>
  <groupId>pl.finsys</groupId>
  <artifactId>hello-docker</artifactId>
  <version>0.0.1-SNAPSHOT</version>
  <parent>
    <groupId>org.springframework.boot</groupId>
    <artifactId>spring-boot-starter-parent</artifactId>
    <version>1.4.1.RELEASE</version>
  </parent>
  <dependencies>
    <dependency>
      <groupId>org.springframework.boot</groupId>
      <artifactId>spring-boot-starter-web</artifactId>
    </dependency>
  </dependencies>
```

```
<properties>
  <java.version>1.8</java.version>
</properties>
<build>
  <plugins>
    <plugin>
      <groupId>org.springframework.boot</groupId>
      <artifactId>spring-boot-maven-plugin</artifactId>
    </plugin>
  </plugins>
</build>
</project>
```

As you can see, we are using `spring-boot-starter-parent` as a parent `pom.xml`. It saves us a lot of work and is excellent for the purpose of this example of having a running Spring Boot application. Our application is built by Maven, so the folder structure needs to resemble the standard Maven application structure. It will contain `pom.xml` file, then `src/main/java` folders. The `java` folder will contain our Java packages. The complete file folders structure will look similar to the following screenshot:

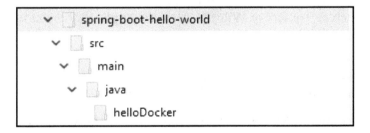

Our first (and only) REST controller will be `Hello.java`, let's put it in the `java/helloDocker` folder:

```
package helloDocker;
import org.springframework.web.bind.annotation.RestController;
import org.springframework.web.bind.annotation.RequestMapping;
@RestController
public class HelloController {
    @RequestMapping("/")
    public String hello() {
        return "Greetings from Spring Boot in Docker!";
    }
}
```

Having this controller saved in the `HelloController.java` file in the `main/src/java/helloDocker` directory, all we need is the actual application—it's starting point. Create a new Java class in the `helloDocker` package:

```
package helloDocker;
import org.springframework.boot.SpringApplication;
import org.springframework.boot.autoconfigure.
  SpringBootApplication;
import org.springframework.context.ApplicationContext;
@SpringBootApplication
public class Application {
    public static void main(String[] args) {
        ApplicationContext ctx =
            SpringApplication.run(Application.class, args);
    }
}
```

This is it; we have a complete Spring Boot application with one feature it will respond to `HTTP GET` call with a message *Hello from Spring Boot in Docker!* Let's build it using Maven first, by executing the `mvn package` command:

mvn package

For this, you will need Maven to be installed and available on the system path. It will take a while, all Maven dependencies will need to be downloaded first and a source of your application needs to be compiled. You should be able to see the following message saying that the build succeeded:

Our application is now packaged as a `helloDocker-0.1.0.jar` file in the target directory of the project. Let's do the trial run and execute the command:

```
java -jar target/helloDocker-0.1.0.jar
```

The spring application will boot and present some log output on the console:

By default, Spring Boot applications listen to HTTP requests on port `8080`; we will expose this port to the Docker image in a while. At the same time, enter the `http://localhost:8080` in your web browser, to verify that our application actually works properly and responds to HTTP requests. You should see the message that we are hoping to see:

If you work on Linux or Mac, or perhaps have `curl` command installed also on a Windows PC, you can also execute it to see the following message:

```
curl http://localhost:8080
Greetings from Spring Boot in Docker!
```

That's it; our application works fine and it's time to put it in the container. We are going to use the fabric8.io Docker plugin for Maven and we already know it from the beginning of this chapter. We will use an existing Dockerfile approach, so let's create a `docker` directory in the `src/main` directory of our project and put the `Dockerfile` inside it. The `openjdk` official repository contains a lot of tags, each with different Java versions packaged for you to pick from. For example:

- 8u102-jdk, 8u102, 8-jdk, 8, jdk, latest
- 8u92-jdk-alpine, 8u92-alpine, 8-jdk-alpine, 8-alpine, jdk-alpine, alpine
- 8u102-jre, 8-jre, jre
- 8u92-jre-alpine, 8-jre-alpine, jre-alpine
- 9-b139-jdk, 9-b139, 9-jdk, 9
- 9-b139-jre, 9-jre

We are going to pick the latest one, which is Java `8u102-jdk`. We will take the inline configuration approach for our image build process, so the plugin section in the `pom.xml` will contain the instructions on how to build an image containing our application. You will need to add the following plugin definition to the `<build><plugins>` section of your `pom.xml` file:

```xml
<plugin>
  <groupId>io.fabric8</groupId>
  <artifactId>docker-maven-plugin</artifactId>
  <version>0.16.8</version>
  <configuration>
    <dockerHost>http://127.0.0.1:2375</dockerHost>
    <verbose>true</verbose>
    <images>
      <image>
        <name>hello-docker</name>
        <build>
          <from>openjdk:8u102-jdk</from>
          <ports>
            <port>8080</port>
          </ports>
          <entryPoint>
            <exec>
              <args>java</args>
```

```
                        <args>-jar</args>
                        <args>/maven/hello-docker-
                          ${project.version}.jar</args>
                      </exec>
                    </entryPoint>
                    <assembly>
                      <descriptorRef>artifact</descriptorRef>
                    </assembly>
                  </build>
                </image>
              </images>
            </configuration>
          </plugin>
```

Now, in order to compile, package, and build your Docker image, execute the following Maven command:

```
mvn clean package docker:build
```

In the output, the maven-docker plugin will output some details, such as specific steps from the process of building images. You will find all your **EXPOSE**, **COPY**, **VOLUME**, **ENTRYPOINT** instructions. All that you have configured either in the external Dockerfile or using the inline configuration in the `pom.xml` file itself. You can see the sample output in the following screenshot:

```
C:\Windows\system32\cmd.exe
[INFO] <<< docker-maven-plugin:0.16.8:build (default-cli) < initialize @ hello-docker <<<
[INFO]
[INFO] --- docker-maven-plugin:0.16.8:build (default-cli) @ hello-docker ---
[INFO] Copying files to C:\Users\jarek\projects\spring-boot-hello-world\target\docker\hello-docker\build\maven
[INFO] Building tar: C:\Users\jarek\projects\spring-boot-hello-world\target\docker\hello-docker\tmp\docker-build.tar
[INFO] DOCKER> docker-build.tar: Created [hello-docker] in 505 milliseconds
[INFO] DOCKER> Step 1 : FROM openjdk:8u102-jdk
[INFO] DOCKER> ---> 96cddf5ae9f1
[INFO] DOCKER> Step 2 : EXPOSE 8080
[INFO] DOCKER> ---> Using cache
[INFO] DOCKER> ---> f964dd9b7501
[INFO] DOCKER> Step 3 : COPY maven /maven/
[INFO] DOCKER> ---> 1c951ae623c4
[INFO] DOCKER> Removing intermediate container 85c7b77dc84f
[INFO] DOCKER> Step 4 : ENTRYPOINT java -jar /maven/hello-docker-0.0.1-SNAPSHOT.jar
[INFO] DOCKER> ---> Running in 82ad1b43f739
[INFO] DOCKER> ---> 204f0ffbd492
[INFO] DOCKER> Removing intermediate container 82ad1b43f739
[INFO] DOCKER> Successfully built 204f0ffbd492
[INFO] DOCKER> [hello-docker]: Built image sha256:204f0
[INFO] DOCKER> [hello-docker]: Removed image
[INFO] ------------------------------------------------------------------------
[INFO] BUILD SUCCESS
[INFO] ------------------------------------------------------------------------
[INFO] Total time: 4.264 s
[INFO] Finished at: 2016-10-18T20:03:38+02:00
[INFO] Final Memory: 31M/426M
[INFO] ------------------------------------------------------------------------

C:\Users\jarek\projects\spring-boot-hello-world>
```

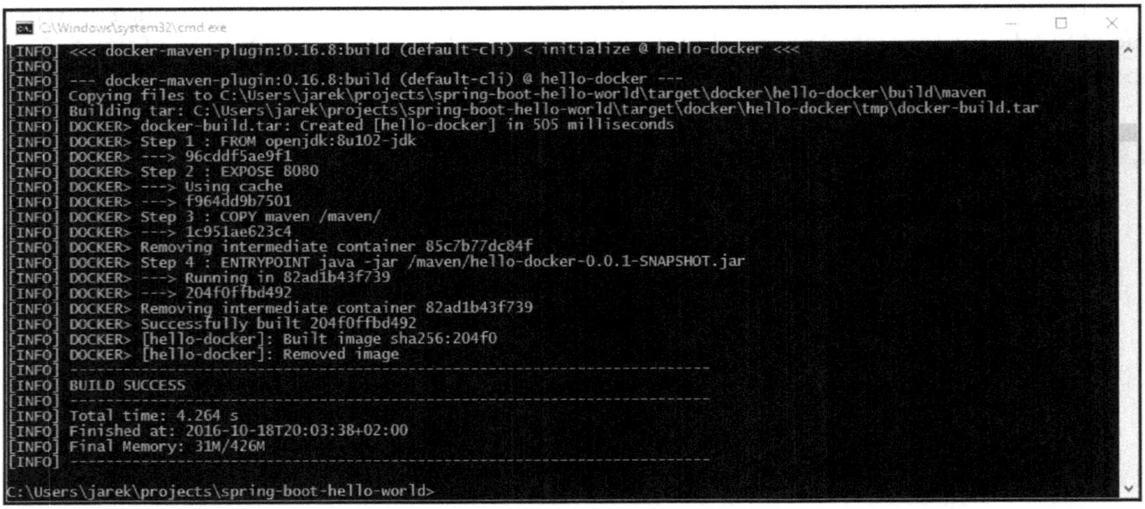

At the end, Docker will output the image ID that was just created. Let's check if our image is on the images list, executing the well‑known docker images command:

```
docker images
```

If everything goes well, you will be able to see your newly created image on the images list, as seen in the following screenshot:

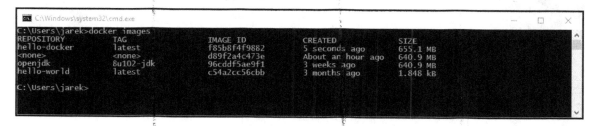

Image is present on the list, let's run it by executing the following command:

```
docker run -it -p8080:8080 hello-docker
```

Note that we have included the -p option to automatically map exposed port into the host's port. As you might remember, we have exposed port number 8080 in our pom.xml configuration. After executing the command, you will see the same output as before, when running java -jar command locally.

However, now it comes from the application contained in the Docker container, as you can see in the following screenshot:

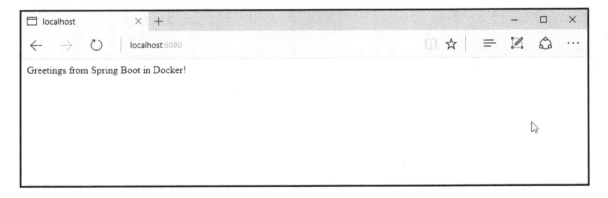

To verify that the application in the Docker container actually works, again, direct your web browser to the `http://localhost:8080` address:

Alternatively, to running docker run by hand, we can include the runtime section into our project's pom.xml file. The whole `<image>` element will look similar to this:

```xml
<image>
  <name>hello-docker</name>
  <build>
    <from>openjdk:8u102-jdk</from>
    <ports>
      <port>8080</port>
    </ports>
    <entryPoint>
      <exec>
        <args>java</args>
        <args>-jar</args>
        <args>/maven/hello-docker-${project.version}.jar</args>
      </exec>
    </entryPoint>
    <assembly>
      <descriptorRef>artifact</descriptorRef>
    </assembly>
  </build>
  <run>
    <ports>
      <port>8080:8080</port>
    </ports>
  </run>
</image>
```

Now you can compile, package, build, and run image in one step:

```
mvn clean package docker:build docker:run
```

Now we have a fully working Spring Boot application packaged as the Docker container. It's ready to be pushed into Docker Hub or your own private registry. Wherever the Docker can run, this application will work the same way. Imagine how much trouble you have saved the users of your application, operating system configuration, Java setup and configuration, the dependency management, and so on. That was a rather simple example, but it should give you an idea of how flexible and useful fabric8.io Docker plugin can be.

Now that we know how to package Java applications, let's do more. We are going to pack sample frontend application. This will be Angular.js frontend running on node.js.

Packaging Angular.js application

In this example, we are going to create a simple Angular.js application which runs on node.js runtime. For the purpose of clarity of example, we are not going to introduce any tests. As it was the case with SpringBoot application, our Angular.js application will be as simple and tiny as possible. We are going to understand how to containerize it instead of diving into Angular.js development. Of course, you are more than welcome to get to know Angular.js if you haven't done this already; it's a wonderful technology. Before you start, you will need to have node.js installed. You can get the installer from node.js website at `htt ps://nodejs.org/en/`.

First, let's divide the structure of our application in two parts. The first one will be frontend, will all the static resources such as Java Scripts and HTML files. The second one will be node.js backed, actually serving our frontend files and responding to HTTP request. The folder structure, having the `angular-docker-example` as a parent directory, would initially look similar to the following screenshot:

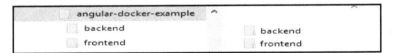

We are going to use Bower to manage third-party JavaScript libraries. Bower uses the `bower.json` file in which you define all the application that need to run. At this time, we only need a single `angular.js` dependency. Here's our little application's minimal `bower.json` file:

```
{
    "name": "hello-docker-angular ",
    "ignore": [
      "**/.*",
      "node_modules",
      "bower_components"
    ],
    "dependencies": {
      "angular": "~1.5"
    }
}
```

We would like all the dependencies to be downloaded into our frontend application folder. So, before we execute bower install, we need to tell Bower where we want those files to go. To achieve this, we need to create a .bowerrc file and put it in the root directory of our project. The JSON content of the file will contain the destination for all the dependencies which are going to be downloaded:

```
{
"directory": "frontend/bower_components"
}
```

Next, you will want to install bower itself first, you can do it globally in your system, by executing the npm install command:

npm install -g bower

Having Bower installed and .bowerrc in place, we can now download all the required front-end dependencies. Execute the following in the root folder of our project to begin the download process:

bower install

After a while, Bower finishes downloading all the dependencies (it will be just Angular.js in our case). They will be present in the frontend/bower-components directory. As it is a single dependency, only one directory named angular will be created in the bower_components directory, as you can see in the following screenshot:

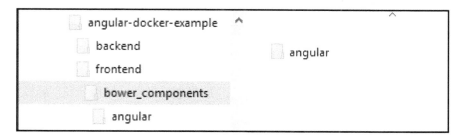

Our `index.html`, which will be an entry point to our application's frontend part, needs to be placed in the root of the `frontend` module, which is `angular-docker-example\frontend` in my case. It will look similar to the following code:

```
<script src="bower_components/angular/angular.min.js"></script>
<script src="hello_world_docker.controller.js"></script>
<div ng-app="HelloWorldApp">
  <div ng-controller="HelloWorldDockerController">
      Your name: <input ng-model="name" ng-keyup="sayHello()">
      <h1>{{greeting}}</h1>
    </div>
</div>
```

We also need do add the controller (it will be `hello_world_docker.controller.js` file) to our application which will react to the keyâ◎◉up event. If you write your name in the text field, Angular will greet you by your name:

```
angular.module('HelloWorldDockerApp', [])
    .controller('HelloWorldDockerController', function($scope) {
        $scope.sayHello = function () {
            $scope.greeting = "Hello from Docker-Angular, " +
                $scope.name;
        };
    });
```

Now it's time to test our application, simply open the `index.html` file in the web browser of your choice and type your name in the text field:

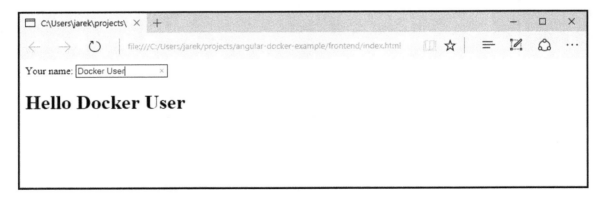

Ok, it's working as intended. Let's proceed to the server part-the web application needs to be served. Of course, our simple application works by running the HTML file directly in the web browser. If you decide to include more Angular features later, for example routing, it will not work by opening directly. Also, the server usually completes the application by responding to HTTP requests, such as REST calls for example. The response taken from those calls can be then used on the static Angular pages. We could use any programming language we like, for example Java and Spring Boot with docker-maven plugin as we did in the previous example. This time, to present the manual way of packaging an application into Docker container, we are going to use node.js runtime as a backend for our application. To get the required node.js dependencies, we will need to create `package.json` file with all the required dependencies:

```
{
  "name": "hello-world-docker",
  "main": "index.js",
  "dependencies": {
    "express": "^4.12.3",
    "bower": "1.7.9"
  }
}
```

The `package.json` file, the same as `bower.json`, needs to be placed in the root directory of our project. If the file is ready, we can run the npmï»¿ install command to download the needed dependencies, which will be Express and Bower in our case. Execute the following command:

npm install

After a while, the `node_modules` folder will be created. It will contain the dependencies mentioned in the `package.json` file and our application will use them. The entrypointï»¿ for our node.js application will be a simple and basic HTTP web server, serving static content from the `frontend` directory. Let's name it `app.js` and fill it out with this content:

```
'use strict';
process.env.NODE_ENV = process.env.NODE_ENV || 'development';
var express = require('express');
var http = require('http');
var path = require('path');
var app = express();
var config = {
    port: 8080,
    root: path.normalize(path.join(__dirname, '../frontend'))
}
app.use(express.static(config.root));
```

```
app.route('/*')
    .get(function (req, res) {
        res.sendFile(path.join(config.root, 'index.html'));
            }
);
http.createServer(app).listen(config.port, function () {
    console.log('hello-docker server listening on %d, in %s mode',
     config.port, app.get('env'));
});
exports = module.exports = app;
```

As you can see in the preceding section, we include node.js Express library to serve our static context, configure port number, and the root path and Express routes. The only specific configured route is `"/*"`, meaning that `index.html` from the `frontend` directory will be sent as a response to every HTTP GET request to `http://localhost:8080/` address.

Every other URL, such as `http://localhost:8080/hello_world_docker.controller.js` or `http://localhost:8080/bower_components/angular/angular.js`—which we include in our `index.html`—will be served as static context. Then we just start the server listening process. This is the last file in or node.js Angular application. The complete structure of files and folders should look similar to the following screenshot:

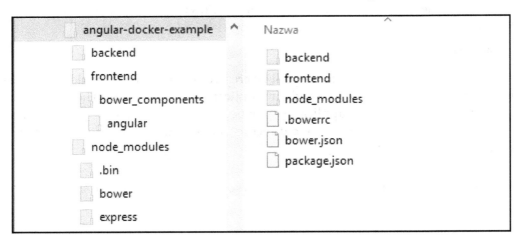

Again, it needs minimal implementation; just enough to make sure it's running and serving our static content. In the normal application you would probably introduce a more complex routes setup, divide the application into modules, and so on.

Let's run our node.js server, by executing the node command in the root of our project:

```
node backend\app.js
```

Then again, fire up your web browser and enter the following address: http://localhost:8080. You should see our application. This time, it will be served from node.js HTTP server:

As you can see our application works properly, it's time to put it into the Docker container. We need to decide the image that we will use as a base image. As always, using official Docker images is highly recommended. The Docker Hub hosts official node.js repository. We are going to use the **long-term support** (**LTS**) version arg on of node available. The node:argon image comes with all the node and npm tools installed, configured and ready to use. The decision about picking up the specific base image gives us the foundation for our Dockerfile. Let's create a Dockerfile in the root of the project and include the FROM instruction:

```
FROM node:argon
```

As the base image contains all the tools we need already, all we need to do is copy our application files and trigger the dependency downloading. The current root directory of our project will be a built context for Docker, so let's create a workdirï»¿ using the following instruction:

```
WORKDIR /usr/hello-docker
```

Now, let's copy the application first. We will use COPY, but we could just also use ADD here. As you remember from Chapter 6, *Creating Images*, ADD can do more than COPY: it allows <src> to be a URL and if the <src> parameter of ADD is an archive in a recognized compression format, it will be unpacked inside the image. That said COPY is enough in our case:

```
COPY backend /usr/hello-docker/backend
COPY frontend /usr/hello-docker/frontend
COPY .bowerrc bower.json package.json /usr/hello-docker
```

Note that the Docker will automatically create a directory with the COPY instruction and hence mkdir command is not needed. As you remember from the Chapter 3, *Understanding Images and Containers* and Chapter 6, *Creating Images*, every separate filesystem command would create another layer in the image. Creating additional, unneeded layers is not the good practice. Skipping mkdir command we can avoid one additional layer.

Now, it's time to run the npmï»¿ install and bower install commands:

```
RUN npm install
```

The last thing to do would be to expose the proper port. Our application listens of port 8080, so we add the following line to the Dockerfile:

```
EXPOSE 8080
The last step will be actually running our node.js server, by
adding the CMD instruction:
CMD ["node", "backend/app.js"]
```

The final version of the Dockerfile is like:

```
FROM node:argon
WORKDIR /usr/hello-docker
COPY backend /usr/hello-docker/backend
COPY frontend /usr/hello-docker/frontend
COPY .bowerrc bower.json package.json /usr/hello-docker
RUN npm install
EXPOSE 8080
CMD ["node", "/usr/hello-docker/backend/app.js"]
```

That's it, our complete Dockerfile is as tiny and simple as our node.js application, but that should be enough. Let's try and build the image, executing the `docker build` command, giving the current directory a build context:

```
docker build .
```

After a long listing of log output, downloading node.js dependencies, adding all the layers related to the instructions in the Dockerfile, we will be given the ID of the image we have just built:

```
Successfully built fa19b25b311e
```

Let's run the fresh image, mapping the port on which node.js server listens for connections to our machine port number `8080`:

```
docker run -p 8080:8080 fa19b25b311e
```

If you now open a web browser again, pointing to `http://localhost:8080`, you will see our greeting application, as seen in the following screenshot:

This time, however, it's being served from inside a Docker container. Again, imagine how much hassle you have just saved for your future customer. Operating system: checked. Node.js setup: checked. All the needed frontend and backend dependencies: also checked. Everything is ready to run everywhere a Docker engine can be run.

Those Java and node.js examples should give you an overview of how you can package your own application into a Docker container. You can use Maven and automate most of the things or you can create a Dockerfile manually. The resulting image will be ready to distribute into the remote registry and it will be also be portable. In the next chapter we will do some kind of a summary. You will be given some useful and high-quality additional resources, which you can use to extend your knowledge about Docker.

Summary

In this chapter, we have been using Docker during the build process of the Java applications using Maven. We know that there are a couple of Docker plugins for Maven and we know their functionality and limitations. To give you an idea of how to package your own applications into the container, we have run Java and JavaScript applications using Docker. Of course, this is just the tip of the iceberg, but I hope you were given some inspirations to package your own applications, no matter what language or framework you use. Having the Docker knowledge you have acquired so far, you will be able to pack any application that you wrote into the container and publish it on the Docker Hub. The world of Docker is enormous today, there's a lot to explore. Further in the book, I will point you to other resources that I find very useful; you can use them to further extend your Docker knowledge base.

More Resources

You have a lot of Docker knowledge at this point. After reading the previous chapters, you can now search and pull the image you need and build your own on top of it. We also know how to package an existing application, let it be a Java web application or a front end Angular.js application working on Node.js. We can do it by hand or use Maven for automating things. There are a lot of places on the Internet where you can extend your knowledge further. I'm going to present the ones I find most useful.

Official documentation

It's hard not to recommend the official Docker documentation, which is of very high quality. You will find it at `https://docs.docker.com`. There is a lot of information here, starting from installing Docker on various platforms and going through pulling images, creating Dockerfiles, building images, and publishing them into the remote Registry. It's a great resource for refreshing the Docker knowledge you already have, but you will also find here a lot of information which was not mentioned in this book. This includes, for example:

- Compose is a tool for defining and running multi-container Docker applications. With this tool you can use a single Compose file to configure your application's services. Then, using a single command, you can create and start all the services from your configuration.
- Universal Control Plane is the enterprise-grade (you can install it behind your own firewall) cluster management solution from Docker. It helps you manage your whole cluster from a single interface.
- Docker Trusted Registry is an enterprise-grade image storage solution from Docker—a secure place to store and manage the Docker images you use.
- The Docker Store, which is the place to find the best-trusted commercial and free software distributed as Docker Images.

Awesome Docker

Apart from the official, very comprehensive documentation, there is an awesome (it's even named that way – Awesome Docker) list of Docker resources available on GitHub `https://github.com/veggiemonk/awesome-docker`.

The list of resources has a good structure and begins with the basics like tutorials explaining what Docker actually is and how to install it on various platforms. The list is divided into main areas, which, among others, include:

- **Useful articles**: This contains a list of articles related to various subjects. Docker networking will list articles related to Docker's networking internals. The Image optimizations section will tell you how to create the smallest possible images and how to create Dockerfiles with the image size in mind. The security section lists resources related to security best practices, auditing, improving container security, and so on. Performance related articles will let you improve the performance of the containers. The Good Tips section is what I found the most useful. It contains a list of tips and tricks, coming from the people who use it in real life – these are very valuable.

- **Tools**: This contains references to a lot of developer and devop tools that are related to Docker. It will include tools for doing continuous integration or continuous delivery, monitoring, and logging; the list is endless, you can find something useful for sure.

- **Slides/Videos**: This holds a list of additional resources available as slides for presentations and a list of videos, webinars, and so on.

- **People, twitter** accounts **and communities**: And last but not least, a catalogue of people important in the Docker world. You will be able to find a list of blogs, and twitter accounts worth following and also a list of Docker related communities you can join.

The Awesome Docker list is updated very often and has a lot of contributors. You will always find a lot of interesting material here. For example, you will find links to the most up-to-date Docker Tips articles and blogs, a list of useful Docker third-party developer tools and recipes for integration with many continuous integration/continuous delivery providers. If you need to host your Docker container, you can get the information about almost all available Docker hosting providers. It's really hard to imagine that you wouldn't be able to find something you are looking for if it's related to Docker. There are even links for running Docker on Raspberry Pi. My advice is to clone the repository to be able to update in the future to find more interesting links.

You can clone the Awesome-Docker list and find the latest changes when doing a Git pull.

If you find something interesting you would like to share with others, you are more than welcome to contribute to the Awesome-Docker-list; the authors appreciate anyone who would like to add something to the list.

 To contribute to the Awesome-Docker list, create a pull request to the repository.

Another resource I would like to mention is the Docker Jumpstart, by Andrew Odewahn. It's also available on the GitHub in the form of mark-up documentation. You can get it at the `https://github.com/odewahn/docker-jumpstart/` address. It's very concise and complete, good for refreshing essential Docker skills.

Training

If you prefer watching videos with webinars, the `http://training.docker.com/` site contains a lot of courses to improve and gain knowledge about Docker. Some of them are self-paced training videos (available at `http://training.docker.com/self-paced-traini ng`). They are free to watch and I highly recommend watching them. Each of the series is a one hour long video webinar. The subjects include:

- Introduction to Docker
- Docker fundamentals
- Docker operations

If free resources are not enough, you can always sign-up to instructor-led training from the Docker team. They have a lot of courses available (paid, of course) at `http://training.doc ker.com/instructor-led-training`. These include specific subjects like:

- Docker administration and operations
- Docker datacentre training series
- Deploying Docker datacenter
- Managing container services with universal control plane

and many others. The paid courses cover more advanced and specialized topics. They contain tips which you will probably not find any where else but they are not mandatory for working successfully with Docker on a daily basis.

There are a lot of Docker related resources available on the Internet; it is impossible to fit them all in here. Most of them are free to access, so your can further extend you Docker knowledge. But the best way of learning is doing – start experiment with your Docker images: pull, create, build and publish. If you introduce Docker in to your daily routine, you will quickly wonder how you worked without Docker in the past. I hope that working with Docker will be as pleasant an experience for you, as it is for me.

Index

A

ADD instruction 133, 134, 135
  examples 134
Amazon
  URL 39
Angular.js application
  packaging 234, 235, 236, 237, 239, 240, 241,
  242
API list
  reference link 214
arbitrary commands
  executing, with exec command 172, 173
ARG instruction 152, 153
Artifactory
  reference link 61
AUFS layers
  reference link 53
Augmented File System (AUFS) 46
automated build
  about 200
  build trigger 206, 207, 208
  setting up 200, 201, 202, 203, 204, 205, 206

B

Boot2Docker utility 13
bridged network 70, 71
build context 200
busybox 57

C

Captain Hook
  reference link 213
CMD instruction 137, 138, 139
  CMD ["executable 137
  CMD command parameter1 parameter2 137
  overriding 170, 171

commands
  overriding, from Dockerfile 170
Completely Fair Scheduler (CFS) 189
constraints
  executing, on resources 186
  memory constraints 186, 187, 188
  processor 188, 189, 190
  updating, on Docker container 190, 191
Consul
  URL 79
container 54, 55, 56
Container Network Model (CNM) 66
  endpoint 66
  network 66
  sandbox 66
container
  changes, saving 56, 57, 58, 59
  executing, in network 72, 73, 74, 75
  identifying 167, 168
  linking 90, 91, 92
  PID namespace mode, settings 168, 169
  UTS namespace mode, settings 169, 170
containerization
  about 9
  versus virtualization 8
COPY instruction 136, 137
curl command
  URL, for download link 207

D

data, in container
  reference link 96
default networks 67, 68
detached mode
  about 165, 166
  executing 165
digest 167

Docker container 9
  events 176, 177
  exit codes 180, 181
  inspecting 177, 178, 179
  logs, viewing 174, 175, 176
  monitoring 173
  restart policy 180, 181
  statistics 179, 180
Docker Distribution toolset
  reference link 199
Docker Hub
  about 106, 107, 108, 122, 123, 124, 125
  account 108, 109, 110
  accounts 107
  automated builds 107
  collaborators 111, 112
  image repositories 107
  integration source code repositories 107
  logging into 113, 114, 115, 116
  organization account 110, 111
  organization teams 110, 111
  organizations 107
  private repositories 112
  REST API 107
  URL 106
  web hooks 107
Docker ID
  reference link 108
Docker image repository
  reference link 203
Docker index 60, 61, 62, 63
Docker Jumpstart
  reference link 245
Docker registry 60, 61, 62, 63
Docker registry REST API
  about 122, 123, 124, 125
  reference link 123
Docker repository 60, 61, 62, 63
Docker resources
  reference link 244
Docker Toolbox 12
  references 23
Docker, credential helpers
  references 115
docker-client

reference link 214
docker-squash
  reference link 52
Docker.DotNet
  reference link 214
Docker
  about 8
  APIs 12
  benefits 10
  bridged network 70
  bridged networking 71
  busybox image, executing without network 68
  compose tool 15
  container, executing in network 72, 73, 74, 75
  containers, linking 90, 91, 92
  default networks 67, 68
  engine 13
  engine client 13
  Git 17
  hardware requisites 20, 21
  host network 70
  immutable infrastructure 11
  installing, on EC2 Cloud 38, 39, 40, 41, 42, 43
  installing, on Linux 35, 36, 37, 38
  installing, on Mac OS 30, 31, 32, 33
  installing, on Windows 21, 22, 23, 24, 25, 26, 28, 29
  Kitematic tool 15
  machine 13, 14
  multi-host networking, creating 76
  network, creating 71, 72
  networking 66, 67
  networking plugins 93
  Oracle VirtualBox 16
  portable build environment 10, 11
  ports, exposing 85, 86, 87, 88, 89
  ports, mapping 85, 86, 87, 88, 89
  reproducible build environment 10, 11
  resources 243, 244, 245, 246
  size 10
  speed 10
  swarm mode 192
  tools 12
  tools, overview 12
  URL, for guidance 245

URL, for installation 21
used, with Maven 218
volume drivers 101, 102
volumes 93
volumes, creating 94, 96, 97, 98, 99
volumes, removing 100
Dockerfile
  about 129
  ADD instruction 133, 134, 135, 136
  ARG instruction 153
  CMD instruction 137, 138, 139
  CMD instruction, overriding 170, 171
  commands, overriding from 170
  COPY instruction 136, 137
  creating 130, 131
  ENTRYPOINT instruction 140, 141, 142, 143
  ENTRYPOINT, overriding 171, 172
  EXPOSE instruction 146
  FROM instruction 132, 133
  HEALTHCHECK instruction 155, 156
  instructions 131
  LABEL instruction 143, 144, 145
  MAINTAINER instruction 133
  ONBUILD instruction 153, 154
  RUN instruction 147, 148, 149, 150
  SHELL instruction 156
  STOPSIGNAL instruction 154
  USER instruction 150
  using 157, 158, 159, 160
  VOLUME instruction 151, 152
  WORKDIR instruction 152
dockerized application 9
dotCloud 7

E

ENTRYPOINT instruction 140, 141, 142, 143
  ENTRYPOINT ["executable 140
  ENTRYPOINT command parameter1
    parameter2 140
  overriding 171, 172
Event Http Collector 175
exec command
  arbitrary commands, executing 172, 173
exit codes
  about 180

  example 181
EXPOSE instruction 146

F

fabric8io Maven Docker plugin
  about 220, 222, 223
  URL 224
foreground mode
  about 166, 167
  executing 165
FROM instruction 132, 133

G

Google Container Registry
  reference link 61
Graylog
  URL 175

H

HEALTHCHECK instruction 155, 156
host network 70

I

ImageLayers
  reference link 51
images 46, 47, 48
  identifying 167, 168
  naming 116, 117, 118
  publishing 197
  pushing 199, 200
  searching 116
  searching, command line used 120, 122
  searching, through web interface 118, 119, 120
  tagging 198
  tags 116, 117, 118
  untagging 198
Infrastructure-as-a-Service (IaaS) 11
InterPlanetary File System (IPFS) 101

J

Java Docker API client
  reference link 214
jq-tools
  reference link 179

JSON parsing jq tool
    reference link 214

K

key-value store
    overlay networking 78, 80, 82, 83, 84

L

LABEL instruction 143, 144, 145
layers 48, 50, 51, 52, 53
Linux version
    reference link 37
log driver
    awslogs 176
    fluentd 175
    gcplogsta 176
    gelf 175
    journald 175
    none 175
    splunk 175
    syslog 175
logs
    viewing 174, 175, 176
Logstash
    reference link 175
long-term support (LTS) 239

M

MAINTAINER instruction 133
Maven
    Docker, used 218
    fabric8io Maven Docker plugin 220, 222, 223
    Spotify's Maven Docker plugin 219, 220
memory constraints 186, 187, 188
multi-host networking
    creating 76
    swarm mode 76, 77, 78

N

networking plugins 93
Nginx Dockerfile
    reference link 146
node.js
    URL 234

non-executing command 133

O

official repositories 116
ONBUILD instruction 153, 154

P

PID namespace mode
    settings 168, 169
Platform as a Service (PaaS) 13
ports
    exposing 85, 86, 87, 88, 89
    mapping 85, 86, 87, 88, 89

Q

Quay
    reference link 61

R

restart policy
    about 180
    always policy 182
    no policy 182
    on-failure policy 182, 183
    unless-stopped policy 183, 184
    updating, on Docker container 184, 185
RUN instruction 147, 148, 149, 150
    RUN ["executable 148
    RUN command 148

S

SHELL instruction 156
splunk
    URL 175
Spotify's Maven Docker plugin
    about 219, 220
    URL 219
Spring Boot application
    in Docker container 225, 227, 228, 229, 231,
        232, 233, 234
STOPSIGNAL instruction 154
swarm mode 76, 77, 78
    about 192
    commands 193, 194, 195, 196

determining 192
node 193
scheduling 193
service 193
swarm 192
swarm manager 192
terminology 192

T

temporary REST endpoint
   reference link 209
traditional virtualization 8, 9
tugboat
   reference link 214
Type 1 hypervisors 8
Type 2 hypervisors 8

U

ubuntu repository, tags
   reference link 125
USER instruction 150
UTS namespace mode
   settings 169, 170

V

version pinning 150
virtualization
   versus containerization 8
volume drivers
   about 101, 102
   Docker Volume Driver, for Azure File Storage
      101
   InterPlanetary File System (IPFS) 101
   Keywhiz 102
VOLUME instruction 151, 152
volumes
   creating 94, 96, 97, 98, 99
   removing 100

W

Webhooks
   about 200, 208, 209, 210, 211, 212, 213, 214,
      215
   build trigger 206, 207, 208
   continuous deployments 208, 209, 210, 211,
      212, 213, 214, 215
WORKDIR instruction 152

www.ingramcontent.com/pod-product-compliance
Lightning Source LLC
Chambersburg PA
CBHW060536060326
40690CB00017B/3508

9 781786 469908